LOCAL HISTORY IN ENGLAND

SOME PRESS REVIEWS OF THE EARLIER EDITIONS

'. . . the student of local history can have no better guide than Dr Hoskins has provided in this admirable book. . . . Written in an unassuming, almost conversational style . . . the book contains an enormous amount of information and yet never makes the reader feel that he is being crammed with facts. It would not be easy to discover anything really important that has been overlooked.'
The Times Literary Supplement

'This book may fairly be described as indispensable to anyone researching in local history. Dr Hoskins puts his learning at the service of fellow workers; not only does he tell them what is to be found and how to go about finding it, he also encourages and directs them to the most profitable kind of inquiry. His book should have a most wholesome influence.'
The Times Educational Supplement

'It is impossible not to be instructed and excited by Mr Hoskins' writing. . . . LOCAL HISTORY IN ENGLAND is an encouraging and practical guidebook to those who would wish to know, and possibly to write something about, where they live. Nowhere in England, not the flashiest shopping arcade on the furthest new 'conurbation' is without interest when seen through the eyes of Mr Hoskins.'
John Betjeman, *Daily Telegraph*

'I think the clue to the enduring value of this book is to be found in the positive way in which techniques and tools are applied to their essential task. . . . This is a new approach to a big subject. It meets a real need.'
E. W. Martin, *Observer*

'As was recognised when it first appeared Professor Hoskins's book is a classic guide to the problems of fieldwork, topography, buildings, and of almost every conceivable facet of the story of English parishes, towns or counties and their sources. A scholar of unequalled experience in this field . . . Professor Hoskins has the ability to excite and instruct in a clear, expressive, almost conversational style.'
Birmingham Post

W. G. Hoskins

LOCAL HISTORY IN ENGLAND

THIRD EDITION

LONGMAN
London and New York

Longman Group Limited
Longman House, Burnt Mill, Harlow,
Essex CM20 2JE, England
Associated companies throughout the world

Published in the United States of America
by Longman Inc., New York

First published 1959
Second edition 1972
Second impression in paperback 1974
Third edition 1984

British Library Cataloguing in Publication Data

Hoskins, W. G.
  Local history in England.—3rd ed.
  1. England—History, Local
  2. England—Historiography
  I. Title
  942   DA1

ISBN 0-582-49413-3
ISBN 0-582-49371-4 Ppr

Library of Congress Cataloging in Publication Data

Hoskins, W. G. (William George), 1908–
  Local History in England.

  Bibliography: p.
  Includes index.
  1. Great Britain—History, Local—Historiography.
  2. Local history.   I. Title.
  DA1.H6   1984   942'.0072   84-4385

ISBN 0-582-49413-3
ISBN 0-582-49371-4 (pbk.)

Printed in Hong Kong by
Wing King Tong Co. Ltd.

CONTENTS

LIST OF ILLUSTRATIONS

PREFACE

The aims and objects of this book on English local history are explained in the first few pages of my first chapter. It is not intended to be a guide to the immense range of sources that are available for the study of local history in this country, for suitable guides already exist to which I make reference in my text. This is mainly a book of advice and encouragement for local historians in any part of England, dealing as fully as possible with those problems and aspects of local history which I think have hitherto been neglected and which to my mind are worthy of attention, and referring only in passing to those aspects which others have dealt with sufficiently. This treatment is especially apparent in the two chapters on towns (6, 7), where I have concentrated on their topography and their social and economic history, and have given virtually no space to their constitutional and parliamentary history. It is not that I consider these subjects less important, but that others have treated of them sufficiently fully to give the local historian all the guidance he needs as to the problems and sources.

It should be noted that I exclude the local history of Wales and London. These require separate books, and also a knowledge that I do not possess. I also exclude prehistoric archaeology for the reasons given in the text, though there is a certain amount about pre-Conquest and medieval archaeology in the chapters on Field-work (8, 9) and elsewhere.

A considerable number of references for further reading are scattered throughout the text of each chapter and in the select bibliography at the end of the book. These lists of references make no claim at all to be comprehensive. If I had attempted to achieve this, they would have added excessively to the length of the book and still would not have given general satisfaction.

This book is based to a considerable extent upon lectures given at Oxford on the problems and sources of English local history, and on the topography and social history of English towns. It could well have been half as long again, but I am anxious that it should reach as many impecunious local historians as possible at a reasonable price. It throws out, I believe, a considerable number of ideas on a variety of subjects which I have not attempted, in most cases, to follow up or to work out completely, believing that most local historians can do this for themselves in the light of their own circumstances. Every local community is unique in some ways, and any general ideas have to be modified accordingly. I hope also that the book will be useful to all teachers of local history, from secondary schools to adult education classes.

It remains only to thank those who have helped me with the various versions of this book. Jack Simmons read the original text in typescript and in proof, and gave me the benefit of his critical sense and of his constructive suggestions. Maurice Barley was kind enough to read the two chapters on Fieldwork in the same spirit, and they benefited accordingly. To Maurice Beresford I am indebted for permission to use his unpublished figures from the 1377 poll tax in my appendix on the Ranking of Provincial Towns, and for checking my own figures from the 1334 tax assessment in the same appendix. Mr C. A. F. Meekings very kindly performed a similar service in allowing me to use his figures from the hearth tax assessment of 1662, and in checking my list for that year. The trouble he and Maurice Beresford took over these apparently simple tables of figures will, I hope, be appreciated by many local historians as well as myself. To Maurice Barley I am also indebted for permission to use his plan of the farmhouse at Boycombe, which he drew specially for my book, a remainder of one of our many pleasant expeditions in the field together. The late Professor H. P. R. Finberg was kind enough to read the proofs of the original edition and to put me right on certain points for which I am duly grateful.

For the present third edition, I owe particular thanks to my former postgraduate student, Dr David Hey. He has given me invaluable assistance in bringing the text up to date, in selecting and commenting upon numerous additional illustrations which have been incorporated, and in compiling the new bibliography of a subject which has grown so enormously since the first edition of this book appeared in 1959. Ill health has compelled me to rely so much for help from Dr Hey that without him I doubt whether a new edition of this book would have been within my powers.

W. G. HOSKINS
6 March 1959/26 May 1983

ACKNOWLEDGEMENTS

Acknowledgement is due to the following for permission to reproduce illustrations: Aerofilms for 1.3 & 4.6; The Bodleian Library for 9.7; The British Library for 2.1; The British Tourist Authority for 5.3; Cambridge University Collection (copyright reserved) for 4.2, 6.4 & 12.3; Alex Chatwin for 3.2 & 6.2; City Hall, Lincoln, for 2.3; C. R. Clemens* for 11.5; Sheila Edwards for 3.3, 5.2, 8.3, 8.7, 8.8, 9.1, 9.6, 10.1 & 13.2; A. F. Kersting for 4.4, 5.1 & 12.4; Leicestershire Museums, Art Galleries & Records Service for 7.1; Leicester University Press for 2.2, 9.4 & 13.1; T. Middlemass, Principal Photographer, Archaeology Dept, University of Durham, for 6.3; The National Trust for 8.1, 8.4 & 9.9; Nottinghamshire County Council for 6.9; the Ordnance Survey for 11.1; The Royal Commission on Historical Monuments for 1.2, 3.1, 6.1, 8.2, 8.5, 8.6, 9.2, 9.8 & 12.1; South Yorkshire Archaeology Service for 12.2; West Yorkshire County Council for 4.7; York Tourist Board for 1.1, 4.5 & 6.6

* Although every effort has been made, we are unable to trace the copyright holder of this print, Mr C. R. Clemens, and would appreciate any information which would enable us to do so.

Ille terrarum mihi praeter omnes
Angulus ridet.

HORACE

It is that corner of the world, above all others,
Which has a smile for me.

I THE LOCAL HISTORIAN TODAY

This book is intended to be a book of advice and guidance to all those who are studying local history and topography anywhere in England, especially those who are hoping to produce their own history of a particular place. There must be thousands of local historians passionately interested in one place—a parish, a village, or a small town. They now form a multitude where once they were a select few.

The local historian, wherever he or she may be, constantly comes up against problems and difficulties in discovering the sources, in using them aright, or in extracting their real meaning; or he* may come up against important periods or problems for which there appear to be no sources at all. All local historians will know these formidable obstacles that suddenly appear in their path, and will also know how often one looks in vain for an answer, for some guidance how to proceed. There is no book to go to.

I have tried to write such a book here, though I would not claim to anticipate all the problems that may arise in all the varied communities of England and certainly not all the answers. However, I have had more than fifty years' experience of studying and writing the history of counties, of towns, of villages, and parishes, and even of farms and streets, and what I have learnt may be of some use to others. I have broadcast often on a variety of approaches to local history and offered advice to unseen audiences; and I have received hundreds of letters which raised difficulties that were

---

* Throughout the rest of this book I shall refer to the local historian as *he* in default of any simpler way of saying what I mean; but I am not unmindful of the fact that women form a large proportion of local historians at work today.

usually of general application and did not relate to one place. Lectures in various parts of England, followed by innumerable questions, have also made me aware of what are the commonest difficulties in the path of those who are devoting themselves to the history of some chosen and beloved place. The time has come to embody this experience, such as it is, in a book of short compass, for I want it to reach all those in need of help and guidance wherever they may be.

In this book I shall be concerned with problems of techniques and methods. I shall discuss also what themes the local historian ought to bear in mind; how he should organise his material so that it presents a coherent whole rather than a miscellaneous collection of facts; how he should tackle and interpret certain particularly difficult but inescapable sources such as Domesday Book; and how he should read maps as historical documents so that they can be made to yield information about dark periods of local history for which there may be no other source. For those particularly interested in town history I have tried to suggest the methods by which they may study the physical growth of a town rather than its growth as an institution: in other words, the town as a town rather than as a borough, for there is plenty of guidance already on the latter aspect. I have also devoted a chapter to the social and economic history of towns. The study of urban history has recently made immense strides in this country and now has its own journal, *The Urban History Yearbook*, which every local historian with a special interest in towns should read.

I also want to give advice on fieldwork in local history. The great scientist Humboldt said that no chemist ought to be afraid to get his hands wet. For the same reasons, no historian—certainly no local historian—ought to be afraid to get his feet wet. I attach so

1.1 Micklegate Bar, York

York's rich history goes back over 1,900 years to the founding of the Roman fort of *Eboracum* in AD 71–74. The Roman defences surrounding the legionary fortress and the *colonia* were strengthened and heightened by each successive group of invaders—Angles, Vikings and Normans—until they achieved their present form during the thirteenth and fourteenth centuries. No other English city has such a remarkable set of walls, towers and bars.

Micklegate was the Viking 'great street', the principal highway from the south and west that curved down the hill to the commercial heart of *Jorvik*. Until 1863 the Ouse could be crossed only this way.

Micklegate Bar preserves its Norman arch, but the upper parts were redesigned in the fourteenth century. Until the late 1820s the entrance was protected by a barbican, which stretched about as far as the front car in the photograph. Micklegate Bar was the scene of ceremonial receptions and the place where the heads of executed traitors were displayed on many occasions in the Middle Ages.

much importance to the visual evidence revealed by fieldwork that I have devoted two chapters to it in this book.* First, on how to study the physical markings on the landscape of the parish and how to interpret what one sees. And second, how to make a record of the buildings of one's chosen territory, for such a survey seems to me to lie very near the heart of the subject of local history: an exact recording of the houses of former inhabitants of a parish or town and of the places where they worked—the early workshops, the water-power factories, engine-houses, lead-mills, or whatever the characteristic local industry may have been. To ignore all this visible evidence because it is not supported by some document in the Public Record Office or the parish chest seems to me an extraordinarily one-eyed view of history. Some of the best documented local histories betray not the slightest sign that the author has looked over the hedges of his chosen place, or walked its boundaries, or explored its streets, or noticed its buildings and what they mean in terms of the history he is trying to write.

This book is not written for the specialist or the professional historian. It is written for the great army of amateurs in this field. Even there I am conscious of talking to readers with very different levels of accomplishment and training, and that some of my advice will be, for some readers at least, superfluous or elementary. I hope they will forgive this necessary approach to the subject and find hints elsewhere in the book that will be of help to them. Not that I think there is only one way of doing these things and that I alone know it. There are many different ways of studying and writing local history. But some ways are to my mind more profitable than others, and I think that local historians ought to make an effort to improve their technique and their knowledge of the sources, however long they have been at it.

On this subject of amateur and professional, there are some pregnant remarks by Samuel Butler: 'There is no excuse for amateur work being bad. Amateurs often excuse their shortcomings on the ground that they are not professional: the professional could plead with greater justice that he is not an amateur.' There is a great deal of truth in this. We always do best those things we are not doing for money, or that we are not obliged to do. The amateur—I hope it is clear that I am using the word in its original good sense—has made a large contribution to English local history in the past, and there is still plenty of room for him (or her) in this vast and still largely

---

* In 1967 I published *Fieldwork in Local History* (Faber), a much fuller treatment of this side of local history.

unexplored field. Indeed, it was amateurs who founded the study of local history and topography in this country, and who nourished it for over four hundred years. One could truthfully say that the professional historian only entered this field when *The Victoria History of the Counties of England* was founded in the year 1899. There will be plenty of room for the amateur for generations to come. He brings to the subject a zest and a freshness, and a deep affection, which the overworked professional can rarely achieve. But he must also take his hobby seriously and go on enlarging his horizon and improving his technique to the end of his days.

Primarily I regard the study of local history and topography as a hobby that gives a great deal of pleasure to a great number of people, and I think it wrong to make it intimidating, to warn them off because they may not have the training of the professional historian. It is a means of enjoyment and a way of enlarging one's consciousness of the external world, and even (I am sure) of the internal world. To acquire an abiding 'sense of the past', to live with it daily and to understand its values, is no small thing in the world as we find it today. But the better informed and the more scrupulous the local historian is about the truth of past life, the more enjoyment he will get from his chosen hobby. Inaccurate information is not only false: it is boring and fundamentally unsatisfying. The local historian must strive to be as faithful to the truth as any other kind of historian, and it is well within his powers to be so.

LOCAL HISTORIANS OF ALL KINDS

Each year as the evenings grow longer and darker some few thousands of men and women, even a few schoolboys here and there, feel the renewed impulse to turn inwards after the outward activity of the spring and summer. They take out once more their notes on the history of their own parish or village, less often their town (for this is a large undertaking), to browse over again, to add a detail here and there, and to wonder how to go on, where to look next for more material, and how to find the answers to questions that have been bothering them winter after winter.

For years perhaps they have been gathering these notes from books in the nearest library, or records in the parish chest, perhaps from central records somewhere in London, and from conversations with people of an older generation who have known an entirely different world. They have set down their notes in exercise books, filling page after page with the past life of their own small piece of country. Nothing is too trivial to them, for they possess that poetic insight which comes from an acute sense of the past, a sense that is very much more general among country people than among towns-men, above all in the remoter provinces of England and Wales. Not that towns have less history: far from it. Every street in an old town is rich in its own peculiar history. But the conditions of life in large towns do not favour generally the contemplative life, and without some leisure for contemplation and reflection this sense of the past cannot be nourished and will not grow.

But whether in town or in country parish these men and women feel an unquenchable desire to know all there is to be known about the past of the small piece of England in which they were born or which they have come to love. They study the map of their chosen place and wonder what secrets it contains if only they could find the key; what history lies in the shape of its boundaries and of its fields and their names; or in the way the streets run and the names they have; or the situation of the farmsteads, their plans and their names, and whether the pattern of the roads and lanes has any meaning which can be unravelled. They study the parish register, turning its fragile leaves crammed with faded brown writing which perhaps they can only partly read. They study the monuments in the church and copy the inscriptions, not forgetting the older headstones in the churchyard and the worn floor-slabs in nave and chancel.

The growing and almost insatiable demand for guidance in the study and writing of local history has been a feature of adult educa-tion classes, especially since 1945. There is, in fact, a shortage of teachers competent to take such classes. It is difficult to explain this remarkable growth of interest in local history. One cannot attribute it even to television, which is partly responsible at least for the equally marked growth in the amateur study of archaeology in this country (and also for much amateur damage to our antiquities). It may be that with the growing complexity of life, and the growth in size of every organisation with which we have to deal nowadays, not to mention the fact that so much of the past is visibly perishing before our eyes, more and more people have been led to take an interest in a particular place and to wish to find out all about it. Some shallow-brained theorists would doubtless call this 'escapism', but the fact is that we are not born internationalists and there comes a time when the complexity and size of modern problems leave us cold. We belong to a particular place and the bigger and more incomprehensible the modern world grows the more will people turn to study something of which they can grasp the scale and in which they can find a personal and individual meaning.

In this book I exclude prehistoric archaeology altogether. This is a distinct branch of knowledge with techniques of its own that require a specialised training for their use. This is not to say that prehistoric archaeology should not interest the local historian, for in some parts of England, for example Cornwall or the Cotswolds or Wiltshire, the history of a given parish may stretch far back into prehistoric times and one cannot separate the history from the pre-history. Christopher Taylor's book, *Dorset: The Making of the English Landscape* (Hodder & Stoughton, 1970) was a remarkable analysis of the extent to which prehistory and the Roman period underlie our modern villages and their fields.

On quite another theme, the Devon Federation of Women's Institutes made a massive survey of the field-names of the county between 1964 and 1970. The coverage was not complete: about half the parishes were completely covered and another sixty-eight parishes in part. This was due to the fact that not every parish possesses a Women's Institute. One parish alone had some two thousand field-names. In fifty-two parishes there was also a complete coverage of the field-names from the tithe maps, and in another ninety-five a partial coverage. In Norfolk the County Federation has compiled a collection of reminiscences of rural life from about 1890 onwards, bringing together much recent local history which would otherwise have perished without anything in writing. Not all human activity and thinking is enshrined in official records (fortunately), and it has to be gathered in other ways.

THE TRAINING OF THE LOCAL HISTORIAN

Anyone who attempts to study and to write the history of a chosen place, whether a town or a country parish or perhaps a whole region, must clearly possess a wide range of historical knowledge. Even if there is no prehistory to cope with, and even if no Romano-British history is involved, one will still require a more or less detailed knowledge of every kind of history—political, ecclesiastical, social, economic, military, and yet other kinds—extending over a period of perhaps 1,500 years, if one is aiming to write the history of a place from beginning to end. I shall suggest later that this is by no means the only kind of local history that one can write. But, assuming that this is the aim, the amount of historical knowledge required may seem intimidating at first.

It need not be so. Obviously a basic knowledge of English history is required. One should have a good grasp of national history into which one can fit and explain a great deal of what is happening locally. But there is no need to carry this encyclopaedic knowledge in one's head. It is often sufficient to know what books to go to for the best guidance and for the best account of a given subject; and one need not, and indeed cannot, anticipate all the books one may have to consult in dealing with the local history of any place.

R. B. Pugh, in *How to Write a Parish History* (Allen & Unwin, 1954) has said that a local historian must know Latin and must be able to read the old handwriting in which most of his sources will be written. This is unnecessarily discouraging advice. A great deal of local history can be completely studied and written up without any knowledge of Latin or palaeography. A knowledge of Latin may present almost insuperable difficulties to those who have not acquired a basis at school If you are obliged to use records written in Latin you may have to depend on some friend who has the necessary knowledge; and there are few local historians so isolated and benighted that they cannot call upon such a friend from time to time. One should say at this point that the local archivist cannot be expected to act in this capacity. He or she is much too busy with routine duties to act as a translator of documents, though they are always ready to give help over particular words or phrases. But it would be wrong to worry the local archivist on a larger scale than this and one should look elsewhere for help.

Similarly, one should not go to the local archivist if one is totally ignorant of palaeography. Much can be done by the local historian to teach himself this knowledge. He will find, if he begins (as I recommend in the next chapter) at the more modern period and works backwards from this point, from known handwriting into the relatively unknown, he will succeed in teaching himself how to read most of the documents written in English for the sixteenth and seventeenth centuries. Many amateurs have trained themselves in this way in a very short time. Before the sixteenth century practically every document was written in Latin, and most legal documents continued to be written in Latin until the early eighteenth century. Here the local historian who has no Latin will have to rely upon his friend. As regards the older English handwriting, the local historian will find it very useful to possess a copy of a handbook published by the Essex Record Office, entitled *Some Examples of English Hand-*

writing, and the subsequent handbook *More Examples of English Handwriting*. He will learn a great deal from these admirable textbooks on the subject, and from handbooks published by other local record offices. But there are still wide fields of local history in which the local historian need not bother at all with palaeography or with Latin.

What he will need, in addition to a basic knowledge of English history and knowing where to go for the answers to questions as they crop up, is great patience and absolute accuracy in copying or in making a précis of record material. He will also need good powers of observation (which can be developed from almost nothing: most people are half-blind all their lives) and a feeling for the past. One should also add a feeling for *the present*, since history is happening all around us and we shall understand the past a great deal better if we realise this clearly. One must train oneself to observe, and as far as possible to understand, the present. As the French historian Marc Bloch says in *The Historian's Craft*: 'Misunderstanding of the present is the inevitable consequence of ignorance of the past. But a man may wear himself out just as pointlessly in seeking to understand the past, if he is totally ignorant of the present.'

BASIC EQUIPMENT AND BOOKS

What is the minimum equipment the local historian should possess in order to work effectively? I am assuming that he is not undertaking anything so vast as the history of a whole county. If he is, he will be too well equipped to seek guidance in this book. I shall assume he is writing the history of a rural parish or of a small town. I must rule out also the man who is attempting to write the history of a large city, for this too is a special case. Leaving such large works aside, the local historian should possess (and not merely borrow) the following books:

1. W. B. Stephens, *Sources for English Local History* (Cambridge University Press, 2nd edn, 1981)
2. W. G. Hoskins, *Fieldwork in Local History* (Faber, 1967)
3. L. C. Hector, *The Handwriting of English Documents* (E. Arnold, 1966)

He ought also to subscribe to *The Local Historian* (published quarterly from 26 Bedford Square, London, WC1B 3HU), which will keep him abreast of current work in the subject and suggest many new lines of enquiry, and he should possess a copy of any special bibliography relating to his own county or chosen area. Most county record offices have now published excellent guides to their archives which the local historian should know about and have on his own work-table. It is a mistake to try to work entirely with borrowed books.

The local historian should also, if he can, possess copies of any earlier histories of his place. Some of these may be scarce works and therefore too expensive to possess nowadays, but they can be borrowed from the local library. There are other standard guides to specialised fields (e.g. vernacular building) which will be referred to later in the appropriate chapter of this book.

The student of local history should also possess as a matter of course the latest edition of the 1-inch geological map for his area; and he should possess, too, the appropriate sheets of the Ordnance Survey maps. If he is writing the history of a rural parish he ought to possess the 1-inch* sheet covering the whole of the surrounding country, because he cannot understand his own parish history without relating it to a considerable area around. If he is working on a town history, he should possess the Ordnance Survey map of the town on the 25-inch (1:2,500) scale, and the sheets of the 1/500 plan for his town which were published some ninety or more years ago. The standard guide to maps in general is *The Historian's Guide to Ordnance Survey Maps*, published in 1964 by the National Council for Social Service—quite indispensable and also inexpensive.

The local historian should have ready access either to E. Ekwall's *Dictionary of English Place-Names* (Oxford University Press, 4th edn 1960) or to the relevant county volume published by the English Place-Name Society, if it exists. There are a number of older books dealing with the place-names of particular counties and districts, but these should not be followed implicitly. The study of place-names has made such great advances in the last sixty years that one may generally say that the older books have been superseded. Every local historian should turn for guidance in these matters to Margaret Gelling's book, *Signposts to the Past* (Dent, 1978), which is the best modern work on the subject.

Another warning should be given at this point. The study of place-names is highly specialised. The meaning of a place-name may look obvious to the amateur and he may think himself safe in making a guess. But even the most obvious guess is quite likely to

---

* In recent years the Ordnance Survey have changed to a 1¼-inch scale (1:50,000).

be wrong, for unless we know the earliest forms of a given name, and the way they have developed throughout history, we cannot possibly know what the original meaning of the name was. Even a simple name like Ashton, which the amateur would assume to mean 'ash tree farm', may well have originated as Easton, meaning 'the eastern farm' in relation to some other and probably older settlement. If, therefore, the local historian encounters place-names within his parish or territory for which he can find no authoritative explanation in print, he should simply record the spellings (with references and dates) as he finds them and leave it to others to decide what they mean. Ekwall's *Dictionary* and the county volumes of the English Place-Name Society are not, of course, infallible. We all make mistakes, and there are some mistaken explanations in the best of books on this subject. The local scholar may well decide after long reflection that he is in a position to offer a more likely explanation of a difficult name than that offered by a scholar who has perhaps never seen this particular parish. But he should state the meaning given by the expert and then his own view, and leave the reader to judge which is the more likely to be right. Few subjects contain so many pitfalls as the study of place-names.

After the place-name, unless there is a Saxon land charter (see Chapter 8), the next major source is likely to be Domesday Book. The local historian should therefore have access to the text of the Domesday survey, which he will generally find most readily in the pages of the *Victoria County History* (though not every county has been covered by this great work). Or it may be that the text for his own county has been published separately by the local historical society, as the Devonshire Association published *The Devonshire Domesday* in two volumes in 1884–92. Phillimore are currently publishing the Domesday survey in a series of reasonably-priced county volumes. The local historian should always go back to the authoritative text, and not slavishly copy someone else's transcription of the text which may well contain errors or omissions. Important and basic material like that in Domesday Book should always be verified in this way. It may well be that the entry in Domesday Book will give rise to a number of questions to which the answers are not easy. I touch on this subject in Chapter 4.

THE THEME OF LOCAL HISTORY

The problems of the local historian will vary not only from place to place, but will also vary in a more fundamental way according to the region in which he is working. For example, the local historian who is working in what the geographers call the Lowland Zone will be studying a very different kind of landscape, with its own historical and topographical problems, from the local historian who is working somewhere in the Highland Zone. Roughly speaking, in the former he will be concerned with the history of a more or less compact village, surrounded by some kind of open-field system with no settlement outside the village until comparatively recent times. In the Highland Zone he may well be studying a parish in which there has never been a true village, but instead a scattering of three or four hamlets and a score or two of isolated farmsteads. Even this distinction is not as clear and simple as all that. In many parts of England a parish may contain mixed forms of settlement: that is to say, a quite 'normal' village somewhere near the centre, and in addition a scattering of hamlets and farmsteads in the surrounding parish.

But there are considerable regional differences even within these very broad divisions between Highland and Lowland Zones. The local historian working in Norfolk faces a number of problems almost peculiar to that part of England, notably the presence of two or three churches within one churchyard, something which must reflect a peculiar social structure dating from early times. Or, if he is working in the wilder parts of Yorkshire and the northern counties generally, many of his basic problems and questions will be very different from those of the local historian working in, say, Hampshire. No one book can give advice and suggest answers to every possible problem arising in all the distinct regions of England. Here one can give only general advice with some regional examples, and throw out ideas that merit consideration. One cannot give the answer to a particular problem in detail, but only suggest some general idea which might prove to be fruitful if applied to a particular local problem.

Is there a central theme round which the local historian should compose his history? In a town or a village his central theme should surely be the origin and growth of his particular local community or society; the peculiar and individual nature of this society and the way it worked through the centuries—that is, the way it solved certain basic political and economic problems, above all the problem of how to get a living for an increasing number of people from the fixed supply of land and other natural resources. In rural parishes the local historian will be very much concerned, on the one hand,

1.2 Hooton Pagnell, Yorkshire

Hooton Pagnell is typical of many of the farming villages of England's Lowland zone. The farmhouses are close together, with their gable ends to the street, so that animals and carts can pass to the farm buildings at the rear. A back lane leads onto the former open arable fields to the east; the common occupied inferior, low-lying ground to the west. Hooton means 'the settlement on the spur of land' and it was distinguished from other Hootons by the name of its medieval lords. The church of All Saints dates from the eleventh-century in its present form, and the adjacent hall from the fourteenth century.

A weekly market and annual fair were established in 1253, but they did not survive the late-medieval contraction of population. Hooton still had a lot of freeholders in the mid-sixteenth century, but 200 years later it had become an estate village. The village has neither pub nor chapel, and all the houses are built in the local magnesian limestone with stone-slate or pantile roofs.

with records about the ownership and occupation of the land; and, on the other hand, with all the records that throw light on population changes over a long period of time. In rural parishes, too, he will probably be concerned with the process by which this local society of his, which was largely self-contained, has disintegrated during the past hundred years or so. This, of course, is not invariably so; but even where local communities appear to survive intact, as in certain small and remote country towns, they are often hollow shells from which the heart and spirit have been eaten away by the acids of modernity. If anyone is inclined to doubt this, let him begin by making a close study of his local directory of a hundred years ago. In three cases out of four he will probably find that his chosen place is considerably smaller in numbers, and diminished in variety, from what it was three generations or so ago. When did this decay begin and why? How did a self-contained community of 1850 reach that size and that particular economic and social balance? Why is the population of the small town or country parish today so often only a half of what it used to be? Some English parishes have fewer people today than they had at the time of Domesday Book. All these and other questions come to mind almost at once.

The central theme, then, is the origin, growth, and (often) the decay of the local society. If the local historian keeps this firmly in mind, he will find that he can discard a multitude of miscellaneous and quite insignificant facts and concentrate upon those that really throw light upon the basic problems of local history. Yet the true local historian will also remember that behind the central theme—which may involve growth rather than decay—there may be many minor themes that are worthy of his attention.

It is clear that when we are studying or writing the history of a town or a village, we are dealing with something which can be, or could have been, called a true society of men, women, and children, gathered together in one place. We can even conceive of certain counties as forming a distinct society, especially those remoter counties on the periphery of England. Dr A. L. Rowse in his masterly study of *Tudor Cornwall* (Cape, 1941) subtitles it *Portrait of a society*; but not all the counties of England would lend themselves perhaps so readily to this distinctive approach.

How far can we assume the existence of such a local society in those parts of England where we rarely find compact villages? Over a great part of the western side of England the local historian will find himself dealing with the history of a parish which may consist of two or three hamlets and a score of farmsteads with no village centre at all. In a sense he is dealing with almost a different civilisation. The great French geographer Demangeon makes some remarks on this point which are equally applicable to England:

When one wishes to explain this fundamental pattern of the peopling of France, one is led to attach less importance to reasons arising from natural conditions (such as the nature of the terrain and the water supply) than to reasons arising from historic facts and from the agrarian structure. Between these two great facets of human settlement lie profound differences of rural civilisation. Some are accustomed to live in groups, others in isolation. It is a matter of very ancient ways of life rooted long ago.

Is it possible, then, to talk about the reconstruction of a local society in a parish of this type? I think it is, for two reasons. The first is that even in the more scattered parishes a unity is often imposed on the parish by the presence of the squire and his estate. Even if he did not own all the land in the parish he may have owned the greater part of it, and to this extent the scattered farms and hamlets are knitted together in a common relationship. Secondly, where there was no squire or any dominant landowner, the parish was still unified by the existence of the church to which all people in the parish, however isolated their farmsteads may have been, were expected to go, and did go, for many centuries.

Nevertheless, it is clear that the history of parishes of this kind will be considerably different from the history of parishes which are centred upon a village. The ownership or occupation of each isolated farm becomes a special problem for the historian of this kind of parish. Yet even here we can apply the formula which I have suggested: that the local historian should take as his central theme the human development of this piece of country which subsequently became an ecclesiastical parish; that he should study among other central problems the way the land has been held, and the distribution of land in relation to population changes within the parish. Even here he may find himself dealing with a parish which has lost a half or two-thirds of its population in the last four or five generations.

In order to clarify in his own mind the fundamental fact that he is dealing with a distinct local society which once had a real existence (and may in rare cases still survive), the local historian might best begin by reconstructing 'the old community' from the records of the nineteenth century. It is far better that he should do this at the outset than that he should wrestle with the fragmentary and ill-understood beginnings of his community as revealed in Domesday Book or an Anglo-Saxon charter, or in pieces of Romano-British pottery.

1.3 Great Waltham, Essex

Great and Little Waltham each have churches that served scattered settlements in typical rambling Essex parishes. This was once a forest area, where hamlets and isolated farmsteads were more common than villages. Great Waltham parish contained eight settlements within five or six miles of each other along the banks of the River Chelmer. North End, Ford End and Hartford End are named in a distinctive Essex manner—other hamlets are named after a tye or green—and Ford End acquired its own red-brick church in Victorian times. Further north, the 'Black Chapel' has served as a chapel-of-ease since the Middle Ages and is still furnished with box-pews, double-decker pulpit and other eighteenth-century fittings. The earliest part of Great Waltham church is the eastern wall of the Norman chancel. Langleys manor house is an ancient structure that was remodelled after 1711, when Samuel Tufnell, a London merchant, bought the estate. The house in the north-east corner of the churchyard with the pairs of tall chimneys dates from 1560.

Before we turn, however, to the materials and methods for the study of local history in the nineteenth century, I wish to say something about those who have studied English local history and topography before us.

2 ENGLISH LOCAL HISTORIANS

THE FORERUNNERS

The study of English local history and topography is five hundred years old. It dates in effect from William of Worcester's itinerary, notes of his journeys made mostly between 1477 and 1480. William of Worcester was born in Bristol in 1415 and was in the service of Sir John Fastolf in Norfolk until the latter's death in 1459. He thereupon retired to his native city and later began his tours of this country, making notes in a pocket-book as he went along. The notes are scrappy and unorganised, but he recorded a great deal of antiquarian detail, distances between towns, sizes of buildings (like cathedrals and monasteries), and so on. He left behind a remarkable description of all the streets and lanes, and many of the buildings, of his native Bristol in the 1470s. No doubt this was a very dull sort of interest at the time, but it now forms the best picture we have of an English medieval town. William of Worcester may rightly be called the founder of local topography in this country, and the study of topography is the foundation of local history. He is the spiritual grandfather of all who read this book.

John Leland (1506–52) was also a topographer rather than an historian. It was his fate to go around England at a bad time, a time like our own of a great social revolution in which much that was good was swept away, year after year, indiscriminately with the bad. The dissolution of the monasteries as carried out by Henry VIII was an act of nihilism: wherever Leland went he saw and recorded the destruction of monastic civilisation, the demolition and pillaging of its buildings, the dispersal and destruction of its libraries and archives. Leland saw and recorded the end of monastic civilisation in England, just as we are witnessing the end of the country-house civilisation which arose almost literally on the ruins of the monasteries, a civilisation which in turn flourished for nearly four hundred years until the year 1914.

Leland went mad in the end; his antiquarian studies overtaxed his brain. But he left behind the manuscript of his *Itinerary*, which had a profound influence upon the study of local history and topography for the next two hundred years. It is the first of the long series of great topographical works that we possess in this country, and we can read it with profit and pleasure to this day. Though it remained unprinted until the eighteenth century, it was handed around in manuscript and read by many scholars. Some of the greatest names in English local history and topography, such as Stow, Camden, Dugdale, and Harrison, all owed much to it.

THE COUNTY HISTORIANS

The earlier writers took the whole of England for their province, and it is not until the 1570s that we have the real beginning of the tremendous stream of local history and topography—surveys of counties, towns, and finally of parishes—that has flowed without interruption ever since.

In 1574 Christopher Saxton began work on the first national atlas to be published in this or any other country, a work which he eventually brought to completion five years later. Saxton's county maps are well known to all students of topography and local history. About the same time—1570—William Lambarde wrote the first county history, or more strictly 'survey', *The Perambulation of Kent*. This was published in 1576 and is still valuable for its topographical information. In the 1590s John Norden was writing his surveys of particular counties. His *Middlesex* came out in 1593, and *Hertfordshire* five years later. Three other counties remained in manuscript for more than a century. It may be said at this point that it is a common fate for local historians to wait for a century or even two for publication. One is in good company.

Lambarde's *Kent* directly inspired Carew's *Survey of Cornwall*, which he began to write in the 1580s. It was not published until 1602. Like so many of these early county surveys, it was handed around in manuscript among friends for a long time before it was published, and it was only the encouragement of 'Master Camden'

2.1 Saxton's map of Sussex and Kent, 1575

Sussex and Kent were among the counties surveyed in 1575 by Christopher Saxton for the first national atlas of England and Wales. The project was sponsored by Thomas Seckford, Master of the Requests at Queen Elizabeth's court, and received the keen support of William Cecil, Lord Burghley. Local JPs were instructed to assist Saxton and 'to see him conducted into any towre Castle highe place or hill to view that countrey'.

The contrasting scenery in Sussex was described by Saxton's contemporary, William Camden, in *Brittania*: 'The sea-coast of this country has very high green hills, call'd the Downs, which consisting of a fat chalky soil, are upon that account very fruitful. The middle part being chequer'd with meadows, pastures, cornfields, and groves, makes a very fine show. The hithermost northern-side, is shaded most pleasantly with woods, as anciently the whole country was, which made it unpassable.'

and the pressure of other friends that led Carew finally to have it printed.

The early surveys bred others by emulation. In one part of England after another, scholarly squires began to devote years of their lives to the compilation of their county histories. So Carew's *Cornwall* gave birth eventually to Westcote's *View of Devonshire*, as Westcote himself tells us:

> Having by ordinary reading, observation, search, and discourse, collected long since some few particulars of the antiquities and other notes and observings of this County, it was my chance (as often I did) to come in presence of an honourable personage (Edward, Earl of Bath), whose eminent virtues assure me he is now with God:—it pleased him in discourse of the state of this Country to propose certain questions to those that were present: to some of them, when I had given a more satisfying answer than he on the sudden expected, he perceived I had a great desire that some one would undertake the Description of this Shire, as Mr Carew had done for Cornwall. He thereupon took opportunity to be the *primum mobile* of this Discourse; and the next fit convenience did powerfully persuade, and he cheerfully animated and seriously required me to undertake this work (as he was pleased to term it *office*); and not to suffer the ancient renown of the generosity of the Province to be any longer neglected and buried in oblivion, which had bred so many famous men in all professions.

In the year 1622 appeared the first history of the county of Leicester, by William Burton, squire of Lindley on the borders of Warwickshire. And this in turn inspired the production of William Dugdale's *The Antiquities of Warwickshire*, a generation later. This history, still one of the most valuable of all county histories, was published in 1656.

William Dugdale had married and settled down at Blythe Hall in Warwickshire in 1626. Shortly afterwards he made the acquaintance of Burton, who lived only a few miles away, and through Burton he was introduced to Sir Symon Archer of Tamworth—'a gentleman much affected to antiquities'. A little later this scholarly circle was enlarged by the addition of the great Elizabethan scholar Sir Henry Spelman (now nearly eighty years of age) and Roger Dodsworth, who may fittingly be termed the father of topographical studies in the north of England, and whose vast collections of transcripts from antiquarian sources of all kinds now repose in the Bodleian Library at Oxford. Spelman and Dodsworth take us far beyond the field of purely local history, but Dugdale's meeting with Archer was immediately followed by their joint embarkation upon a History of Warwickshire, towards which Archer had already made extensive collections. These he made available to Dugdale, 'being desirous to preserve the Honour of their Families by some such publiq' work as Mr Burton had done . . . in Leicestershire'.

Thirty years after he had settled at Blythe Hall as a young man, Dugdale produced his great history of Warwickshire, which won immediate fame and was indeed a remarkable performance. Anthony Wood said that his 'tender affections and insatiable desire for knowledge were ravished and melted downe by the reading of that book' which had turned his life into 'a perfect Elysium'. A more weighty critic said to the author: 'Seriously, you have drawne the bridge after you and left it impossible for any man to follow you.' And Richard Gough much later said that 'Dugdale must stand at the head of all our county historians.' His *Warwickshire* is Dugdale's greatest claim to fame, much more so than the *Monasticon*, which bears his name but which was pre-eminently the work of Roger Dodsworth.

Dugdale was a country gentleman, and his interpretation of the history of his county reflects this strongly: it is dedicated to 'the gentry of Warwickshire' and has a strong genealogical interest for the county families and no others. But it marked a great advance with its copious and accurate use of authorities, and in the presentation of results, which made it vastly superior to any earlier history of a similar kind. In turn it inspired another great county history, deliberately constructed on the same model—Thoroton's *The Antiquities of Nottinghamshire*, which appeared in 1677. Dugdale's *Warwickshire* and Thoroton's *Nottinghamshire* are the two greatest county histories that the seventeenth century produced. Soon very few counties lacked a history. More than twenty-five county histories were produced between 1622, when Burton's *Leicestershire* appeared, and the middle of the eighteenth century. Between 1750 and 1800 twenty-two more appeared, and only seven counties awaited a chronicler when the nineteenth century opened.

These county histories, some of them of monumental size, like Colt Hoare's huge history of Wiltshire, varied greatly in historical value. Not all by any means showed Dugdale's command of record sources, or his orderly presentation. One of the most disappointing of all county histories is Polwhele's *Devon*. The general historical chapters represent a miserable level of performance, though the parochial descriptions are valuable. Even so, Polwhele covered only a small part of the county and the work as a whole is third-rate. Polwhele was a parson and a representative of a new class of local historians. The squires were still the most numerous class, but the eighteenth-century parson with his ample leisure, his university education, and his more ready access to manuscript sources, joined the ranks of local historians in considerable numbers. It is probably true to say that during the nineteenth century the parson took the place of the squire as the likeliest historian of his county, his town, or his parish. But in general his work showed the same bias and narrowness of interpretation: socially he was often one with the squire, a member of the same class or dependent upon him, and his notion of local history therefore continued to be a history of the descent of landed property and of the genealogy of the county families.

Despite this, the scope of English local history was greatly widened in two ways. One was through the work of a band of notable men during the seventy years that followed the Restoration, whose labours laid the foundations of Anglo-Saxon and medieval scholarship in this country—Rymer, Madox, Hearne, and a host of others—who made available in print the vast manuscript sources of English history which local historians have used ever since. The other was the slow growth of interest in the history of the towns, as distinct from the counties, which introduced whole new fields of record material and historical problems quite foreign to those of the county historians.

Of the labours of the English scholars who provided, throughout the seventeenth and eighteenth centuries, such solid and extensive foundations for the local historian to build upon, there is no room to speak here: moreover, they belong to the field of national rather than purely local history. But the extension of the study of local history to towns calls for some comment.

TOWN HISTORIES

London naturally attracted the first attention, and as early as 1598 John Stow produced his famous *Survey of London*. This was, as Stow tells us, inspired by Lambarde's *Perambulation of Kent*. In the following year came a history of Great Yarmouth by Thomas Nash—*Nashes Lenten Stuffe, containing the description and first procreation and increase of the towne of Greate Yarmouth in Norfolk.** But further growth in this field of study was slow. Somner's *Canter-*

* John Hooker's *The Description of the Citie of Excester* was compiled between about 1580 and 1600 but was not published in its entirety until 1919. A portion seems to have been published about 1583.

bury appeared in 1640, Butcher's *Stamford* in 1646, William Grey's survey of *Newcastle* in 1649, and a history of *Scarborough Spaw* in 1660. But most English towns, even anciently important cities like York and Norwich, had to wait for a history until the eighteenth century, many until well into the nineteenth; and many still await anything that remotely resembles an adequate history. Moreover, most of the towns selected by the earlier historians were the seats of bishops; their ecclesiastical interest often outweighed the historical. The histories were not reasoned accounts of municipal development, but more or less valuable collections of documentary and archaeological materials. Though they greatly widened the field of English local history and made available an ever-growing mass of record material of new kinds, these town histories still suffered from the same fundamental defects as the county histories. They were still too narrow in their view of what constituted history, and they were still presented as more or less undigested compilations of materials—the materials for a history, not the history itself, the uncooked potatoes and not the finished meal. This criticism applies, too, to much of the local history being published today, with some notable exceptions.

When the historian, J. R. Green, was travelling along the Italian coast near Genoa in the year 1871, he wrote to a friend in England:

> Roaming through these little Ligurian towns makes me utter just the old groans you used to join in when we roamed through France—groans, I mean, over the state of our local histories in England. There isn't one of these wee places that glimmer in the night like fireflies in the depth of their bays that hasn't a full and generally admirable account of itself and its doings. They are sometimes wooden enough in point of style and the like, but they use their archives, and don't omit, as all our local histories seem to make a point of doing, the history of the town itself.

Green's great contemporary, Freeman, was interested enough in local history to edit and bring out a series of short histories on *Historic Towns*, beginning in 1887. He was pre-eminently a national historian, and mainly interested in local history—in certain towns—in so far as their history could throw light on national political development. Nor did he read the original records for himself, and spend laborious days in ill-lit and dusty muniment rooms deciphering the manuscripts wherein the true history of a town or a parish lies secreted. His *History of Exeter*, in his own series, exhibits these two fundamental defects throughout. Both these defects—the treatment of local history as only national history writ small, and the failure to use the original local records in which England is so astonishingly rich—still run through a very great deal of English local history as it is studied and written today.*

It was left to the great Cambridge historian Maitland, in his masterly studies of borough history in the 1890s, to lay the real foundations for the study of urban history—as he laid the foundation of so much else for the local historian to build upon. How often one goes back to Maitland even now for the essentials of some problem in local history, and with increasing admiration for his scholarship and his presentation! And he in turn inspired students such as Mary Bateson, whose editing of the municipal records of Leicester was a landmark in this field of study. Her three volumes of the borough records, published between 1899 and 1905, remain among the best of all the published volumes of town records, and a tribute to the enlightenment of the corporation of that time—those leisurely, more cultured, late Victorian days—which engaged her to edit the records and spent so much civic money on publishing them.†

PARISH HISTORIES

As the mass of record material available to the local historian increased—both in his own neighbourhood and in the national archives—and as, too, the notion of what constituted History widened with every decade (the development of economic and social history during the nineteenth century must alone have doubled the size of the local historian's task)—so in sheer self-defence the local historian, like the national historian on his own level, was obliged to narrow his field of study. He chose a smaller area, but he cultivated it more deeply and intensively. It became impossible even to contemplate writing the history of a county so as to embrace all the new fields of interest and all the manuscripts that lay behind them. The day of the great county history was over; that of the small town or the country parish had begun, though not in tall folio volumes any more. For one thing, the costs of printing were now too high for such lavish presentation; and for another, the class of wealthy patrons who could afford ten, twenty, or thirty guineas

---

* On the other hand, it ought to be said that Freeman was one of the earliest professional historians to take notice of local history. Some of his local history, within the limitations I have noted above, was very good, especially his *English Towns and Districts*.

† Since then the borough records have been published down to the year 1835, edited by G. A. Chinnery and published by the University of Leicester Press.

for a local history had acquired other interests and no longer supported scholarship in such numbers as they had once done.

With the parish we reach the smallest field in the study of local history, though by no means the least interesting or valuable. As William of Worcester founded the study of English topography and antiquities on a national scale, and Lambarde was the first of the long line of county historians, so White Kennett founded in 1695 the study of parochial history.* As a country vicar in that year, introducing his *Parochial Antiquities attempted in the History of Ambrosden and other adjacent parts*, he wrote:

> Next to the immediate discharge of my holy office, I know not how in any course of studies I could better have served my patron, my people and my successors than by preserving the memoirs of this parish . . . which before lay remote from common notice and in few years had been buried in unsearchable oblivion.

He was the first of the long dynasty of country parsons who busy themselves to this day with a similar fond enquiry into the parochial antiquities of their own small corner of the English countryside, many of whom could turn back with profit to their founder, White Kennett, for inspiration and guidance.

His example was not followed immediately. Nearly two generations seem to have gone by before another parish history appeared, though probably many were written and never published.† One of my own discoveries, in a little bookshop just outside Waterloo Station during the war, was *The Antiquities and Memoirs of the Parish of Myddle* (in Shropshire), by Richard Gough, written in 1700 but not printed until 1834, and then only imperfectly. The first complete edition did not appear until 1875. Richard Gough lived on his own small estate in the parish of Myddle and amused himself in his latter years in writing the history of his parish according to a remarkable plan. First of all he describes the parish in full and the various places of interest in it—the church, the castle, and so on—and then he proceeds to give an account of the different families who had lived in the parish within his recollection. He gives the plan of the seating in the church, as allotted to different farms in the parish, followed by a systematic account of the occupants of each pew, with many scandalous and lively stories. I do not know

---

* Thomas Fuller's history of Waltham Abbey may possibly be regarded as the first parish history (published in 1655), but Fuller was mainly interested in the abbey and not in the parish, though there are some parochial details.

† An anonymous history of Sutton Coldfield in Warwickshire appeared in 1762, but I know of no others so early as this.

any other book in English which gives such a complete and detailed picture of everyday life in a seventeenth-century parish. In 1968 the Centaur Press reprinted this marvellous local history in full, and I had the pleasure of writing an introduction to a book I had found on a dirty bottom shelf nearly thirty years ago.

Another early parish history, but one written on an entirely different plan from Gough's, is the history of Warton in north Lancashire by John Lucas, a schoolmaster at Leeds, between 1710 and 1744. Warton was his native place, and for more than thirty years in his Leeds exile, he wrote about it. His book was a huge rambling production, full of enormous digressions on every conceivable subject, in which a great deal of interesting local history and topography was embedded. Its length and rambling nature deterred anyone from publishing it until two scholars edited it in 1931, cutting out great tracts of universal history and leaving only the purely local. What is left is a most valuable account of a remote north of England parish in the early part of the eighteenth century.

SOME CRITICISMS OF LOCAL HISTORICAL WRITING

In the course of the nineteenth century a steady stream of parish histories appeared in print. Even so, it is doubtful whether more than one parish in ten has anything remotely resembling an adequate history. Most of the authors of these parish histories were parsons who carried on a tradition of local history writing initiated by the seventeenth-century squires. This fact gave a decisive twist to the writing of local history. It resulted in a lopsided view of what local history is about, a view which was apparent even in the volumes of the *Victoria County History* until recent times. It was apparent above all in the excessive space given to the minutiae of manorial history, and at the same time in the almost complete neglect of the

2.2 Myddle Castle, Shropshire

Myddle was a marcher lordship only a few miles from the Welsh border, and its castle was one of the many fortifications that were designed to subjugate the Welsh in the wake of Edward I's campaigns. Built in 1308 by Lord Strange, it was already 'veri ruinous' when John Leland visited the area c. 1540. The last keeper was 'Wild' Humphrey Kinaston, a riotous and dissolute man who ended his days in a Nesscliff cave after being outlawed for debt. Richard Gough could remember that when he was a boy some of the old walls were still standing; the castle was arranged around a courtyard and surrounded by a square moat, with an adjacent moated area that was entered through a gatehouse. Myddle castle was set in the corner of a deer park, close to St. Peter's church, whose seating plan formed the basis of Gough's remarkable local history.

history of the village itself. This preoccupation with the descent of manors and other considerable landed properties, and with the pedigrees of landed families and their heraldry, has also bedevilled much local history published by antiquarian and archaeological societies all over England. The dead hand of the seventeenth-century squire still guided, until recently, the hand of the living antiquary.

An even more fundamental criticism may be levelled against local history as it is often written today: that it is preoccupied with facts and correspondingly unaware of problems. With very few exceptions, local histories are written by antiquarians and not historians.

Local historians have not yet succeeded in emancipating themselves completely from the tradition of the great antiquaries of the past. Valuable as their monumental works were, and are, they remain enormous collections of facts, the raw materials for history and not history itself. Many local historians go on writing in this tradition, without perceiving the fundamental questions which they should be engaged in answering. All the facts about the past life of their village or parish have for them an equal value; and their histories therefore become a series of chapters without any unifying central theme, and each chapter an assembly of more or less unrelated facts, without any of the narrative to which the writing of national history lends itself.

One must except from this criticism some admirable town histories, notably Sir Francis Hill's four volumes on Lincoln (Cambridge University Press, 1956, 1965–66, 1974). One has only to read the bibliographies, reviews and 'research in progress' in the *Urban History Yearbook*, already mentioned, to see the immense amount of scholarly work now being done on town histories. Much of this impetus has come from Professor H. J. Dyos of the University of Leicester, whose book, *Victorian Suburb: Camberwell* (Leicester University Press, 1961) was a landmark in urban studies in this country. In what may be called non-urban history, too, there has recently been an enormous advance in standards among what one still likes to think of as amateurs, even as antiquarians.

The wide gulf between the antiquary and the historian has been narrowed in recent years. It will never be closed, but it is perhaps not desirable that it should be. The purely antiquarian study of a particular parish or district may make delightful reading. It is a type of English writing that has long traditions behind it, and no one would wish to see it perish entirely, for all its faults. But it cannot be regarded as local history.

2.3 Lincoln

The magnificent cathedral that towers over the ancient city is one of eastern England's most famous landmarks. It stands high on a limestone ridge, facing the Norman castle, on a site that had already been occupied for several hundred years. Its western facade is a late-eleventh century creation, but the rest of the Norman building had to be taken down after a severe earth tremor in 1185. A hundred years or more of rebuilding produced one of the finest cathedrals in England. The central tower was crowned by Europe's loftiest spire, which fell in a violent storm in 1548; the spires on the western towers were taken down in 1807.

Lincoln's place-name is derived from the Celtic word *lindo*, a pool or lake, undoubtedly the Bayford Pool at the bottom of the hill 200 feet below the cathedral. Visible remains of the Roman *Lindum Colonia* include the Newport Arch, which still takes traffic out of the town. After the withdrawal of the Romans, Lincoln became in turn the capital of Lindsey, one of the five boroughs of the Danelaw, a shire capital and a Norman cathedral city. Its history is traced through to Victorian times in Sir Francis Hill's four volumes.

3 THE OLD COMMUNITY

There is no necessity for local historians to start their studies of places at the beginning, especially as this usually involves wrestling with the relevant entry in Domesday Book which is by no means an easy document to understand. Further, it means that one then goes on immediately into the obscure and difficult period of the medieval centuries. One may become bogged down in more or less unrelated detail and discouraged in the early stages. There is a great deal to be said for studying the history of a place backwards, that is, beginning with the most recent period. I need hardly say that one would not write the finished history in this way.

In one of his books Eric Gill says:

> The men and women of the nineteenth century witnessed the destruction of a world, a material world as old as man himself. Up to the nineteenth century . . . men had depended on their own exertions to win a living from the earth. . . . This world, a world dependent upon human muscular power, the muscular power of draught animals, was a product of many thousands of years of development. It was not a primitive world, it was not an uncivilised world, above all it was not an uncultured world. All the primary needs of humanity, material and spiritual, were met and met adequately . . . it was a hand-made world throughout, a slow world, a world without power, a world in which all things were made one by one.

It is this largely self-contained world, in which local communities were still mainly self-sufficient, that the local historian might well begin by reconstructing.

In other words, he should concern himself with recreating a community which in most places has largely disintegrated. This is not true, of course, of big towns, nor of villages in 'the commuter belt' around the urban centres, but it is largely true of the majority of country towns and villages throughout England. There is a simple test of the truth of this statement: if one looks at the census figures for 1851 and those for 1951 one will generally find—away from the neighbourhood of large towns—that the population of most country towns and parishes has fallen during the century, sometimes by as much as half. At the best they may be stagnating.

In this old community, which takes us back perhaps a hundred years, there was a sense of place, of belonging somewhere. There was also a much greater sense of the family as an institution. 'For a family to maintain itself,' says Lewis Mumford, 'it must have a permanent headquarters, a permanent gathering place.' This is what most families still had in England up to the early nineteenth century, and it is this kind of world that the local historian might well seek to re-create as a start.

LOCAL DIRECTORIES

I shall suppose that he or she is concerned with the village, the parish, or the small town, that is, an area of manageable size. In order to obtain the first picture of such a chosen place, one should go to the old directories of the nineteenth century and the early twentieth. Most local libraries will contain a set of these directories. One should also consult J. E. Norton, *Guide to National and Provincial Directories of England and Wales, excluding London, published before 1856*, which was published by the Royal Historical Society in 1950. These directories generally give a useful introductory note about the size and site of the place, followed by a list of the principal inhabitants and tradesmen and craftsmen. So we get a partial picture at least of the social and occupational structure of the place throughout the second half of the nineteenth century and the first half of the twentieth. Some of the most valuable directories of this kind are those published by William White, beginning with Yorkshire in 1831, Nottinghamshire in 1832, Sheffield in 1833, and so on. There will not be anything like an annual series of directories for most places, but this is not necessary for the local historian's purposes. Thus in Devon we have White's Directories for 1850, 1878, and 1890, after which Kelly's Directories took over, the last of these being issued in 1939. From these directories one not only gets a static picture of a place in certain years, but it is also possible to draw some preliminary conclusions about the way the place has changed in the last hundred years or so: for example, whether its population has declined or risen, or remained more or less stagnant, and whether certain old trades and crafts have died out and when. Directories, then, give us a good start for reconstructing the kind of community which existed over a period of about a hundred years from the 1830s to the 1930s. But it is only a start. In chapter 11 I show how small a sample the earlier directories at least give of the total population, even in truly rural parishes.

CENSUS SCHEDULES

The directories do not give anything like a complete list of the inhabitants of a place. To obtain this one must go to the Public Record Office in London, where are preserved the original census schedules from 1841 to 1881. These are the enumerators' books, compiled as they went from house to house. They list every household, the head of the household and the names of all the others, their relationship to him, their ages, and their occupations. In the 1841 census ages over fifteen were rounded down to the nearest five years, but from 1851 onwards the ages were supposed to be exact and the place of birth was also recorded. Here then we have a complete record of the inhabitants of a place a hundred or more years ago and of all their occupations, and one could almost write a chapter on the conclusions to be drawn from the census schedules and the directory. If one is unable to visit the Public Record Office in person, a letter stating the name of the parish and the county one is interested in will produce an estimate for photographing one or other of these schedules, so that the historian can work upon the photographic copy at home. In recent years many record offices and libraries have acquired microfilms of census schedules, and the local historian ought to check whether these are available locally. The South Yorkshire County Record Office, for instance, has complete microfilm coverage of the 1841 to 1881 census returns for its area, and Derbyshire county library performs a similar service for its county. The microfilming of central records is a great boon to students of local history.

CENSUS REPORTS

One should obtain from the printed census reports the population figures for the parish or town for every census from 1801, when these figures begin.* The trend of population exposed by these ten-yearly figures may well reveal to the local historian one of the basic problems he should be concerned with for that period. If, for example, he finds that the population of his chosen place has halved since 1851 he must seek to find out what has happened to bring about this dramatic fall in population and then to trace the consequences of this fall.

These three classes of record alone will give the local historian a great deal to go on with. In considering the 1851 census schedule, for example, he might well work out how many of the families who were living in the place in that year are still living there today. He might also work out how many of the heads of families in 1851 were born in that parish or in an adjoining parish. This is not just an antiquarian detail, but may be a fact of considerable sociological significance. A village in which the great majority of people have been born and have married within the parish will be an infinitely more closely knit society, and much more difficult to disintegrate, than a place in which the majority of people have come in from some distance away. In other words, the proportion of people born in the place in which they are living is a measure of the strength of the social cement that holds the community together. One might also study, though this is rather more tedious, the interrelationships of village families with the aid of these records and of the parish registers. Some communities are much more strongly interrelated than others. I remember a Leicestershire woman some forty years ago telling me that when she got married she immediately became related to every other family in the village. This close interrelationship has its personal disadvantages, but it is certainly also a powerful cement which binds together the local society.

To pursue the same theme, though it takes us well back before the nineteenth century, one ought also to study the longevity of families in a parish—how many families last for a hundred years, two hundred years, three hundred years, and so on, and what is the rate at which families tend to disappear? One could do this with the aid of the parish registers of baptisms, marriages, and burials, and

---

* Here the local historian will find useful *A Comparative Account of the Population of Great Britain in the Years 1801, 1811, 1821, 1831*, published as a parliamentary paper in 1831.

of the fuller taxation returns, and of certain manorial records where they exist. It is a popular delusion that families in the past tended to stay rooted in the same spot for centuries on end. A few did, especially if they were small freeholders, but the majority of families seem to have moved about from century to century to a much greater degree than we generally believe. They did not move far, mostly within a radius of ten miles perhaps, but they rarely lasted more than a hundred years in one place. It is not always easy to trace the movements of these lesser families who have no records of their own, but I have given some suggestions about the kind of records one should use for this purpose in Chapter 11, on The Homes of Family Names.

OLD NEWSPAPERS

Another valuable source for the reconstruction of the old community is that provided by newspapers. These are obviously more likely to exist in the larger towns, but sometimes quite small places possessed their own newspapers in the early nineteenth century and these should be sought out as an invaluable mine of local material. Many people will know *News of a Country Town*, compiled by James Townsend and published in 1914. This gives a picture of a little Berkshire town (Abingdon) drawn from Jackson's *Oxford Journal* over the period 1753–1835. It should be said that there is a great deal more to be got from local newspapers than would appear even in this excellent little book. The advertisements, above all, are particularly valuable for a detailed picture of the life of a small town during the period covered by the newspaper. In general the very early newspapers devoted themselves to news of national importance and rarely gave local news except in the form of a few advertisements.

3.1 Northampton, All Saints Church

The old town was destroyed by fire in 1675, but by Defoe's time it was 'finely rebuilt with brick and stone, and the streets made spacious and wide'. Defoe thought the public buildings, especially All Saints Church (seen here in an early photograph) and the Sessions House, were 'the finest in any country town in England'. Northampton was an elegant county capital with large town-houses for gentry and professional families in the main streets and on the outskirts. It was a great thoroughfare town, where major roads from the north and the west converged on London, and it held the most famous horse fairs in England. It's inns, especially the George, the Peacock and the Red Lion, were large and commodious, the centres of local commercial, social and public life.

The *Northampton Mercury* was founded by William Dicey in 1720 and sold throughout the midlands, as far south as St Albans, north as far as Sheffield, west as far as Worcester and east as far as Cambridge. Its advertisement pages are a mine of information for local historians.

In my experience, purely local news begins to appear in the newspapers in the closing years of the eighteenth century and not much before, though there may be local advertisements from a much earlier period.

For catalogues or lists of early newspapers one should consult *The Times Handlist of English and Welsh Newspapers 1620–1920*. Other sources for tracing old newspapers are referred to in the select bibliography at the end of this book. Local newspapers will be found preserved in various places. For example, there is a complete set of the *Northampton Mercury*, one of the oldest newspapers in England, in the public library at Northampton, running from 1720 to the present day. Where these early newspapers still survive today, the offices of the newspaper may have more or less complete files in its possession. The British Library also possesses a vast number of files of local newspapers for the whole of England. The pre-nineteenth-century collection is available in the Reading Room, and the nineteenth- and twentieth-century collection is preserved at Colindale, near Hendon. The Bodleian Library at Oxford also has a considerable collection of English newspapers for the period 1622–1800.

Newspapers are of the greatest value for a variety of local history. One cannot write the political and parliamentary history of a town without using systematically the files of the local newspapers. A first-class example of this kind of history is *Radical Leicester* by A. Temple Patterson (Simpkin Marshall, 1954), which was based to a very considerable extent on the close reading of four sets of local newspapers. Another excellent example is Robert Newton's *Victorian Exeter* (Leicester University Press, 1968), which covers the period 1837 to 1914. The extensive bibliography of this book shows the wide range of sources, in addition to local newspapers, which are available to students writing a town history over a limited period.

Newspapers are also invaluable for the study of the topography of towns, the development of new streets, and of important new buildings. We learn the names of the men who built the new Georgian terraces and crescents, for example, and the way in which the town came to look as it does. For towns which were ports we frequently have weekly sailing lists giving the names of the ships, their destinations or ports of origin, and their principal cargoes. We also learn a great deal about the social and cultural history of a town from the columns of the newspapers, and about the administration of the poor law or the vicissitudes of public health. There is hardly any limit to the value of newspapers as a source for the local historian. The chief danger is that he will be side-tracked into reading a great deal of interesting material which is not really relevant to his immediate purpose.*

REMINISCENCES

Nor must one overlook the reminiscences of old people, either printed or verbal, in the reconstruction of the former local society. These reminiscences obviously require checking at every possible point. People's memories, and especially the memories of old people, are notoriously faulty. But such evidence of past history is not to be dismissed altogether merely because it is difficult to check its complete authenticity. A well-informed, elderly professional man can often give one a view of the inner social history and business history of the town which one would never get from any printed or written records. Provided that oral testimony is treated as rigorously as written evidence it can make a real contribution to the study of neglected aspects of local history. The books of George Ewart Evans show what can be done in rural communities, and those who pursue this special approach now have their own journal, *Oral History*.

LOCAL RECORDS: PRINTED AND MANUSCRIPT

In a town of any size, there is likely to be a considerable mass of both printed and manuscript material relating to various aspects of borough affairs. One should find a complete series of the annual borough accounts from 1836 onwards and the annual reports of the medical officer. At Leicester this latter series is complete from 1855. It is invaluable for the study of the physical growth of the town, and of its public health, and of the incidence of epidemics, etc. It is impossible to discuss here the full range of printed materials available for research during the nineteenth century, but the historian who is working in this field may ascertain from the borough librarian what is available in his own locality.

There will, of course, be a great range of manuscript records in the nineteenth century for both towns and country parishes. The

* For the range of subjects covered by a typical local newspaper, see Chapter 12 also.

records available for a town cannot be described in detail here, but the local librarian or local archivist, as the case may be, will be able to say what is available in any given place. In many rural parishes it is possible that not much manuscript material will be available. When I wrote the history of a Leicestershire village, as *The Midland Peasant* (Macmillan, 1957), I made the surprising discovery that there was almost no surviving manuscript material for the nineteenth century, anywhere in the parish, until the year 1894, when the urban district council was set up. With the breakdown of parish government in the early nineteenth century it seems that most of the work of administration was carried on by a few ill-paid part-time officers, if one can call them that, who when they left office carried away their meagre records with them. At Wigston Magna, therefore, I found the nineteenth century was the leanest century since the fifteenth for manuscript records, for this and other reasons. Other local historians may have this unfortunate experience. Most of what survives should be in the parish chest and the parson will know where this is to be found. There should, of course, be church-wardens' accounts, the accounts and other records of overseers of the poor, perhaps vestry minutes, and other miscellaneous documents.* Many parishes have now transferred their records to the greater safety of their county record offices, where they have been listed and made much more accessible. Every county in England has now set up a record office, and many have published full guides to their contents. These cover infinitely more than parish records, as an inspection of a good guide will soon show. Kent has also published a series of inexpensive books on a variety of subjects based on its own record sources. The publications of the Essex Record Office have long been a byword of enterprise along these lines: but one must not become too invidious in these matters. A list of *Record Repositories in Great Britain* has been published (HMSO, 1968), giving addresses, hours of opening and other basic information.

PARLIAMENTARY PAPERS

Parliamentary Papers are a valuable source of information for the local historian. The bigger the place he is interested in, the more

* The indispensable guide to parish records in the nineteenth century, as well as for earlier periods, is W. E. Tate, *The Parish Chest* (Cambridge University Press, 1946; new edition 1969).

is he likely to find in this source; but in certain reports there may be much purely parochial material, above all in the minutes of evidence that are usually printed as appendices to the reports. Thus the Report of the Special Assistant Poor Law Commissioners on the Employment of Women and Children in Agriculture (1843) contains a great number of what would be called today 'case studies' relating to various parishes in south-western England, eastern and south-eastern England, Yorkshire, and Northumberland. Reports on emigration, education, public health, housing, agriculture, and the working of the poor law, should all be examined, and, of course, reports upon any purely local industries or social problems. It is impossible to list all the headings under which a search should be made for relevant material: the local historian must be guided by the general history of his own area.

The Parliamentary Papers cover an enormous range of subjects and it is not always easy to track down material for a particular place. The preliminary and indispensable guide for such a search is the *Select List of British Parliamentary Papers 1833–1899*, compiled by Professor and Mrs Percy Ford (Blackwell, 1953). The earlier period is covered by *Hansard's Catalogue and Breviate of Parliamentary Papers, 1696–1834* (Blackwell, 1953). Before embarking upon this vast field of exploration, the reader who is unaccustomed to their use might well study *A Guide to Parliamentary Papers: What they are: How to find them: How to use them* (Blackwell, 1955) by the same writers. Other useful guides include M. F. Bond, *Guide to the Records of Parliament* (HMSO, 1971) and W. R. Powell, *Local History from Blue Books* (Historical Assoc., 1962). Reprinting by the Irish Universities Press has made parliamentary papers much more available.

MAPS

Old maps are a most valuable source for the local historian, especially in towns where changes have been relatively rapid. It may be difficult to find a parish map before the first edition of the 6-inch sheets of the Ordnance Survey. As regards maps or plans of towns, the local library should possess a complete set of whatever has been published. The historian of a town might well make a composite map for himself from a number of old maps showing the topographical growth of the town during, for example, the nineteenth century and the early twentieth.* The 6-inch and 25-inch maps of the Ordnance Survey will be familiar to all students of local history. It is advisable to use the first edition of these maps since they often give information that has since been obscured or has perished.

There is one town plan, however, which seems to be almost unknown to local historians and is of the greatest value as a document. A great number of English towns, even comparatively small ones, were surveyed on the very large scale of 1/500. Some early plans were done on a scale of 1/1056 and 1/528, but from 1855 onwards the scale of 1/500 was settled on. These maps, which were published between 1855 and 1895, show an immense amount of detail, down to every lamp-post and every pillar-box, even paths in people's gardens, and one could almost write an essay on the town at a given date from this plan alone. A great number of now vanished features are shown, such as cab stands, horse-tram tracks, numerous public houses and inns, and so forth. For those who are particularly interested in the minutiae of topographical research in a town, the 1/500 plan is essential. The towns covered by these large-scale plans are given in the *Historian's Guide to Ordnance Survey Maps*, already mentioned, on pp. 29-30. Let me say again that this booklet is quite indispensable to the local historian, both in town and country.

For some towns there may be a tithe map in existence which will give a picture of the town as it was in the 1840s. There are also, of course, some thousands of tithe maps for rural parishes made at about the same period. The Tithe Commutation Act was passed in 1836 and resulted in the first accurate survey we have for thousands of parishes, in order to achieve the commutation of tithe in kind into money charges on land.

The tithe map, where it exists, gives the names of all owners and occupiers of land in a parish. It gives the names of the farms and of every field and piece of land contained in them, the acreage of every separate piece of land, and the use to which it is put. This is the most complete picture of a parish since Domesday Book and is infinitely more detailed than that record. There should be three copies of every tithe map and award: one copy should be in the possesssion of the parish (probably in the vestry or parsonage),

---

* For an example of what can be done in this respect, see the maps showing the physical expansion of Leicester in *V. C. H. Leicestershire*, vol. iv, pp. 196, 252, 261, 275, 292.

another copy in the diocesan records,* and a third copy in the central records. The Tithe Redemption Office, formerly in Finsbury Square, E.C.4, and now transferred to Worthing, Sussex, possesses a copy of all the tithe maps and awards that were ever made and should be resorted to if the local maps cannot be found. For most people, however, it would be easier to use the parish copy or the diocesan copy.

Not all parishes possess a tithe map and award. There may be a complete set for a particular county, or you may find that in your county only about one-third of the parishes appear to have been surveyed in this way (for example, Leicestershire). The coverage in Cornwall, Devon, Kent and Shropshire is practically 100 per cent, but in Northamptonshire it is less than one-quarter. The reason for this is that in those counties where the parliamentary enclosure movement was prominent the opportunity was taken at the enclosure of the open fields to extinguish the great and small tithes at the same time. Tithes in kind were converted into an equivalent allotment of land. In such parishes, therefore, the Tithe Commutation Act of 1836 would not apply and therefore there is no map and no award. The enclosure map and award usually belong to an earlier period, generally speaking between about 1750 and 1820, though some enclosure awards are earlier and some are later than this. These are considered more fully in the next chapter.

LAND TAX ASSESSMENTS

Another fruitful class of records which enable us to construct our picture of the parish as it was, are the land tax assessments. These will be found among the county records. Although the land tax was established in its present form by the act of 1692, detailed parochial assessments are rarely found before 1773. Most counties possess a complete series of such annual assessments from 1780 to 1832.† They usually give the owners and occupiers of all the land in the parish, with the names of farms where these are scattered about the parish, and the amount of tax chargeable on each farm or holding,

* Most of the parish and diocesan copies have now been transferred to county record offices, where they are much easier to use.

† Some county record offices possess a few earlier assessments and some have gathered in many of a later date from solicitors' offices. Thus Devon now possesses a fairly complete coverage down to 1939, though the more recent ones may not be available for public search.

house or cottage. One cannot use these assessments in order to arrive at the acreages of land owned or occupied by particular people any more than one can use the poor-rate or church-rate assessments for this purpose. Nevertheless, the land tax assessments give essential information about the distribution of land in the parish in the last generation of the eighteenth century and the first generation of the nineteenth. By relating the assessment for 1832 with the house-holders listed in the census schedule for 1841, one can also arrive at some idea of the number of families in the parish who neither owned nor occupied any land. It is true that these two dates do not exactly coincide, but they are the nearest one can get for the purpose of this particular information.

ILLUSTRATIONS

The local historian in town or village should obviously collect or at least have access to all old photographs, drawings, or engravings of his chosen place. These will often reveal information which is not otherwise recorded. The local library of the town, or the county library, will probably possess collections of illustrations and these should be consulted. Many old photographs and drawings may still be in the possession of private persons. Even old picture-post-cards have become a valuable record of village scenes or town-streets which have long since disappeared. It is regrettable that so much material of this kind seems to have perished completely. This is particularly true of old towns in which ancient streets were swept away in slum clearance orders in the 1930s without any record being made, other than occasional picture-postcards which are no longer in print.

Miss Joan Wake, in her admirable guide *How to Compile the History and Present Day Record of Village Life* (Northampton, 1935), makes the point also that old photographs are bound to fade and in the end to become valueless. They should, therefore, be rephoto-graphed before it is too late, and carbon prints made.

For most counties, too, there are important collections of draw-ings in the British Library, notably the Buckler drawings.* These often show buildings and street scenes, many of which have since disappeared. The local historian should therefore consult the

* There are important collections of Buckler drawings in various places, such as the Bodleian Library at Oxford, in the Hertfordshire County Record Office, at Taunton Castle, and elsewhere.

3.2 Wednesfield Road, Heath Town, Staffordshire

Old picture-postcards are now collected avidly and special Postcard Fairs attract enthusiastic crowds. Collections of old photographs with suitable captions make a popular contribution to local history, for the changes that have occurred over the last two generations have been greater than in any previous period. The first twenty years of the present century was the most productive time for the picture-postcard industry, and many everyday scenes were recorded. Picture-postcards were by no means confined to pretty rural villages, as this example from the Black Country shows. Heath Town originated as an eighteenth-century squatter settlement for metal-workers, but by the time this photograph was taken a few years before the First World War it had become part of the conurbation that linked Wolverhampton to Walsall, Dudley, West Bromwich and Birmingham.

Department of Prints and Drawings at the British Library to see whether it possesses any drawings (or maps) relating to his own place. M. W. Barley, *A Guide to British Topographical Collections* (Council for British Archaeology, 1974) gives a brief description of drawings, prints and photographs that have been collected in national and local repositories, and ought to be consulted.

A little-known but valuable collection of drawings, plans, and notes for nearly every county in England exists in the public library at Northampton. This is the Dryden Collection, of which a catalogue was issued in 1912. The Dryden Collection covers every county in England, some counties much more fully than others. Thus for Cornwall there are only thirteen parishes for which Sir Henry Dryden left material, and the material itself varies considerably in usefulness today. The collection is naturally very full for Northamptonshire and the counties adjoining it, but the catalogue should be consulted by local historians in whatever part of the country they may be working. Another magnificent special collection of photographs, prints, and drawings is that housed in the National Maritime Museum at Greenwich. This is of particular interest to local historians concerned with old ports and, above all, perhaps, with shipbuilding, and it is essential for such historians to consult this collection in some way, either by a personal visit or by correspondence.

DIARIES, LETTERS, AND ACCOUNT BOOKS

The value of old diaries and letters for the nineteenth-century historian cannot be over-estimated, though the deficiencies of such material from the historical point of view will be obvious enough. They represent a record made at the time and, being unofficial, they probably reflect more of the truth of the event than an official and edited version is likely to do. On the other hand, the diarist or letter writer is likely to be giving a highly subjective impression of an event or a person and such a record should be treated with the proper caution and reservations. There are a great number of diaries deposited in the British Library. It is always possible that the local historian will make what amounts to a brilliant and original discovery of a local diary which no one has hitherto thought of looking at. Such was Dr A. L. Rowse's discovery of the diary of William Carnsew, a Cornish gentleman, for 1576–77, which he used with great effect in his book *Tudor Cornwall*. Another was *The Diary of James Clegg* (an eighteenth-century dissenting minister and doctor in the Peak District), which Dr Vanessa Doe has edited in three volumes for the Derbyshire Record Society (1978–81). There must also be a vast number of diaries lying around in private houses which might well be tracked down by an assiduous searcher. They would throw much light upon town, and village, and parish life in the nineteenth century. Parsons' diaries are particularly valuable in this respect and occasionally one finds good diaries kept by farmers, such as that of Cornelius Stovin, a Lincolnshire Wold farmer in the early 1870s.* Old account books give one a vast amount of information about the prices, materials, and housekeeping of past generations. Much valuable material of this kind still lies unknown or disregarded in private houses.

---

* See J. Thirsk, *English Peasant Farming* (Routledge, 1957), pp. 323–33.

3.3 Chinley Chapel, Derbyshire

'Our new place was finished in the year 1711 and at first multitudes flocked to it and I hope some good was done', wrote James Clegg (1679–1755), the Dissenting minister and medical practitioner. The chapel served the scattered farms and hamlets around Chapel en le Frith, high in the Peak District, in what Daniel Defoe called 'the most desolate, wild, and abandoned country in all England'. Despite these difficulties Clegg spent a lifetime travelling on horseback throughout Derbyshire in pursuit of his spiritual and medical duties. His diary provides vivid insights into many aspects of country life two-and-a-half centuries ago.

AUCTIONEERS' CATALOGUES AND SALES NOTICES

The catalogues of sales of land, with maps and plans, which have been issued by auctioneers for the last hundred and fifty years would, if they had been systematically collected, have formed a mass of useful material for the agrarian historian of the period since 1800. A few libraries and record offices possess collections of such records but it is rare to find anything like completeness. Such records are particularly valuable for the period in which great estates were being broken up and sold off. This was going on all through the nineteenth century as well as in our own time, and the parish historian will be fortunate if he can find an auctioneer's catalogue and maps for the break-up of some large estate in his own territory in Victorian days. Many record offices and public libraries are now making a collection of all such catalogues and sales notices. So much of this material has been destroyed in the past as ephemeral but it has now become of considerable historical interest.

As an example of how valuable and comprehensive such business records may be, the Devon county record office recently acquired several hundred files from an old-established auctioneer's business, covering the period 1880 to 1925. These relate to a very wide range of farms and house property in north-east Devon. The records include inventories of household goods, of factory stock, of farm goods and stock, and also detailed surveyors' notes on hundreds of farms, field by field. One need hardly stress the importance of such a collection for many kinds of historian.

4 PARISH, MANOR, AND LAND

SOME DIFFICULTIES OF DOMESDAY

For the great majority of places the first documentary record will be Domesday Book (1086). If we are fortunate, we may possess a Saxon land charter which tells us something about our chosen territory several generations before the Norman Conquest. If we are particularly unfortunate we may not have even a reference to our chosen place in Domesday Book. Local historians in these counties will already know that the great survey excludes Northumberland, Durham, Cumberland, and northern Westmorland. Here our first record of a particular place may not appear until the twelfth or thirteenth century; but this is not to say that it did not exist before that time. In other parts of England covered by Domesday Book we may still find that our particular town or parish is not mentioned by name. This may be because it did not exist in the late eleventh century. Many English towns were not founded until the great age of borough creation in the twelfth and thirteenth centuries, and there are not a few villages also which did not exist until this period. There is, however, another possibility which the local historian should bear in mind, and that is that his village or parish is silently included in the Domesday entry under another heading. We find a great number of the large manors in Domesday Book which must include, and often are known to include, a considerable tract of the surrounding countryside with all the villages, hamlets, and farms dotted about it. The vast episcopal manor of Taunton in Somerset is a case in point. So, too, is the episcopal manor of Crediton in Devon, and there are similar examples all over England. Sometimes we can be quite certain that a particular village about which Domesday Book is silent was already in existence because it is referred to in a document of the Anglo-Saxon period, or because it has an archaic place-name which could have come into existence only at a very early date.

Domesday Book is the most remarkable document of the eleventh century in Europe. It makes a wonderful starting-point for the recorded history of most English towns and villages, but it is full of pitfalls and difficulties despite the apparent clarity of its language. That is why I have suggested in an earlier chapter that most local historians would be well advised not to begin their study of their chosen place by copying out the relevant entry or entries from Domesday Book, but to begin by studying the recent past.

There comes a point, however, when the local historian has to face the intricacies of this great record and to make up his mind what the entry means in relation to his own piece of territory. It is impossible in this book to discuss all the difficult questions that arise from the close study of this survey, even if one knew the answers to all these questions. The anxious reader will find Mr Pugh's pages on the subject of Domesday Book a clear and valuable introduction. He refers the enquirer for further enlightenment to the classic book of F. W. Maitland, *Domesday Book and Beyond* (1897), but in my experience most local historians find this great work too difficult to understand; or rather they generally find it does not appear to answer the questions which they are putting to it. I would prefer to direct the local historian in the first instance to Ballard's *The Domesday Inquest* (1906). This book, with all its faults, is more readily intelligible to the majority of local historians and provides more direct guidance.

It is quite true that simple answers to difficult questions, especially questions about the meaning of Domesday Book, are likely to be misleading. There are so many questions arising from this record that seem to be simple to the local historian who is asking them but can only be answered with a number of qualifications and in the light of the special local circumstances. But however much the professional historian may deplore anyone trying to give simple answers to difficult questions, the fact is one cannot leave the local historian completely in the dark. One must make some attempt to guide him through the first stages, provided he realises that in a great number of instances the answer he is getting is only the first approximation to the truth and that his own prolonged enquiries may throw more light on an obscure subject before he has finished.

Each region in England has its own difficulties of interpretation, and the local historian must bear this in mind wherever he may be.

In the south-west of England, for example, we not only have the general difficulty that Domesday Book does not refer to a number of villages and hamlets which we know existed generations earlier, but we face the special difficulty that a great part of the south-western landscape has never been settled with villages as we know them in the Midlands. It was settled with isolated farmsteads and hamlets from the beginning. Just as the great episcopal or royal manor may silently include, under the heading of the principal manor, a number of other villages, so in Devon and Cornwall, and possibly in west Somerset and west Dorset also, a comparatively small manor may, and probably does, silently include a number of single farmsteads. These farmsteads may not appear separately by name until the public records begin to grow in volume round about the middle of the thirteenth century, but there is good reason for believing that they already existed at the time of Domesday and for several generations before that.

A specific example will help to make this point clear. In the hilly country to the west of the middle Exe valley in Devon, where there are very few villages but hundreds of scattered farms, we find a manor in 1086 called *Bovelia*. This can be identified beyond question with a farmstead called Great Bowley which still exists as a separate farm. We are told that on this manor William de Poillei 'has in demesne one virgate and one plough and the villani have one virgate and one plough. There William has four *villani* and three slaves'. The entry goes on to give some other information which does not concern our immediate purpose. The questions we have to ask ourselves about this entry are: what kind of settlement have we to envisage at Bowley in 1086? Was it a hamlet with the villein farms clustered together in one group? If so, why and when did the hamlet disintegrate so that all we have left today is a single farm?

There is no doubt in my mind that the Great Bowley of today represents the demesne farm of William de Poillei worked by the three slaves who are recorded on the manor, and that the four *villani* were farming separate farms in the adjacent countryside. This theory is simpler than one which supposes there was once a hamlet which for some unknown reason distintegrated; and it is to my mind strongly supported by the fact that all around Great Bowley we have farms called West Bowley, Middle Bowley, East Bowley, and Little Bowley. Middle Bowley has in fact disappeared from the landscape, but it is shown on the tithe map of the parish of Cadbury in 1842.

All these other Bowleys are recorded in various ways back to medieval times, and there can be little or no doubt that they represent in fact the four villein farms of the eleventh century. We obviously have here a piece of countryside with the general name of Bowley, meaning 'the curved *leah* or clearing in a wood'. The tithe award shows that this property covered about 420 acres in all, Great Bowley being by far the largest farm of the group, as we should expect. It looks from the tithe award as though the lesser Bowleys, which I have identified with the villein farms, were in the region of fifty acres each. The four villein farms covered rather more than two hundred acres between them, and the demesne farm of Great Bowley slightly less than two hundred acres. This agrees remarkably well with the assessments recorded in the Domesday entry, where the demesne farm was assessed at one virgate and the villein farms at one virgate together.

I have given this example at some length because I am convinced that this is the general picture we must look for in many hundreds of Domesday entries for small manors in the south-west of England; and I give it also to show how one can use much later record material in order to throw light upon the precise meaning of the Domesday entry. Such a method of approach has its obvious dangers. We must use it with caution and make quite clear what is fact and what is opinion in building up our theory. I have elaborated the whole argument in an essay entitled 'The Highland Zone in Domesday Book', published in *Provincial England* (Macmillan, 1963). The Domesday survey for eastern England presents yet another set of topographical problems which I would not venture to comment upon. Only those familiar with the detailed topography of the present landscape are competent to elucidate the Domesday entries for this part of England.* Here the local historian is helped in a general way by H. C. Darby's five volumes on Domesday geography (Cambridge University Press, 1952–67). These volumes are valuable not only for the history they contain but also because they place Domesday Book firmly in its geographical setting, and at this period especially the geography of a place is absolutely essential to the understanding of its history. Even so they leave many topographical and other problems unsolved.

---

* See, for example, Miss F. G. Davenport's *The Economic Development of a Norfolk Manor, 1086–1565* (1906) for a discussion of the complicated Domesday material for the village of Forncett and a detailed comparison of this with a manorial survey of 1565. Local historians in Norfolk and Suffolk would do well to study Miss Davenport's book for guidance in this difficult field of enquiry.

SITE AND EARLY GROWTH

Supposing that one has arrived at certain conclusions about the nature and size of one's chosen place as recorded in 1086, one is then led to enquire at what point in pre-Conquest times the settlement came into existence and in what ways it had grown in the first unrecorded centuries of its history. Here we are on even more difficult ground, often without a single document to support us. Yet we must face the difficulties. It is absurd to begin one's history in 1066 or 1086 when the village may already have been in existence for three, four, or five centuries, as long a period of time, perhaps, as separates us from the Civil War or the Wars of the Roses. Even if we cannot give a single specific date for any event in this long period of time it is obviously essential to say something about it.

We must examine the one-inch geological map (if it is available in print) in order to see why our settlement began exactly where it did—in other words, its relationship to drinking water, to a dry soil for houses, to a reasonably fertile soil around for farming purposes, and its aspect in relation to the prevailing winds and rain of this country. The siting of compact villages in the Somerset Levels, still heavily flooded every winter, is beautifully brought out on the geological map (drift) where the settlements were founded in pre-Conquest times on the dry soils known as the Burtle Beds. These form small islands rising some 20 or 30 feet above the flood-plain (Fig. 4.1).

Even if there are no documents for the long period before 1086, there are certain types of evidence that may help us to say something about the earlier centuries. Over the greater part of the Lowland Zone of England we find a good deal of archaeological evidence from the Anglo-Saxon period. This consists in the main of cemeteries of the heathen period, producing grave-goods which can usually be dated to within a century or less. These, where they exist, are clear evidence of an occupation of that site (or somewhere very near it) within the preceding generation or so. In this way we can take the beginnings of many village histories in the Midlands and Eastern England back to the fifth, sixth, or seventh centuries. For this period the local historian would do well to consult the keeper of antiquities in his nearest museum, or some other competent archaeologist. Most counties now employ at least one archaeologist, who is responsible for compiling an up-to-date index of all known sites and finds in his area, as well as directing fieldwork and excavations.

4.1 Village-sites in the Somerset Levels

Often, too, the meaning of the place-name will throw some light on the history of a site. It may be an archaic place-name such as Naseby (Northamptonshire) which suggests a settlement on this site in the very early days of the Anglo-Saxon migration into this country; or it may be place-names like Harrow (Middlesex) or Weedon (various counties) which go back to the heathen period of the Anglo-Saxon conquest, and so give us an approximate date for the first settlement. At the other end of the time scale, a place which is called Newton in 1086 and which has only a handful of inhabitants at that date, may be assumed to have come into existence within the preceding generation or two, some time perhaps in the first half of the eleventh century.

There are various other clues and hints to be derived from the study of the meanings of place-names. These will often help the local historian to place the origins of his settlement within a century or two. Place-names of Danish or Norwegian origin can, of course, be dated fairly precisely, though one must beware even here of the

4.2 Wye, Kent

Wye is one of 40 to 50 place-names that go back to the earliest years of English settlement and which signify a heathen shrine. Such places either incorporate the Old English elements *wēoh*, *wih* or *hearg* or they are named after the heathen gods *Woden*, *Thunor* and *Tīw*. Harrow (North London) and Wednesbury (Staffordshire) have dramatic hill-top churches which may have been built on previous pagan sites. Wye was a centre of local importance from the earliest days of Jutish Kent, both as a parish and as the head of one of the country's original lathes. It ranked as a small market town in the Middle Ages, and was described by John Leland *c.* 1540 as 'a pratie market townelet' with a great fair on St Gregory's day, but it has since declined to village status.

possibility that an Old English village may have changed its name when a Danish overlord took over in the ninth or tenth century. We know this has happened in some cases—for example, Derby (a Scandinavian name) was formerly called Northworthy (an Old English name). Many other examples of this change of name are known and there must be hundreds of which we have no knowledge. All this may be rather disconcerting to the local historian but at least he should be aware of the pitfalls even in simple names. I say nothing of the other awful possibility that an Old English settlement may have had a Celtic place-name at an earlier period. A few examples of this kind are known. We know, for example, that the hamlet of Biddisham (Somerset), an Old English name, formerly had the British name of Tarnuc or Ternuc. A record of 1065 specifically refers to '*Biddesham quod Tarnuc proprie appellatur*'.

This introduces the very difficult problem of the continuity of a site from Romano-British times into the Anglo-Saxon period and hence down to the present day. Whether or not such a continuity can ever be proved satisfactorily remains to be seen. I have no doubt in my own mind that there must be many villages and hamlets in this country which have had a continuous existence since Romano-British times, but this difficult question still exercises the minds of national historians and is very far from being settled. The local historian will do well, unless he has the most striking evidence for continuity, to avoid speculating upon the subject. One does not wish to warn the local historian off this field entirely, because it will most likely be he, with the necessary detailed local knowledge, who will succeed in establishing such a continuity here and there. I myself think the village of Cassington in Oxfordshire presents great possibilities in this respect. But this is clearly not a field into which the local historian should venture unless he is singularly well equipped.*

One can also discover something about the antiquity of a given settlement from a study of the mother-churches in the district, combined in some cases with the inspection of the pattern which the boundaries of the ecclesiastical parishes make on the map. A mother-church almost invariably indicates a parental settlement, the oldest settlement in that particular neighbourhood, and the

---

* Local historians who are interested in this field of enquiry should read Dr H. P. R. Finberg's *Roman and Saxon Withington: a Study in Continuity* (Leicester University Press, 1955) in which a wide variety of different kinds of evidence is brilliantly marshalled and discussed. Christopher Taylor has discussed the same subject with considerable persuasiveness in his *Dorset* (1970), esp. pp. 72–5.

daughter-churches generally, if not invariably, represent settlements which have hived off from the parent settlement at a later date. If we can discover the existence of groups of mother- and daughter-churches we have gone some way towards working out the chronology of settlement in the district. Many of the early mother-churches were called *monasterium*, a word which comes down to us as the place-name ending of 'minster'. We may regard all places whose names end in 'minster' as the oldest settlements in their immediate district.

Occasionally, also, place-names embodying the element 'church', if they are so recorded in Domesday Book (or earlier), indicate the existence of an earlier minster. There were far more minsters in pre-Conquest times than are commemorated today in 'minster' place-names. It is likely, for instance, that the place-name Cheriton, which occurs in several counties and means 'church village', also indicates the existence of a mother-church and therefore a parental settlement. There are, however, many place-names which end in 'church' and not all of these must be taken to be mother-churches, even if they were churches in 1086. Churches were founded not only by missionaries going out from the central minster, but, in the late Saxon period especially, by private landowners, and many of these private churches, as we may call them, would not necessarily indicate a parental village. In some cases it can be shown that they are themselves daughter-settlements. Thus we find the place-name Honeychurch in mid-Devon, recorded in Domesday Book and telling us beyond any doubt that the church—'Huna's church'—existed in late Saxon times. It is perfectly clear, however, from a scrutiny of the ecclesiastical parish boundaries in this district that the tiny parish of Honeychurch was originally carved out of a corner of the great parent-parish of Sampford Courtenay. On the subject of minsters and private churches, the local historian will find two publications by Canon Addleshaw indispensable reading. They are *The Beginnings of the Parochial System* and *The Development of the Parochial System from Charlemagne (768–814) to Urban II (1088–99)*, both published by St. Anthony's Hall, York. All serious students of local history in the pre-Conquest and early Norman period should possess them as a matter of course.

Even without clues such as place-names embodying the element 'minster' or 'church', a careful reading of the map often enables us to recover the boundaries of large pre-Conquest estates which have subsequently been divided into a number of ecclesiastical parishes. When we succeed in reconstructing such a large estate for which

4.3 An ancient estate in North Oxfordshire, showing later division into ecclesiastical parishes

This group of parishes clearly fit together to form an original whole, centred upon Fritwell. Somerton, in the middle Cherwell valley, originated as a summer pasturage when the river meadows became usable. It was clearly the 'summer *tun*' of Fritwell, which then included Souldern also. It is significant that these three manors were all held together by Rainald Wadard in 1086 (though under two different overlords), suggesting again that they had constituted a single large estate in pre-Conquest times.

In 1086 Souldern had no district name, but is recorded as one of the two Fritwell manors. It was then very small in population (only five households, and a slave on the demesne). It was probably developed systematically during the first half of the twelfth century, for we first hear of it (in the cartulary of Eynsham abbey) under the name of Souldern between 1152 and 1161. Extensive Norman work in the parish church supports the belief that it became a separate parish with its own church about the middle of the twelfth century.

Here, then, is a good example of a conjunction of different kinds of evidence: the 1-inch map (1:50,000), Domesday Book and later documentary evidence, and the structural evidence of the parish church. Such examples can be worked out in hundreds of other cases all over England.

there may be no other evidence but that of the map, we are often in a position to decide which church in this large area is the mother-church, and hence which is the oldest village in the district. The evidence yielded by the map in this and other ways is just as valuable as the evidence obtainable from any other kind of document. The Ordnance Survey maps of England are in fact magnificent documents in themselves and we must learn to read them as such. They are difficult to read aright, not only because there are no rules to guide us in this particular study, but also because they are palimpsests; that is, documents which have been written upon over and over again. They contain written evidence of several different periods, unlike the great majority of documents which have been written on once and whose date may be precisely known; and the local historian's task is to disentangle, if he can, the various writings from each other.

THE MANOR

So far I have been speaking mainly about early estates and ecclesiastical parishes. There is another very important element in the local history of the countryside and that is the manor. The manorial organisation of England was superimposed at a comparatively late date upon a countryside originally divided into more or less large estates. We are fortunately not called upon here to enter into the difficult question of the origins of the manor. It appears more or less fully developed by the time of Domesday and the local historian from this date onwards will find that it bulks very large in his history for a number of centuries.

There is a great variety in the types and sizes of manors even in the eleventh century. They may or may not coincide with the boundaries of the ecclesiastical parish. In some parts of England there is a tendency for the manor and the parish to coincide; but in other parts one may find two, three, or more manors inside a single parish, often overlapping untidily into adjacent parishes. In thirteenth-century Oxfordshire the parish and the manor coincide in two cases out of three. In the counties of Warwickshire, Buckinghamshire, and Huntingdonshire, about one in every two coincide. But in the north of England, East Anglia, and the West, manor and parish very rarely coincided and the pattern is one of great complexity. Each local historian must unravel this complexity for himself and it is in fact one of the more fascinating problems of local topography. If the local historian is fortunate enough to possess

4.4 Athelhampton Hall, Dorset

Athelhampton is a small parish of only 480 acres, dominated by the fine hall of the Martyn family, half a mile east of Puddletown. Sir William Martyn, a Dorset man who became Lord Mayor of London in 1483, used the wealth he had gained from commerce and his post as Collector of Tonnage and Poundage in the city to build a house in creamy Portersham stone, an excellent oolitic limestone. His building was entered through a porch and screens passage, with a service range to the right and a great open hall to the left. The attractive oriel has an archway which presumably led to a parlour wing, which was later completely rebuilt by Robert Martyn, who owned the house from 1525 to 1550. Robert used golden Ham Hill stone for the dressings and lit his attics with gabled dormers. He also built a gatehouse and connecting walls which have since been demolished.

The timber roof of the great hall is basically that constructed for Sir William. The five principal trusses rise from corbels to sturdy collars and are strengthened by elaborate cusped braces that immediately catch the eye upon entry. All the woodwork is heavily moulded and the purlins are decorated with leaf bosses. The house was carefully restored in the 1890s; the linenfold panelling in the hall is not original.

An early sixteenth-century circular pigeon cote stands in the grounds to the rear of the hall. The Martyns also had a deer park of about 160 acres, of which part of the enclosing bank and ditch remains.

for his particular district a Saxon land charter, he may be able to show the precise relationship between this large pre-Conquest estate and the manor or manors recorded in the same area in Domesday Book, and further, to show its relationship to the ecclesiastical parish. One would like to know a great deal more about the way in which the manorial pattern was superimposed upon the existing landscape and property rights, and it is here that the local historian, with his special detailed knowledge, may again be able to make an important contribution to a difficult subject.

Many small manors recorded in Domesday Book disappear as such in later centuries. They become absorbed into a larger manor, probably through some accident of ownership, and other manors or 'reputed manors' may come into existence at a comparatively late date. These later 'manors' usually result from a common ownership over a number of scattered small estates. Thus Plympton Priory, in South Devon, had lands scattered over at least fourteen different parishes, and these lands came to be known as the 'manor of Plympton Grange' after the Dissolution. It was an entirely artificial grouping of lands but it remained almost intact in Crown hands until the early seventeenth century. Similar groupings are found on secular estates.

Having established what manors lay within his parish or chosen territory, the local historian then has the task of tracing the descent of the lordship of each. The records enabling him to do this are discussed by Mr Pugh in *How to Write a Parish History* (pp. 51–53). The reader who is anxious to pursue this particular subject is also referred to the parish histories in the *Victoria County History*, where the footnote references to the section on manorial history form the best possible guide to the material available.

In my own view (and it is a purely personal view) it is possible to spend too much time upon the minutiae of manorial history. It is true that no other country in western Europe has such a magnificent range of sources for this study, but there comes a point when one feels that the minor details, especially where manors become split up among a number of heirs, are not really significant for the history of the community, above all where these changes are taking place in the overlordship. Villagers must often have been completely unaware of changes at this level, which can have had no effect upon their lives. Such detailed manorial history is a nice exercise in historical scholarship and detection, but for the average parish history it can be as tedious and unrewarding as an unnecessarily detailed account of family relationships. The local historian would be well advised to confine his treatment of the history of the descent of the manor to those changes which can be shown to have had a direct impact upon the parish or the village. He may safely ignore many of the minor variations which he may come across in odd records. As the French historian Marc Bloch says: 'there is no waste more criminal than that of erudition running, as it were, in neutral gear, nor any pride more vainly misplaced than that in a tool valued as an end in itself'. He is not saying this specifically of English manorial history, but the cap often fits.

Apart from this warning there are one or two other remarks which it may be useful to make about the manor. Some local historians will be aware of these already; others may not. In the first place, the lordship of a manor did not necessarily involve the ownership of all the land within the manor. Indeed, it was rare for it to do so. The lord of the manor might own a considerable part of the land within the manorial jurisdiction which he could either farm himself (a home farm or demesne) or which he would let out to the customary tenants and/or leaseholders. But there might well be several hundred acres of land within his manor which belonged to other men who would be styled 'free tenants of the manor' and from these the lord might collect only a token rent of a few pence or a few shillings a year. Sometimes these free tenants might own more of the land between them than the lord himself. In manorial rentals and surveys the holdings of the free tenants are almost invariably dismissed in a cursory fashion, simply because the lord had no appreciable income from them or interest in them. The names of the free tenants are usually listed in such rentals or surveys together with the small nominal and fixed rent which they are called upon to pay. We are not told anything about the size of their tenements, and the chief rents, or high rents as they are often called, are no guide to the size of the holding in terms of acres. We have to discover, if we can, the size of these free tenements from other sources. If all else fails, we may have to turn to the tithe award of the 1840s to give us some idea of their size, though we must bear in mind that after so many centuries there may well have been changes in the original size of such tenements.

In villages where there were two or more manors, especially in the open-field part of England, there was a strong tendency for the village meeting to be the active governing body rather than the manor court. Where an open-field village was divided between a number of manors the individual manors did not have their own open-field systems. Their lands lay intermixed in the fields. This is

exactly what we should expect when we remember that the open fields, in origin, were very much older than the manorial framework that was superimposed on them. So in villages of this kind, which are common in the Midlands, we might well find strips lying side by side in various furlongs which appertained to different manors. In such cases the practical details of regulating the farming in the open fields could not possibly be laid down in two or three different manorial courts. The village had to manage its fields as a whole, as in fact it had always done before the manor had ever been heard of. Hence in these parts of England we often get interesting collections of village by-laws, governing every detail of the management of the fields, arable, meadow, pasture, and commons.

This subject has been exhaustively covered by the American historian W. O. Ault in *Open-Field Husbandry and the Village Community* (American Philosophical Society, Philadelphia, 1965). After a long and fascinating introduction he gives numerous examples of every kind of by-law from 1270 to 1608. There is also a splendid subject index to the by-laws. Our ancestors in the open fields had far more practical sense than they are often credited with by urban-minded historians.

CHURCH LANDS

A considerable proportion of all the land in England has belonged at some time to the church, either to the monasteries or to bishops and cathedral chapters, or to the parish clergy, or to a number of other religious foundations. The grants of land made to a particular ecclesiastical foundation were often copied for reasons of safety and convenience into registers called cartularies. A great number of

4.5 Fountains Abbey

In 1132 thirteen Benedictine monks from St Mary's Abbey, York, moved to a remote site marked by springs or fountains on land provided by Archbishop Thurstan in Skeldale and began a new life according to the Cistercian rule. Fountains became and remains one of the most famous monastic foundations in England. The surviving architecture is mostly twelfth and thirteenth century, though Abbot Marmaduke Huby added a tower in the reign of Henry VIII. The monastery was dissolved in 1539 and some of the stone was used by Sir Stephen Proctor to build his Jacobean hall. During the 1720s and 1730s John Aislabie of nearby Studley Royal laid out beautiful gardens leading to a wonderful view of the abbey ruins.
The Fountains cartulary was edited by W. T. Lancaster and published in two volumes in 1915. In 1981 the Yorkshire Archaeological Society Record Series (ed. D. Michelmore) published *The Fountains Abbey Lease Book*, a register of leases and indentures from the late fifteenth century to the dissolution, which gives many insights into the workings of a great monastic estate.

these cartularies survive in various repositories. Should you wish to trace a particular cartulary the standard guide is now *Medieval Cartularies of Great Britain* by G. R. C. Davis (Longmans, 1958). This lists not only the cartularies of religious houses but also the more limited number of secular cartularies which are known to exist. One will also find large collections of records relating to episcopal lands in the appropriate diocesan registry (unless they have been transferred to some local Record Office) and to the lands of cathedral chapters in the appropriate cathedral library. It need hardly be said that the records of bishops and of deans and chapters form entirely distinct collections. All lands formerly belonging to bishops, or to cathedral chapters, were transferred in 1836 to the Ecclesiastical Commission, now known as the Church Commission. In their offices at Millbank, London, S.W.1, the Church Commissioners have an enormous collection of records relating to these transferred lands.

In 1535 the Crown caused to be made a great survey of all the ecclesiastical property in England and Wales. This is known as the *Valor Ecclesiasticus*, the text of which was published in six volumes by the Record Commission in 1810–34. The survey covers not only monastic lands, bishops' lands, and cathedral lands, but also the lands of hospitals and other religious foundations, and the glebe lands of the parish clergy. Every parish historian should consult this important source. Where monastic lands are concerned, their history after the Dissolution may be traced through a variety of records in the Public Record Office, some of which are well known to local historians while others are not. While the monastic lands remained in the hands of the Crown their revenues were carefully recorded and collected by bailiffs. The financial details of monastic estates in this period are recorded in the *Ministers' Accounts* in the Public Record Office. When the lands came to be sold by the Crown they were always carefully surveyed and a proper purchase price fixed in the light of this information. These detailed surveys of ex-monastic estates coming up for sale are recorded in a class of records (also in the P.R.O.) known as the Particulars for Grants. These Particulars are of the greatest interest to the local historian and topographer and are not as well known as they should be. Those for Devon for the period 1536 to 1558 have been calendared and published by the Devon and Cornwall Record Society (see Additional References at the end of the book). This volume contains a valuable introduction about the machinery for the handling and disposal of monastic lands with special reference to the Particulars for Grants, and it also draws attention to a number of other classes of record in the Public Record Office, relating to the same subject, which the local historian ought to know about.

MANORIAL RECORDS

We have a brief description of each manor as it was in 1086. Are there any other records which enable the local historian to follow up this account? Occasionally there are valuable surveys, mainly of ecclesiastical lands, during the twelfth century. The existence of these special surveys, many of which are in print, will be known to the local historians in the regions concerned and cannot be satisfactorily listed here. In the middle of the thirteenth century there begins an invaluable series of documents known as the Inquisitions Post Mortem. These were returns made to the chancery on the death of any tenant holding directly under the Crown. Even if such a tenant held only a small proportion of his property directly from the Crown (as tenant-in-chief) the return will list all his lands. Abstracts of these Inquisitions from their beginning in 1216 down to 1384 have been published by the Public Record Office. The Inquisitions for the reign of Henry VII (1485–1509) have also been printed in the same series. In many counties local societies have indexed the inquisitions down to the time when they end in 1649.* These records are invaluable for the compilation of the history of the manor, but going with them in a great number of cases is the even more valuable class of record known as Extents. These are really rudimentary surveys of the manor (or other estate) and despite their brevity they often give us a kind of picture of the countryside as it was at that date. Occasionally the essential details of these Extents are to be found in the published calendars, but in far too many cases these have not been printed and one is merely told that an Extent of a certain manor or other piece of property exists.

It is essential for the parish historian to obtain a transcript of all the Extents that exist for his chosen territory. They are likely to be difficult documents to read and to interpret, and it is probably best to get the transcript done by an authorised searcher at the Public Record Office. By the sixteenth century, with the development of

---

* Most of the original record material of all kinds published by local historical societies and other special record societies, has been listed in *Texts and Calendars*, edited by E. L. C. Mullins for the Royal Historical Society (1958). I say 'most' because this valuable work of reference is now inevitably out of date.

the art of surveying, we get much more elaborate surveys of manors and these form a considerable class of records throughout the seventeenth and eighteenth centuries. If one is particularly fortunate there may be maps of the manor or estate made at an early date. Maps of private estates are known in the closing years of the six-teenth century, and became fairly common thereafter. But one will generally find them only where the estate belonged to a large landowner who had the means to employ surveyors and map-makers, and whose estates were sufficiently large and complex to call for such large-scale maps. Where land belonged to an Oxford or Cambridge college, for example, one is very likely to find old estate maps besides all the more usual material (rentals, leases, etc.).

Manorial surveys vary considerably in the degree of detail they give. Many of these have been put into print. A good example of this type is *The Surveys of the Manors of Philip, First Earl of Pembroke and Montgomery, 1631–32*, published by the Records Branch of the Wiltshire Archaeological and Natural History Society. Besides the manorial surveys we may find rentals of a manor or an estate at any date from medieval times onwards. These are less informative than full-blown surveys, usually consisting only of the names of the tenants of the manor and the rents they pay.

Nor must we forget the class of records known as *custumals*. These set out in some detail the customs of the manor which all tenants were obliged to observe under penalty of forfeiting their tenements (in serious cases) or some monetary fine for more trivial breaches. Manorial custom had the force of law on each particular manor, and was enforced in the manor court. Customs varied, often widely, from manor to manor, even on the same large estate. Not many such custumals survive. They were usually made as a result of some dispute between a lord and his tenants, or later (especially in the sixteenth and seventeenth centuries) to forestall possible disputes. On many manors the customs were never com-mitted to writing. They rested on oral tradition, handed down from generation to generation, and are now lost to us for ever. Such custumals, where they were drawn up, may be found either locally (for example, in the archives of the Dean and Chapter if they in-volved cathedral property) or in the central records in London, where they may have been deposited in some legal dispute in past centuries and never returned. Fortunate is the local historian who can find such a record for his own particular place, for it will give him much valuable everyday detail about the management of the manor, its farms and its fields.

Finally there are the manor court rolls. These are a record of the decisions of the court. They not only give details of various petty crimes, but, much more important, information about the manorial tenants and the succession to their farms. Some manor court rolls date from the thirteenth century. Those of Hales in Worcestershire have been published for the period 1272–1307, those of Wakefield in Yorkshire for 1274–1333 and 1348–50, and those of Chalgrave in Bedfordshire for 1278–1313. From these published rolls the local historian will get a good idea of the kind of information contained in this class of record. Not many rolls are as old as this, and some manors have no surviving rolls or records of any kind. Generally speaking, the later rolls are much less valuable and informative than the medieval ones, but they should nevertheless be read carefully. One never knows when they will suddenly boil up from a bald run of entries to something spectacular that is worth having. A register of the whereabouts of all known manor court rolls, and other manorial records, is kept at the National Register of Archives, in Quality Court, London, W.C.2, where it may be consulted on request. The N.R.A. may also be consulted for its typescript lists of private estate papers and records. Some of these private collections may not be available to searchers, but the bare lists are often very informative. The best general introduction to manorial records of all kinds is still Nathaniel Hone, *The Manor and Manorial Records* (2nd ed. 1912), a book which is to be found in all good libraries.

LATER RECORDS RELATING TO LAND

Besides the rentals and surveys of private landowners we must not overlook the value of parish rate books for the history of land-ownership and occupation. Detailed assessments for the church rate or the poor rate often exist for the seventeenth and eighteenth centuries, and in parishes consisting mainly of scattered farmsteads they may supply us with a complete directory of owners and occu-piers together with the names of the farms and the amount at which they are rated. At Bovey Tracey (Devon), for example, there is a full church rate made in the year 1596 containing no fewer than 160 assessments—seventy-five on houses in the borough, and eighty-five on 'land' in the surrounding parish. The latter gives the names of the owners or occupiers and the farms they then held. Here we have not only what is virtually an Elizabethan directory but also a complete picture of the distribution of the land at that time. The parish of Flitton (Beds) possesses a complete rate assessment for the year 1598. Late sixteenth-century assessments are not uncommon, but such records become more numerous as the generations go by. Occasionally, too, one finds parish assessments made on the live-stock (mainly sheep and cattle) which give us valuable information about the pastoral side of farming.

In the last quarter of the eighteenth century one begins to get a complete series of the assessments for the land tax, year by year, down to 1832, and often far beyond. The nature and whereabouts of these records has already been discussed (see Chapter 3).

PARLIAMENTARY ENCLOSURE

Most local historians are already familiar with the fact that the open-field system of farming prevailed over the greater part of the Lowland Zone of England and above all in the great Midland Plain. It used to be thought that this kind of agrarian pattern had never existed in the Highland Zone, but we now know that it was originally found in medieval times in such counties as Cornwall and Devon, in the south-west; in Lancashire, in the north-west; and also in Kent and Essex, in the south-east. It had disappeared from all these regions by the middle of the sixteenth century, except for a few small remnants here and there, and this had led to the belief among historians that it had never existed. The truth seems to be that in these peripheral regions of England the open-field system was established around a great number of villages (and often hamlets had their own small open-field pattern), but that this pattern covered only part of the landscape. The open fields were probably

4.6 Pattern of ridge-and-furrow in the Midlands

In certain parts of England, particularly in the extensive Midland Plain, patterns that were created by ploughmen centuries ago are preserved in today's landscape. Comparisons of aerial photographs and old estate maps have shown that these patterns are often correlated precisely with the former open-field system of farming. Individual ridges formed strips or 'lands', groups of ridges were arranged into flatts or furlongs, and access was provided along unploughed balks or headlands. The land was ridged to help with drainage, and the varied pattern seen here followed the different slopes. In this parish, as in many parts of the Midlands, the old landscape is overlain with the quickset hedges of parliamentary enclosure; the fields have long been put down to pasture and have not therefore been subject to modern deep-ploughing methods which have destroyed ridges in other areas. In some parts of the country ridge-and-furrow patterns are the result of post-enclosure ploughing, but in such cases the ridges are narrow and straight and are broken by hedge boundaries.

islands of varying size in a sea of more or less enclosed country. In these regions the greater part of the landscape was probably culti-vated from the first in small hedged fields such as we have today. The local historian in these regions must therefore be on the watch for traces of both systems of land-holding—open-field and severalty. It may be added as a further hint for the local historian to follow up that in these regions where the open-field system was not the universal pattern it seems to have been transformed into enclosed country at a very early date. We have evidence of this happening in Devon, for example, in the thirteenth and fourteenth centuries, and the same is possibly true of other anciently enclosed counties. The reasons for this enclosure by mutual agreement among the medieval farmers would take us far beyond the scope of this book.

Elsewhere in England the open-field system remained the char-acteristic pattern until the time of George III, when the enclosure movement initiated by private acts of parliament made its greatest headway. Even in the heart of the Midlands, however, there was much enclosure of open fields and common pasture during the fifteenth and sixteenth centuries. In a great number of cases this has resulted in the total disappearance of the village from the face of the landscape. The local historian who is working in these parts of England must refer for his background information to a good general economic history of the period. The enclosures of the Tudor period produced a great deal of rural agitation and outcry, and rightly so at the time, but they were concentrated in the inner counties of the Midlands and were highly localised even within that region. In point of fact the seventeenth century is probably much more important than the sixteenth for the amount of enclosure of open field and common pasture which took place. Seventeenth-century enclosure was carried through by private agreements between lords of manors and other owners of land, and in many cases the tenants also. Many of these private agreements were enrolled among the Chancery records in the P.R.O. and are not easy

4.7 Enclosure of the Wastes, Yorkshire

The landscape of hill-country such as the Pennines was transformed dramatically during the era of parliamentary enclosure. The rectangular fields seen here were designed on a surveyor's drawing board and then enclosed with high stone walls, under the terms of the Langsett enclosure award of 1814. It is thought that the semicircular walls were designed to protect sheep from inclement weather. The straight road that crosses the picture is part of an ancient highway that was turnpiked in 1741. It was given its present character by the enclosure commissioners.

to locate. The local historian who has reason to suspect that his parish was enclosed during the seventeenth century and is anxious to trace the sources available for this crucial event should refer to Appendix I of vol. ii of the *Victoria County History* for Leicestershire. This gives a list of Leicestershire parishes enclosed before the parliamentary period, the date of enclosure (where known), and the sources for this information. He should also consult Joan Thirsk, ed., *The Agrarian History of England and Wales, Vol. IV, 1500–1640*, (Cambridge University Press, 1967) and the forthcoming volume V (1640–1750) for general background.

Despite this early enclosure, millions of acres of open field remained to be enclosed by private Act of Parliament, mainly during the second half of the eighteenth century. Most county record offices will have copies of the private enclosure acts for their counties, and they will also have the enclosure awards eventually made under the act by the Commissioners. Some counties, such as Berkshire, have published special catalogues of the enclosure maps available in their Record Offices. The standard reference work is the late Dr W. E. Tate's *Domesday of English Enclosure Acts and Awards*, edited by M. E. Turner (Reading University, 1978).

It will be clear from what has been said above that a great number of English counties possess no private enclosure awards relating to open field. On the other hand, such counties usually possess a considerable collection of enclosure awards and maps dealing with commons and wastes. Their open field had disappeared centuries before, but since these counties are in the Highland Zone they contained extensive commons and wastes which remained unenclosed until well into the nineteenth century. Indeed, vast stretches of upland waste still remain unenclosed. These enclosure awards relating to wastes, commons, etc., should be carefully studied by the local historian, though they obviously have nothing like the importance of an award relating to open fields, which usually effected a complete transformation of the landscape of the whole parish and initiated profound social changes in the village.

The latter type of award calls for intensive study by the parish historian. From it he can build up the picture of landownership in his parish at a certain date in the eighteenth century or the early nineteenth. The parliamentary enclosure movement is still a source of considerable controversy among economic historians, whether in fact it was responsible for some of the great social changes attributed to it. The student of a particular parish may find that many of these profound social changes had begun decades or generations earlier, and that the parliamentary enclosure award merely set the seal upon them. In other words, there may well have been a class of absentee landlords owning a disproportionate share of the land of the parish long before the enclosure award was ever made; the owner-occupier of land may have been a rare figure even in 1700; and there may have been a considerable class of landless house-holders a generation or two before the award. The local historian will find that parishes vary remarkably, however, in these respects. In some places he will find that his parish contained a large class of true peasant farmers right down to the date of the enclosure award; in other places that the peasant farmer had already disappeared in favour of the big landlord and the tenant farmer. He may also find, after the enclosure had been carried through, that the number of small owners of land actually rose, contrary to the fairly general belief that the small man was crushed out of existence at this time. The local historian should therefore approach these controversial questions about the precise effects of enclosure upon his parish, his village, and the community as a whole, with a completely open mind and see for himself by a detailed scrutiny of the records what really happened.

By studying the award closely he will be able to ascertain the number of absentee landlords, who they were, and how much of the parish land they owned. He will be able to find out the number of owner-occupiers and the proportion of land farmed by them. Less easily, he will be able to find out the proportion of families in his parish who neither owned nor occupied any land, but were in fact a landless proletariat. He can do this if by some means he knows the total number of families in the parish at the time. By subtracting from this total the names of all the families owning or occupying some land, he is left with the residue, the landless. He can also calculate to what degree there was inequality in the ownership of land. There may be fifty owners of land specified in the award, but one may find that five of these owned perhaps two-thirds of the parish. It is possible to construct a table to show facts like this. If the local historian finds this kind of picture in his parish at the time of the enclosure, he must then seek to explain when and why these profound changes had taken place; and he may find that they are to be associated with the rapid growth of the population of the parish at some earlier period, coupled with the steady engrossing of farms by a few thrusting, energetic, and acquisitive families whose history would call for some special examination. It is clear from all this that a close examination of the enclosure award may raise all sorts of questions which will set the local historian at work upon the records of the seventeenth century and even earlier. In other words, the enclosure award shows him what kind of questions require answering for the preceding century or so.

What happened after the enclosure? Did the small farmer lose his farm, or did he succeed in hanging on? Where the enclosure award falls in date within the range of the land tax assessments, the local historian is in a very good position to see precisely what happened at the enclosure. He will have a picture of ownership and occupation before the revolution, so to speak, and he will have an annual picture of his parish for decades after the revolution. This should suffice to tell him pretty exactly what really happened in his parish. I have discussed many aspects of this question in *The Midland Peasant*, to which the reader may be referred for some general ideas. He may find that his own parish was quite unlike that of Wigston Magna, which I was dealing with, but the book may nevertheless offer some suggestions about the line of approach to the subject. For some parishes which underwent parliamentary enclosure there may be other valuable records relating to the enclosure. In some places one may be fortunate enough to find the minute-book of the enclosure commissioners, and (more rarely) the 'strip map' of the open fields of the parish, prepared for the commissioners before they set to work to redistribute the land.

FARMING

All that has been said so far relates to the ownership of land or its occupation and says nothing about the ultimate purpose to which the land is put. I have remarked elsewhere, and may perhaps be allowed to say it again, that

> historians have tended to study the *manor* rather than the *village*, the legal concept rather than the physical fact, and to be more interested in tenures and rents than actual farming: to give elaborate consideration to questions of land ownership and land occupation and to give little consideration to land use: to be interested in short in the details of the machinery and to forget what the machinery exists for. . . . All these things—manorial history and organisation, land tenures and so forth—are important. I am not attacking them as subjects for enquiry . . . but let us remember all the time that we are dealing with actual men and women who have struggled to get a living off a

real piece of country that we can go and walk over today, to keep in mind the facts of soil, climate, and topography, rather than the nice distinctions of copyhold tenures, the workings of the manor courts, the heriots, fines, and amercements. Let us, while taking account of the machinery of the land ownership and occupation, devote more thinking to the actual use to which the land has been put. Let us in fact get down to Earth.

What sources exist for the study of farming practice and land-use in a given area? Where the tithe map and award exist for a parish it is possible to construct a complete picture of land use— arable, pasture, meadow, woodland, orchards, and so on—at that date. This may be compared with the picture of land use as it is today and will provide an interesting short chapter on changes in farming practice and land use during the past century.

For the earlier period there are a few literary sources, notably the writings of Arthur Young and William Marshall and the reports to the Board of Agriculture which were made by various writers between 1793 and 1817. These reports took the form of subjective *General Views*, but they contain much useful local information. Some counties have two reports, written by different people at different times. Other local printed information may exist of which the borough or county librarian will have knowledge.

For the sixteenth and seventeenth centuries we have an in-comparable class of records, the probate inventories. These records were made for the purpose of proving a man's will. The Probate Court required the production of a true and perfect inventory of all the goods and chattels of the deceased before any distribution of his estate was made. This was designed to safeguard the administrators of the will and also to protect the next of kin from fraud. The great bulk of these probate inventories naturally relate to farmers of all classes and degrees of wealth, as one would expect in a predomi-nantly agrarian society. The records vary in the amount of detail they give, but if one examines every inventory for a given parish, one obtains enough information to write a detailed account of farming practice, implements, crops, and livestock over the best part of two centuries. An example of such a study is provided in an excel-lent paper on 'Kirdford inventories 1611 to 1776', by G. H. Kenyon in *Sussex Archaeological Collections*, vol. xciii. Mr Kenyon found no fewer than 210 inventories for his parish during this period, the great majority of which related to yeomen or husbandmen, and the result is a full picture of farming in a Wealden Clay parish for the best part of two centuries. At Wigston Magna in Leicestershire, farmers' inventories run from 1529 to 1826, though they thin out considerably after about 1730.*

From these inventories one can generally discover the crops that were grown, and in what proportions, the numbers of livestock kept, the implements used on the farm, and occasionally other details of farm practice. We can often ascertain the arable area of the farm, but the inventories do not give us much idea, if any, of the grassland area. We can only gather some idea of the balance of the farm as between arable and pasture by noting the relative values in the inventory—for example, the total value of the arable crops as against the total value of the hay and the livestock. There are a number of other difficulties in using these records for this purpose, but one often finds that information which is missing from one inventory is provided in another. Most of the difficulties in handling these records can be resolved by common sense and by an elementary knowledge of the farming year which most local historians in a rural parish will have. To get the true value of the crops, for example, one should ideally have an inventory made just before harvest or just after it. On the other hand, inventories made in the early spring frequently tell us how many acres had been sown under the different crops, which gives us a good notion of the relative importance of the crops from a different angle. Similarly, the numbers and value of the livestock shown may well vary according to the time of the year. In all these matters the local historian will use his common sense, and he may also derive considerable help from the practical knowledge of farmers in his parish who may well be able to explain to him facts which are at first sight mysterious or baffling.†

In recent years a number of useful studies have appeared in which inventories have been used in bulk to identify farming regions and to examine many aspects of provincial life. Barrie Trinder and Jeff Cox, *Yeomen and Colliers in Telford* (Phillimore, 1980) is a particularly instructive example. In those areas of England which were farmed on an open-field system historians should also consult Professor Maurice Beresford's paper on 'Glebe Terriers and Open-Field Yorkshire' in vol. xxxvii of the *Yorkshire Archaeological Journal* for guidance on how to use these records in a farming context.

---

* See *The Midland Peasant*, especially pp. 153–77, 234–36.

† For inventories as a source of local history see the articles under the title by O. Ashmore and J. J. Bagley in the *Amateur Historian*, vol. iv, nos. 4, 5, 6, and 8 (1959–60).

It is extremely difficult to obtain any accurate information about farming practice and land use before the probate inventories begin. Very occasionally one finds a medieval farmer's inventory by chance among some ecclesiastical records, but no coherent picture of the farming in the medieval village is generally possible. The main exception to this statement is where we have a considerable estate, belonging to a big landlord, which was farmed by a bailiff. The annual accounts of the bailiff for this estate will enable some picture of farming in the medieval period to be constructed. Monastic records are a particularly fruitful source in this respect.

The interpretation of manorial accounts of this kind is not so straightforward as might appear. The accounts tell us a great deal about the state of the stock in corn and beasts each year, and what has been happening in the way of sales and purchases, but they were not intended to be as comprehensive as a modern balance-sheet. Before embarking on the use of accounts of this kind, should they exist, the local historian would be well advised to familiarise himself with N. Denholm-Young's book, *Seignorial Administration* (new edn, Cass, 1963), and the late Miss Levett's article on 'The financial organisation of the manor' in her *Studies in Manorial History* (Oxford University Press, 1938; rep. 1963; Merlin Press)—not easy reading, but it is a difficult subject. For manors which had no such elaborate organisation as this we are usually entirely without information about the farming of the medieval period except such incidental information as we may glean from their agrarian by-laws (see p. 64).

The attention of the local historian should also be drawn to the value of farm accounts and manorial rentals and surveys in providing some elementary information about land use where other records are lacking.* Not all rentals and surveys are informative in this respect, but occasionally one finds a fuller statement than usual about individual farms. Thus the rental of the Devonshire lands of Cecily, Marchioness of Dorset, made about 1524,† gives such information as the following:

> Grenelynche [Greenslinch in Silverton parish] Agnes Richards widow, tenant-at-will, holds there by indenture dated 10 April 20 Henry VII the whole farm of Grenelynche by the lease of Sir John More, with

* The best-known farm accounts are those of Robert Loder for the years 1610 to 1620 (edited by G. E. Fussell, Camden Society, 3rd Series, vol. iii, 1936), but there are many others still unprinted and unused.

† Public Record Office. Augmentation Office Miscellaneous Books, no. 385 fos. 112–208.

appurtenances, consisting of 25 closes containing 195 acres, of which 60 acres are arable worth 8d an acre, 2 acres are meadow worth 10s, 60 acres are heath worth 8d an acre, and 73 acres are pasture worth 10d an acre. Also an orchard and garden.

Such information as this for the year 1524 might usefully be compared with that given in the tithe award in 1842.* Here Greenslinch appears as a farm of 125¼ acres, of which about 86 acres were arable, nearly 31 were pasture, and about 8 acres consisted of orchards and copse. It appears that about 70 acres had been lost to neighbouring farms between 1524 and 1842 (unless the size of the acre varied between the two documents, which is a factor the local historian must never overlook). However this may be, it is possible to remark on some considerable changes in land use on this farm in the course of three hundred years.

* Devon County Record Office, Tithe Awards and Maps, Silverton.

5 CHURCH, CHAPEL, AND SCHOOL

THE PARISH CHURCH: THE FABRIC

The date of the first foundation of a parish church, in so far as it can ever be discovered, has already been discussed in the previous chapter. Few churches, however, retain in their fabric anything as old as the earliest documentary or other reference to them, though this occasionally happens with churches founded in the eleventh and twelfth centuries. At Weaverthorpe, in the East Riding of Yorkshire, the village church built by Herbert the Chamberlain between 1108 and 1121 still stands in its original state. At Tugby, in the uplands of East Leicestershire, the parish church has a pre-Conquest tower of late date. On structural grounds one would put it in the eleventh century. Now, Tugby means 'Toki's village or estate', and on turning to Domesday Book we discover that 'Tochi (or Toki) son of Outi' held Tugby as part of a larger estate in the year 1066. There can be little doubt in this instance that it was Toki, the lord of the village in the middle decades of the eleventh century, who built the first church at Tugby (of which the lower two stages of the tower alone survive) about the middle of the century. Generally, however, the existing fabric in most parish churches shows few or no traces of the first building on the site.

In many cases the font provides the best clue to the date of the earliest church on the site. The right to baptise was a cherished one, and where a church was rebuilt in later centuries there was a strong disposition to retain the old font as tangible evidence of this ancient right. Most such fonts date from the twelfth century, though occasionally they go back to pre-Conquest times. We do not know, of

5.1 St Mary-le-Wigford, Lincoln

An Anglo-Saxon inscription cut into a stone near the door on the west face of the tower is translated as 'Eirtig had me built and endowed to the glory of Christ and St Mary'. The tall, simple tower is characteristic of a Lincolnshire type dating from the late-tenth or the eleventh century. A similar tower can be found nearby at St. Peter-ad-Gowts and another (rebuilt in the reign of Charles II) at St Benedict's. All three stand by the High Street which follows the line of the old Roman Ermine Street, one of the major ancient routes from London to the North.

course, whether there may not have been a Saxon font and a Saxon church before ever the Norman font came into existence, and this possibility must always be borne in mind. The font must not be treated as absolute evidence of the first building unless there is other evidence to support it or to suggest it. Thus at Honeychurch, in mid-Devon, the surviving font dates from the second half of the twelfth century, when the church was rebuilt. But a church certainly existed in late Saxon times on this site, since the name means 'Huna's church' and is so recorded in 1066.

The local historian is obviously called upon to write a description of his parish church from an architectural standpoint. There are numerous books which will help him to date the fabric of churches, though it is not always as easy as it looks, and unless one has a good working knowledge of the styles and local chronology of church architecture it is as well to find someone more expert to provide the necessary description.

Even when this has been done, the subject is far from finished. Over the space of several centuries the fabric of the church has suffered and has been repaired, sometimes extensively, and there is a good deal of documentary evidence about the architectural history of parish churches which the local historian should use in order to complete his account of the structure. In the medieval period we have such documentary evidence as Domesday Book, the Taxation of Pope Nicholas IV of 1291,* and bishops' registers. It should be observed that Domesday Book does not set out to record the existence of all churches. It does in fact record the existence of several hundred, particularly in the east of England, but there were undoubtedly great numbers of other churches in existence in other parts of England. The Taxation of 1291 gives us the names of all the churches which existed at the end of the thirteenth century and is a much fuller record in this respect. It is, however, rather late in time,† and the bishops' registers of the earlier thirteenth century sometimes provide additional evidence for the existence of particular churches. There may also be casual references in other records of the twelfth and thirteenth centuries to particular churches. Another valuable source for the history of a building may be found in the indulgences issued by the bishop of the diocese to all those helping in the rebuilding or repair of particular churches. The fifteenth-century bishops' registers in the diocese of Exeter contain a great

---

* Published as *Taxatio Ecclesiastica*, by the Record Commissioners in 1802.
† There is also *The Valuation of Norwich*, made in 1254.

number of such indulgences. These enable us to date many churches in Devon and Cornwall with a considerable degree of precision. Medieval wills are also a valuable source of evidence for new building. Many of these wills, particularly of ecclesiastics, will be found in the bishops' registers, but the local historian must not overlook the great collection of wills in the Prerogative Court of Canterbury which begins in the year 1383. Pre-Reformation wills abound in references to the fabric, furniture, and other contents of parish churches.

Churchwardens' accounts are often of great value in this respect. Sometimes they cover the complete rebuilding of the parish church as at Louth (Lincs) in the early sixteenth century, and at Bodmin (Cornwall) in the rebuilding of 1469–91. Such accounts covering a complete rebuilding are rare; the majority of accounts merely refer to more or less repair work.

The records of visitations by bishops or archdeacons frequently contain references to the state of the church fabrics. The records of the archdeacons of Leicester (now in the city muniment room at Leicester) contain a number of Inspection Books setting out the defects of church fabrics, and the repairs needed and effected, for many dates between 1619 and 1842. In the diocesan registry at York there are 324 bundles of terriers which give remarkably detailed evidence for the condition, endowments, and furniture of the parish churches of the whole province of York. There are in every diocesan registry also Faculty Books giving information about alterations to the fabric and fittings of parish churches for which approval had been granted by the bishop. It seems to be rare to find Act Books or other evidence of faculties before 1600. A great deal of work was done to the fittings and furnishings of churches in the seventeenth, eighteenth and nineteenth centuries, and here the Faculty Books are an invaluable source of evidence. Another source of evidence for dating extensive repairs are the briefs granted for authorised collections in other places for the repair of churches damaged by fire or storm.

Later sources for the structural history of churches will be found in the records of the Incorporated Church Building Society, founded in 1818. These are rich in plans and elevations of churches built or altered in the nineteenth century. In the nineteenth century also we should consult the files of *The Builder* from 1842 onwards, and the volumes of *The Ecclesiologist* from 1841 to 1868. Local newspapers also contain useful accounts of the rebuilding of old churches, or the building of new ones, in the nineteenth century, especially in towns; and it need hardly be said that all diocesan registries contain a mass of papers relating to the rebuilding and alteration of churches and chapels (Anglican) in the eighteenth and nineteenth centuries. Often there are the plans for a complete rebuilding, with other details of architectural interest. There are also papers relating to the rebuilding of parsonage houses, again often with plans. Thus the diocesan records of Exeter (now housed in the Devon County Record Office) contain a plan and survey report on the old vicarage at Kentisbury, on the edge of Exmoor, made in 1779. There is also a proposed plan of the new vicarage, with estimates, made in the same year. Earlier descriptions of rectory and vicarage houses will be found in the glebe terriers from about 1600 onwards, and occasionally slightly earlier.

Even when the local historian has described his parish church in purely architectural terms he has not completed his task. He must try to interpret the building historically, precisely as I suggest in a later chapter he should interpret the secular buildings of his parish or his town. If, as at Honeychurch, already cited as an example, a Saxon church was completely rebuilt in the twelfth century, what is the significance of this in terms of manorial or parish history? Was there some change in the ownership of the manor about this date which would suggest a reason for the rebuilding? Or what is the significance of the widespread rebuilding of parish churches in the Midlands in the twelfth and thirteenth centuries in terms of regional, or perhaps purely parochial, history?

The parish historian may have to look outside his own small territory to discover important changes in the agrarian history of the whole region in which his parish lies. The unbroken line of magnificent churches one finds along the southern side of the Wash, from Spalding as far as King's Lynn, mainly dating from the twelfth and thirteenth centuries (with a later enlargement in many cases), is to be attributed almost without exception to the prosperity of the whole Marshland and Fenland region during these generations, when new dykes were being built year after year, and more and more of the rich, virgin soils brought into use by an active and intelligent society of landlords and peasants.* Sometimes the explanation of a particular church is mainly to be sought in agrarian changes over

---

* For a most fruitful study of the agrarian development of the Lincolnshire side of the region in this period see H. E. Hallam, *The New Lands of Elloe* (Leicester University Press, 1954), and the same author's *Settlement and Society: a study of the early Agrarian History of South Lincolnshire* (Cambridge University Press, 1965).

a wide region, as in the Marshland of Lincolnshire and Norfolk; sometimes it lies in purely parochial or personal changes, as in the lordship of the manor. Or it may be a mixture of both sorts of history.

A neat example of the purely manorial kind comes from the village of Kegworth in north Leicestershire. Here we find what the guide-book describes as 'a large and almost faultless village church . . . built, with the exception of the lower part of the tower, at one date, the late Decorated'. Churches such as this, built as a whole in one style, clearly call for a special explanation. The manorial history of Kegworth supplies the answer in this case. Sir Henry Greene, a successful member of a local family, who acquired property in several counties after a lucrative judical career, went to considerable trouble and expense to buy both the manors into which the village of Kegworth had long been divided. This he accomplished in the year 1354. He died fifteen years later. The rebuilding of the parish church to one design for nave and chancel, in a style consonant with this period, was more than probably due to the initiative of, or was at the expense of, the new lord of the manor between 1354 and 1369.*

In the sixteenth century and later we sometimes find that a church has been reduced in size by walling up one arcade, so dispensing with one aisle. Such a change as this probably reflects a notable fall in the population of the parish, and raises a problem which the local historian should try to solve. At this point it is appropriate to remark that the size of a parish church has no necessary connection with the size of the population of the parish, especially where medieval churches are concerned. Churches were built for the greater glory of God, and parishes rivalled each other in the size and splendour of their churches without regard to the size of the local population at the time, but simply spending all the money that was available. On the other hand, reductions in the size of churches probably indicate a fall in the parish population over a long period.

CHURCH GOODS

So far we have been concerned with the fabric and fittings of churches. We can obtain information about church goods (princi-

---

* I have to thank Dr D. Stein of Kegworth for the detailed working out of this apt illustration.

pally the church plate and vestments) from pre-Reformation wills, and from the inventories of church goods, made in 1552, which are now in the Public Record Office. Some of these Edwardian inventories have been printed either in volume form or as articles in the *Transactions* or *Proceedings* of local historical societies. Glebe terriers often contain lists of church plate and other goods and fittings during the seventeenth and eighteenth centuries. Churchwardens' accounts will also contain numerous references to the purchase and repair of vestments, plate, service-books, and other 'goods'.

INCUMBENTS AND BENEFICES

An essential part of any parish history is a list of the incumbents of the parish church. Such a list is often made for display in the church and not as part of a parish history; but it is rare to find lists which contain all the particulars they should contain. It is not always an easy and straightforward task to compile such a list of incumbents. Those who wish to do so should consult an invaluable essay by the late Professor A. Hamilton Thompson entitled 'Ecclesiastical benefices and their incumbents', published in the *Transactions of the Leicestershire Archaeological Society*, vol. xxii (1944–45). This essay also explains the distinction between rectors and vicars, and the importance and significance of the patron. From the Reformation onwards the Crown became interested financially in benefices all over the country, and the almost unbroken series of Institution Books in the Public Record Office should be consulted as the most convenient means of tracing the names of incumbents and patrons.

Lists of incumbents are of value not only for the names. They are, as Professor Hamilton Thompson says, a most valuable testimony of the historical continuity of the parish and its church, and they may well suggest questions for the local historian to consider, even if he cannot always answer them. What, for example, happened in the parish at the Reformation? Does the list of incumbents show that the same incumbent survived throughout the Reformation period, or were there any significant changes at this time? Was there, even more important, a significant change in the patron of the living? Did the advowson fall into the hands of a Protestant-minded gentleman, or one who was likely to be influenced by a great Protestant personage like the earl of Huntingdon (in Leicestershire) or the earl of Bedford (in Devon)? In the eighteenth and nineteenth centuries one often notices a growing tendency for rectors to remain for long periods of time. This must have been an element making for great stability in the parish; but before jumping to such a conclusion one must be certain that the rector resided in his parish and that his duties were not in fact being carried out by a succession of ill-paid curates. In this and other ways a list of incumbents and of patrons can throw much light on the religious life of the parish at different periods.

The local historian should also pay some attention to the material endowments of the benefice in the form of tithe, glebe lands, and offerings. The value of the benefice may be ascertained at certain dates such as the Taxation of Norwich (1254), the Taxation of Pope Nicholas IV (1291), and the Inquisition of the Ninths (1341). None of these great records is complete for various reasons. The Taxation of Norwich survives for only five English dioceses; the Taxation of Pope Nicholas IV exempted benefices not exceeding six marks in value, and for certain areas the return is wholly lacking; and the Inquisition of the Ninths survives for the greater part of twenty-seven English counties only.* In 1535 a new valuation of all ecclesiastical property was prepared, known as the *Valor Ecclesiasticus*, which has been referred to elsewhere. Later details about the material possessions and value of vicarages and rectories will be found in the glebe terriers which generally begin in the late sixteenth century or the early seventeenth. The reader is also directed to some valuable pages in Mr Pugh's *How to Write a Parish History* (pp. 72–80).

SPIRITUAL LIFE OF THE PARISH

So far we have not touched on the reason for which all this machinery existed, that is to say, the worship carried on in the church. We have very little recorded evidence of this for particular places before the Reformation, though occasionally a medieval will informs us that a parish church had a certain number of altars and gives us their dedications. A number of pre-Reformation churchwardens' accounts survive and these sometimes throw light upon the services and service-books in the pre-Reformation church. A list of extant churchwardens' accounts will be found in J. Blain, *A List of Churchwardens' Accounts* (Ann Arbor, Michigan, 1933).

* Published by the Record Commission in 1807 under the title of *Nonarum Inquisitiones*.

Of more value, perhaps, are those churchwardens' accounts which cover the period of the Reformation, for they tell us by implication what happened through all the changes and counterchanges of the years between Henry VIII and Elizabeth I. At Sheriff Hutton in Yorkshire the churchwardens' accounts cover the period from 1535 to about 1580, and also contain a full inventory of the ornaments and furniture of the parish church in the year 1524. In these accounts we see the exact impact on the parish of the successive changes under Henry VIII, Edward VI, Mary, and Elizabeth I. At Morebath (Devon) the accounts of the churchwardens have been printed for the period 1520–73 (Exeter, 1904). They are particularly valuable in that they were all written by one person, the vicar, Christopher Trychay, who remained in his cure throughout the whole period. For the Elizabethan period and afterwards, there are the visitation books of archbishops or bishops or archdeacons. In the diocese of York, for example, the visitation records of the archbishops and archdeacons begin in 1563 and are exceedingly rich in material down to the present day. In Essex there is an important visitation book for the archdeaconry of Essex dating from 1565 which shows, among other things, the delay in carrying out the terms of the Elizabethan settlement. Besides the various visitation records one also finds in diocesan registries the answers from parishes to questionnaires sent out by the bishop relating to the number and kind of services held in the church and to a number of other matters. There is a particularly valuable survey of all the parishes in Devon and Cornwall for the year 1744 in the Devon County Record Office. The answers to these episcopal queries throw a good deal of incidental light on the state of nonconformity in the various parishes, though such evidence, coming from Anglican clergy, must be used with caution. Excellent examples of the kind of record available for the state of the church and church services and schools, in the nineteenth century, are *Bishop Wilberforce's Visitation Returns for the Archdeaconry of Oxford in the year 1854*, published by the Oxfordshire Record Society (1954) and the returns for the diocese of Exeter in 1821 published by the Devon and Cornwall Record Society (1958, 1960).

THE NONCONFORMIST CHAPEL

Few parishes in England are without a nonconformist chapel of one kind or another and many parishes contain several chapels of different denominations. The history of nonconformity in England is an exceedingly complicated story and to trace the development of various chapels is no easy task. D. J. Steel (ed.), *Sources for Nonconformist Genealogy and Family History* (Society of Genealogists, 1972) is an invaluable guide to the records, as useful to the local historian as to the person tracing his family tree. The standard published work for the early history of dissent is G. Lyon Turner, *Original Records of Early Nonconformity* (three volumes, 1911–14). One should also consult Alexander Gordon, *Freedom after Ejection* (1917), which prints the valuable returns by counties on the state of Presbyterian and Congregational nonconformity in 1690–92. A third source of considerable value is A. G. Matthews's *Calamy Revised* (Oxford University Press, 1934), which is a revision of Edmund Calamy's *Account of the Ministers and Others Ejected and Silenced 1660–62*. Walker's *Sufferings of the Clergy during the Grand Rebellion 1640–60* is a classic work; this, too, has been revised by A. G. Matthews under the title *Walker Revised* (Oxford University Press, 1948).

For the eighteenth century there is much valuable record material in Dr Williams's library in London, including a statistical survey of the dissenting churches in 1715 and the following years (Evans MS), and a survey of the dissenting congregations in each county in 1773 (Thompson MS). There are other statistical surveys in the same library for the eighteenth century; and in the nineteenth century we have the series of official year-books of the various churches. The national census of 1851 embodied a mass of ecclesiastical information which has never been completely printed. These returns cover all places of worship, including dissenting churches, and when they were founded and the size of their congregations. This record is in the Public Record Office (H.O. 129).

There are numerous local records relating to the history of nonconformity in each county, above all, perhaps, the registers of meeting-places which were kept after the Toleration Act of 1689. County archivists are, however, best able to direct the local historian to the sources for nonconformist history in the county records and there is no need to elaborate the subject here. Even with the central records and the local public records, the sources for the history of nonconformity are still not complete. Nonconformist churches were jealous of their independence and kept their own congregational records. Much of the material, therefore, for the history of nonconformity must be looked for in the possession of individual ministers and chapel secretaries. Nor should the local historian

5.2 Bullhouse independent chapel, Yorkshire

This chapel holds a special place in the history of Nonconformity, for independent services have been held here for nearly 300 years. A datestone over the door shows that the building was opened on 18 April 1692; its external appearance has hardly changed since.

During the seventeenth century the Rich family were minor gentry with firm puritan beliefs. William Rich was a captain in the parliamentary army and his son, Sylvanus, built the main part of Bullhouse Hall in 1655. Sylvanus's son, Elkanah, extended the hall in 1688 and built the chapel alongside. The name Sylvanus appears in several of St Paul's letters, while Elkanah was the name of Samuel's father and means 'God hath acquired'.

In 1689 Nonconformists were granted the freedom to worship as and where they pleased. Elkanah Rich sat in the family pew in Penistone church 'until they carried things so high and were so full of ceremonies that we resolve to provide a better way of worship at home'. His new chapel was licenced at the quarter sessions in April 1692. It has a simple one-up, one-down cottage for the minister at the rear, and in John Evans's *List of Dissenting Congregations* in 1715 the congregation was said to number 200.

forget that many early nonconformist chapels are worthy of a careful architectural description, though in general their buildings are deplorable.

Nothing has yet been said of another kind of nonconformity— Catholic nonconformity. There is a vast literature on these subjects in the form of books and articles which it is impossible to survey in a brief space. Reference should be made for these periods to the *Bibliography of British History*, of which the three volumes so far published cover the period 1485–1789 (Oxford, 1933–51). Much has appeared in print since these volumes were published, principally perhaps in the Proceedings or Transactions of local societies with which the local historian will be familiar. Notable amongst this work is that of Professor A. G. Dickens on Yorkshire recusancy and on the Marian reaction in the diocese of York. Reference should also be made to the volumes of the Catholic Record Society. A good general account of the type of local sources that are available is contained in M. Greensalde's paper 'Sources for Post Reformation Staffordshire Catholic History' in *Staffordshire Catholic History*, vol. 1 (1961).

SCHOOLS

The history of schools is an important aspect of local history everywhere, and there is a vast amount of material both in print and still in manuscript on this subject. In medieval times schools were usually associated with religious houses or with chantries. With the sixteenth century our information about small and local schools becomes more copious. From 1562 onwards the clergy and all those who wished to practise as schoolmasters had to give evidence of religious orthodoxy. This evidence is contained in the Subscription Books to be found in diocesan records. From 1604 onwards all schoolmasters were required to be licensed by the bishop. Hence the visitation records and the Subscription Books together form a most valuable source of information for the existence of local schools. Other small schools may come to light incidentally as the result of proceedings in the ecclesiastical courts. The kind of sources available for the study of schools can be best ascertained from such books as Brian Simon's *Education in Leicestershire 1540–1640* (University of Leicester Press, 1968) and from articles published in the journal, *History of Education*. The existence of a schoolmaster in a given place at a particular time may not be evidence of a continuing school. Small local schools came and went, and they are sometimes difficult to trace. On the other hand, many had a long history even though little is known about them. The village school at Wigston Magna in Leicestershire was in existence in the 1580s as we learn from some proceedings in the court of the archdeacon of Leicester, and it continued to exist until 1839 when the National School opened up in the village. During this long period we know almost nothing of this useful little school beyond occasional references in the church-wardens' accounts to the raising of money to pay the schoolmaster's salary.

Sometimes we can discover facts about such schools from the registers of Oxford and Cambridge colleges which tell us from what schools their students came. Unfortunately, most of these college registers are still unprinted. Those that have been printed show that boys often went on direct from the most remote little village schools to Oxford or Cambridge colleges. Occasionally boys attended a larger school between the village school and the university. In the seventeenth and eighteenth centuries many schools were founded and endowed by private persons and the history of these will be found amongst the reports of the Charity Commissioners and others, especially the reports of the Brougham Commission. Information about the kind of teaching given can be found in the diocesan records, and is often very entertaining. At Northam, in North Devon, teaching was carried on in 1724 by three 'infirm sailors' who were discovered to be unlicensed and were ordered by the bishop to desist from teaching. At Ilfracombe in 1729 the only schoolmaster was a boatman who had other duties as well. These took up so much of his time that he had not taught in the school for ten or twelve years. Most schools taught reading, writing, and arithmetic, but occasionally there were special subjects such as the principles of the Church of England for girls, and the art of navigation for boys in coastal towns and villages.

With the early nineteenth century came the foundation of the National and the British Schools Societies. We have consequently two complete surveys for the whole country, made in 1816 and in 1835. Reference should also be made to the parliamentary papers, especially to the *Select List of British Parliamentary Papers 1833 to 1899*, under the heading of Education. Among these parliamentary papers the reports of the Taunton Commission in 1867–68 are particularly interesting as throwing light upon the state of the endowed local schools. Other sources for the history of smaller schools will be found by consulting the more recent topographical volumes of

5.3 The village school at Hawkshead, Cumbria

Hawkshead grammar school was founded in 1585 by Edwin Sandys, Archbishop of York, who had been born at nearby Esthwaite Hall. Twelve 'charity boys' were given free education, clothing and accommodation, and fee-payers were attracted from many parts of north-west England. Up to sixty boys were lodged in a boarding house supervised by the headmaster, and others found cottage accommodation in the town and surrounding hamlets. In William Wordsworth's time about 100 boys were taught classics and mathematics. A quotation from Wordsworth's *Personal Talk* has been painted around the walls.

the *Victoria County History*, which contain sections on the history of local schools in the various parishes. The history of larger schools in towns is a somewhat more complicated subject, and here reference may be made to the pages on primary and secondary education in vol. iv of the *Victoria County History of Leicestershire* which deal with the history of schools in the city of Leicester. The sources used for this article are of general value for the history of schools in any town.

The writing of the history of individual schools is usually an act of piety. Such histories are rarely of any general interest and tend to be rather arid compilations, of interest here and there only to former pupils. This need not be so, especially where the school survived, possibly as a re-foundation, through the critical period of the Reformation. In this critical period, schools played a most important part. England was largely converted from Catholicism to Protestantism in two or three generations, to a considerable extent through the indoctrination of the younger children, a technique used with effect down to the present day for the instillation of particular political ideologies. An excellent essay which brings out the vital importance of schools at this period is *The Free Grammar School of Leicester*, by M. Claire Cross (Leicester University College, 1953). This history is valuable not only for the light it throws upon the working-out of the Reformation in one English provincial town, but also for the variety of sources which were used in its compilation.

The great value of school 'log-books' should not be overlooked, both for the history of education and to some extent for the social history of villages and small towns. These records were kept by the head teachers of schools founded in the nineteenth century and reveal, often in great detail, the ordinary routine of the school and the untoward events and happenings from time to time. Such records, where they survive, should always be consulted. A good idea of other sources that are available for the history of local education may be gathered from the section on Education in *English History from Essex Sources 1750 to 1900*, published by the Essex Record Office in 1952.

6 TOWNS: TOPOGRAPHY

When I began this chapter in 1958 I could truthfully say that 'the writing of town history has been much neglected in this country'. This is no longer true: the study of urban history has made great advances in recent years. The bibliography of the subject is now immense, as is evident from reading the various issues of the *Urban History Yearbook*, already referred to. Yet most of the cities and towns of England still lack a good history, and despite the massive array of professional historians now writing in this field there is a vast territory still for the local historian to work on. Above all this is true of the smaller towns, which generally do not attract the academic historians and are also more within the compass of the trained local historian. I do not wish by these remarks to make invidious divisions between professional and amateur: there are no precise boundaries, and I would be the last to try to draw them.

Towns of pre-Conquest origin may be viewed as military, administrative, and commercial centres. They may also be viewed as physical organisms, in other words as human communities of which we can study the origin and growth in terms of physical facts. Mr Pugh, in his *How to Write a Parish History* (pp. 90–97), has an excellent discussion of the problems arising in urban history from the administrative aspect, and the sources for dealing with them, and the reader is referred to these pages for this side of town history. Indeed, it would be true to say that English towns have been more adequately served on this side than on any other, as witness the classic book by Tait on *The Medieval English Borough* (Manchester University Press, 1936). This book is the only guide, and a somewhat difficult one, to the constitutional side of town history. In this

6.1 Blandford Forum

After a disastrous fire in 1731, this old Dorset market town was rebuilt under the direction of two local builders, the brothers John and William Bastard. The medieval market place had been encroached upon by tradesmen's stalls and rows, but after the fire this central space was left uncluttered to give the town a grander appearance. Otherwise, the new buildings followed previous street lines and property boundaries. Blandford remains a remarkable eighteenth-century period piece, for later developments did not affect the town-centre.

On the north side of the market-place the church (1733–39) and town hall (1734) provide focal points. Portland stone (which had become fashionable after Wren had chosen it for rebuilding the city of London) was used for tht town hall. Nearly all the houses are of brick, often with walls of continuous headers of a hard blue glaze, complementing the varied reds of the quoins and the opening surrounds. The houses between the church and town hall form a homogeneous group with common eaves lines and symmetrically-placed sash windows; they were the shops and residences of middling tradesmen. The wealthiest merchants were housed on the outskirts of the town, and the artisans lived just off the market area in pairs of houses with a common central entrance and passage.

and the following chapter I shall discuss towns from two other aspects—that of topography, and that of social and economic history. This is not because I think the constitutional and political side of urban history is less important, but because that side has been adequately treated in print already, and there are handy guides to the sources in this field of enquiry.

URBAN ORIGINS: SOME PHYSICAL FACTS

Some towns are of Roman origin, others came into being at various periods in Anglo-Saxon times (mostly rather late) and many more did not come into existence until early medieval times. Many towns, of course, came into existence for the first time with the Industrial Revolution of the period 1750 onwards, and these require special treatment from their historians.

Where the earlier towns are concerned, that is, towns founded before the fifteenth century, the local historian should try to answer a number of specific questions about them. To do this, he must also be something of a geographer and a geologist, because the factors of water supplies, soils, strategic position, and so on, all enter into the siting of an old town. One need not labour this point, for it is fairly obvious. Nevertheless, it is curious how many local historians do not stop to ask why the town or the village was founded precisely on a particular site and not somewhere else. In a town especially, one tends to overlook the importance of water supply, though it was a serious and continuing problem in a growing town, much more so than in most rural areas, where growth was slower and access to fresh water in general easier.

Since access to adequate supplies of water is the primary physical fact about the siting of any settlement, let me give an example or two of its importance in urban history. Everyone knows that before the present city of Salisbury was founded in the year 1225, Old Sarum, its predecessor, had occupied the top of an isolated chalk hill about two miles to the north. On this constricted site, wells were sunk into the chalk, the remains of some of which can still be seen. But this supply of water became inadequate by the twelfth century and was one of the reasons for the abandonment of the town for a new site in the meadows of the Avon below.

The Roman city of Exeter derived its water supply from wells sunk through the gravel capping of the hill, and this seems to have been sufficient throughout both Roman and Saxon times. But with

6.2 Wolverhampton in 1914

Some of our industrial cities, such as Birmingham, Liverpool, Manchester, Newcastle on Tyne and Sheffield have long histories as urban centres, going back to the early Middle Ages. Some can trace their ancestry back to Anglo-Saxon times as minor settlements. Wolverhampton was a market town by the late twelfth century and a medieval borough centuries before it was created a county borough in 1888. St Peter's fine parish church was rebuilt in the late-fifteenth century at the height of the town's fortunes from the wool trade, but its history goes back at least another 500 years, for it was mentioned in a charter of 994; the fourteen-foot high pillar cross that stands in the churchyard has been dated to the mid-ninth century. The original settlement was known simply as Hampton until Wulfrun's name was attached to it after she had acquired the estate in 985. The town underwent a radical transformation during the course of the nineteenth century; by 1901 its population was over eight times larger than it had been in 1801. But the photograph shows that on the eve of the First World War the central market retained its former vitality and that the horse still provided the principal means of transport.

the more rapid growth of the city in the twelfth and thirteenth centuries there is evidence to suggest that this simple form of water supply was becoming inadequate. It is possible that with the growth of population and the greatly increased consumption of water, the water-table beneath the gravel dropped to such an extent that some wells at least began to run dry. We know that in the first years of the thirteenth century the city was obliged to construct underground conduits in order to bring in water from springs well outside the city to the east. This suggests that the problem had become acute by the end of the twelfth century and there is indeed one specific piece of evidence from the year 1136. In that year, the strong castle at Exeter, held by Baldwin de Redvers, was besieged by King Stephen in person. There is a graphic description of this siege in the chronicle known as the *Gesta Stephani*, which tells us that the fate of the castle was more or less decided when the well within its walls, which had never been known to fail, ran dry. Some distance away, a copious spring which took its rise immediately under the south wall of the Cathedral, and was perhaps a specific reason for the siting of the Saxon monastery here in the seventh century, also seems to have been running dry by the thirteenth century, if not somewhat earlier. Thus the underground conduits of the early thirteenth century were a bold attempt to overcome what might have been a drastic shortage of water inside an important walled city. This new supply seems to have been adequate until the closing years of the seventeenth century when it, too, proved inadequate for the greatly enlarged population. Then we find new schemes for bringing water up to the city direct from the river.

There is another piece of evidence about the water supply of medieval Exeter. The underground conduits served only a limited number of people and limited areas in the city. For example, one passage ran to the cathedral, another to St Nicholas's Priory. The majority of the population probably derived little or no benefit from this supply. They may not have required much water either for drinking or for sanitation, but they certainly required some. Moreover, the poorer houses almost certainly had no wells. It is significant that as early as the middle of the thirteenth century we find a reference to Waterbeer Street, which probably means 'the street of water carriers'. These carriers brought up water from the river in barrels and buckets and sold it from door to door. At Sandwich in Kent one can still see the broad open conduits by which water was brought in from outside. In the newly founded city of Salisbury streams of fresh water were carried down gutters along all the streets, as one sees to this day in the streets of Wells in Somerset. One could see the same thing until recently in a number of East Devon towns and villages. Water was obviously of fundamental importance in the growth of the town. The local historian should take it into consideration when he discusses why a town was sited exactly where it is, and what happened when the town increased in population and the immediate water supply became inadequate.

There are many other physical features involved in the siting of a town, some of them involving special military considerations, others what may be called mainly economic considerations. In this connection, the local historian should view his town from two points of view: first, its immediate site, and second, its wider setting in relation to the surrounding countryside. This is quite obvious when one is considering, for example, the history of a town which became a great seaport, such as Bristol. It would be fantastic to attempt to write the history of Bristol without considering, even in the early days, its relationship to the Severn estuary, to Wales, and above all to Ireland, not to mention its relationship to the countryside behind it.

But even a small inland town must be considered from this dual point of view. Thus Stamford in Lincolnshire was one of the most important towns in England from the eleventh century to the fourteenth. It was a flourishing industrial community, making its own well-known cloth, and it was also an important meeting-place for merchants from southern and western Europe. It began life in all probability as a small farming village in the closing years of the fifth century. The site of this village was chosen by some of the earliest Anglo-Saxon immigrants, who were using the River Welland as one of the broad corridors by which they penetrated into the heart of the English midlands. At Stamford the dry limestone plateau slopes sharply to the banks of the river on both north and south. The sloping ground on both sides of the river gave a narrow crossing with no alluvial flooding or bogging-down.

There was, moreover, at this crossing point, a ford with a hard, stone bottom. The name Stamford means 'stone ford' and this must have struck the early settlers as the basic fact about the site of the place. The first settlement, therefore, grew up on the little plateau above the north bank of the river. The limestone gave dry sites for building and shallow wells provided the necessary domestic water supply. Behind, to the north, stretched the fertile limestone uplands which were to become famous for their sheep and corn. In the later Anglo-Danish wars, the site of Stamford, controlling both sides of the river, also became of military importance, and in the tenth century there were earthworks on both sides in order to bar the river against the Danish armies. All these were more or less immediate factors involved in the site of the early settlement. A settlement had also grown up on the southern slope leading down to the river, on the Abbot of Peterborough's land, before the tenth century. We hear of a mint in this monastic suburb in the reign of Edgar.

Why, however, did Stamford become so important in the early Middle Ages that it had one of the four great international fairs of medieval England? Here one must consider the wider implications of its site, though the first immigrants had no knowledge of these when they arrived in the fifth century. In fact, though they did not know it, the town of Stamford, as it had become by the tenth century, lay at the junction of two wealthy regions—the oolitic limestone uplands to the west, and the fenland to the east. We can still get the feeling of this today. If we walk four or five miles eastward out of Stamford along the road to Market Deeping we enter the Fens. The air is colder, the skies open out, and the long and level drains stretch far away in front of us. Stamford is set a little way back from the open fen, but the east wind blows bitterly cold through its streets in the early spring. The oolitic limestone uplands were, well before the eleventh century, carrying vast flocks of sheep and were also producing much corn. To the east, the Fenland itself was one of the richest regions in England. It is one of the commonest delusions that the Fens were little more than a swamp before Vermuyden arrived in the seventeenth century. One has only to explore the country to the west and to the south of the Wash, with its magnificent series of churches dating from the twelfth century onwards, to see immediately how rich this region must have been from soon after the Norman Conquest. Stamford lay, therefore, at the junction of two important but quite dissimilar regions, and from the twelfth century onwards its fair must have been important not only for cloth but for the exchange of every kind of agricultural produce. One cannot, therefore, see the history of Stamford in its true meaning unless one's vision extends over a wide tract of country all around it. The urban historian above all must take this large view of his chosen subject.

6.3 Durham Cathedral and fulling mill

Durham has been a great ecclesiastical centre for almost a thousand years, ever since the relics of St Cuthbert of Lindisfarne were brought here in 995 and the seat of the bishop transferred from Chester le Street. Durham's name was originally Dunholm, an Anglo-Scandinavian compound signifying the great rock upon which the city was built. The bishop was given extensive estates between the Tees and the Tyne, and after the Norman conquest this 'land of St Cuthbert' was made into the county palatine of Durham. As the see lay near the dangerous Scottish border the bishop was also made an earl, and he ruled Durham like a Continental prince.
The cathedral was begun in 1093 and completed within forty years, though the towers were heightened later. Sir Nikolaus Pevsner has described it as 'one of the most perfect and also historically most interesting buildings in Europe'. Many of the associated monastic buildings survive (for Durham was a monastic cathedral like Canterbury or Ely), and so does much of the bishop's castle, which since 1833 has housed the University. This memorable grouping of medieval buildings, perched high on the rock within a loop of the River Wear, forms one of England's finest historic scenes.

URBAN ORIGINS: SOME HISTORICAL FACTS

Whenever a town originated, these physical factors must be taken into consideration. They arise in a Roman town as much as any other. One cannot suggest every local problem which may arise in research of this kind. The intelligent local historian will gradually see for himself the questions that require answering. There is rarely a document to tell us about the beginnings of a pre-Conquest town, though such documents occasionally exist for a medieval town. We may be able by a close inspection of the geological map and of the contours of a site to say why a town should have grown up on a particular spot, but that will not tell us *when* the town appeared there or *where* exactly the original nucleus of the town was sited. Towns of Anglo-Saxon origin are occasionally mentioned in the Anglo-Saxon Chronicles. This may give us some sort of date for their foundation, though we must remember that a town may have existed as an agricultural village many generations before it is noticed in any record. Many towns which grew up in the pre-Conquest period are not recorded in any document until the Domesday survey. In some cases, however, we have the evidence of coins for their earlier existence. Thus the earliest evidence we have for the existence of both Bristol and Norwich is the appearance of coins minted in these places. There are Norwich coins dating from about 930, and Bristol coins from the reign of Ethelred II (978–1016). The little Somerset town of Langport is first evidenced on coins of about 930 and the Devonshire town of Totnes is first noticed as a name on coins in the reign of Edgar (959–75). It is likely that all these places, being royal mints, had existed for some time before even the coins appeared and had already acquired some commercial importance, but this is as far as the evidence will take us.

Sometimes we can use Domesday Book to ascertain roughly when a new town came into being. At Okehampton (Devon) we have in Domesday Book a detailed description of a large rural manor which ends with the information that Baldwin, sheriff of Devon, had also four burgesses and a market paying four shillings a year. Here we have the very beginnings of the town of Okehampton, which was founded on a new site away from the Saxon village shortly before 1086. The origin of the town of Launceston in Cornwall can similarly be pinned down fairly precisely from the entry in Domesday Book.

It is sometimes possible in towns that started life as villages in the pre-Conquest period, to ascertain exactly where everything began. At Plymouth, Old Town Street undoubtedly marks the original street of the Saxon village of Sutton from which the medieval town of Plymouth eventually sprang. At Bristol we may feel equally certain that in the High Street, rising northwards from Bristol Bridge, we are standing in the very street where the first merchants who congregated at the north end of the bridge assembled to do their trading. In some towns it may be the market-place, perhaps at the gates of a castle or of a monastery, where the town began its life. If we can pin-point the nucleus of a town in this way, we may then be able to say something about its subsequent growth by an intelligent dissection of the large-scale map, and by the use of such early medieval property deeds as exist in the town archives.

I have said above that occasionally there is a specific document in the medieval period which tells us about the precise origin of a town. An inquisition was held in 1290 following a complaint from the men of Grimsby that their trade was being captured by the town of Ravenserod in the estuary of the Humber:

> In the reign of king Henry [1216–72] the father of the present king, at first by the casting up of the sea, a certain island was born which is called Ravenserod. And afterwards fishermen dried their nets there and men began little by little to dwell and stay there, and afterwards ships laden with divers kinds of merchandise began to unload and sell at the town. And now, inasmuch as the island is nearer the sea than our town of Grimsby and ships do unload more easily, nearly all ships do stay, unload, and sell there.
>
> Asked what time men had lived at Ravenserod, the jury say that forty years ago a certain ship was cast aground at a place where there were no houses built, and a certain man took the ship and made a cabin out of it, to live in, and dwelt there, selling food and drink to merchants whom he received there, and so others came there to dwell. But thirty years ago there were not more than four dwellings.
>
> And now Isabella de Fortibus, Countess of Albemarle, is the lady of the island and takes the profits there and men freely buy and sell. The market is not held on any fixed day. The men of Ravenserod also take tolls as if the place was really a borough.

The men of Grimsby were unsuccessful in their complaint, but having drawn attention to the existence of this flourishing new town, the king in 1299 charged the men of Ravenserod £300 for the privilege of having a borough charter. By this they acquired among other things thirty fair days a year and two market days a week. In 1304 they sent two representatives to Parliament. But the sea which had cast up the original banks of sand and stone now began to wash it all away. By the 1340s two-thirds of the town had gone and people were moving out daily with all their possessions. Another twenty years and the town was under water again, having lasted barely a hundred years. The destruction of Dunwich on the coast of Suffolk is better known. In an inquisition of the year 1354 there is a graphic account of the steady destruction of this large town by the sea since the time of Edward I.

The Calendars of Miscellaneous Inquisitions, which have now reached the date 1422, contain a great deal of valuable historical material relating to towns. Thus the most recent volume contains information about the impoverishment and decay of towns like Lyme Regis, Melcombe Regis and Winchelsea in the early years of the fifteenth century. Lyme was described in 1405 as wasted by the sea, by enemy attacks, and by pestilence, so that scarcely one-twentieth of the town was now inhabited. The Winchelsea inquisition of 1415 gives a particularly long and detailed description of the topography of the town, following a petition to enclose a smaller area within a new wall because the site was much too large for the remaining inhabitants.

The site of the town of Great Yarmouth in Norfolk is traditionally supposed to have been cast up by the sea like the site of Ravenserod, but at an earlier date. The tradition is that the sea cast up a bank of sand upon which a few fishermen settled. It is even said that the first of these was called Fuller and his name still survives in part of the town called Fuller's Hill. The sandbank increased in size and strength and the population grew. By the time of Domesday, Yarmouth was a sizeable town with seventy burgesses. If the tradition is correct, as it very possibly is, we may date the beginnings of Yarmouth as round about the year 1000.* There can be little doubt that it was the rich herring fishery in the North Sea which led to the first huts being built on the sandbank and subsequently to the appearance of a town. The inquisition made in the year 1378 says:

> The town of Gt Yarmouth is charged with a yearly payment of £60 to the king, and pays £100 when fifteenths and tenths are demanded. In like manner it sustains many other burdens. Unless it regains the liberties granted to it by Edward III in the 46th year of his reign, it cannot bear these burdens. . . . Since the revocation of the charter the town is impoverished, a great part of the people gone away, and many buildings in ruin and deserted. It used to be a strong bulwark

---

* There is, however, some archaeological evidence for earlier habitation on this site. Local historians should familiarise themselves with the work of archaeologists, and with the archaeological material in their own and neighbouring museums, wherever they may be.

well filled with men, and was mainly founded from ancient times on the profit of a free fair for herrings and other merchandise from Michaelmas to Martinmas, as the town has no lands, meadows, rents, or services, whereby it might otherwise be sustained. The fair was brought to an end after the revocation of the charter, to the great damage of the town and neighbourhood, as while it lasted the country people used to sell their corn and other victuals there. For these reasons the liberties in the said charter should be restored.

From the middle of the fourteenth century, Yarmouth, like many English towns, went into a long decline which according to Manship* lasted about 220 years. Then, from about 1570 onwards, began a great rebuilding of 'void grounds' and an expansion of the former built-up area so that by 1610–19, when Manship was writing, he could say that it was about a quarter larger than it had ever been in medieval times. The remarkable piece of town planning which produced the Rows is certainly a subject for the attention of the local historian and topographer. My own view is that it is likely to be medieval in origin, and to have been devised for military purposes.

LAYOUT AND BUILDING MATERIALS

Many towns evolved gradually from agricultural villages without any particular plan or foresight. But often the lord of a rural manor, seeing what was happening, and seeing the prospect of a considerable increase in income from the growth of the town upon his lands, issued a charter granting to the nascent community certain rights and privileges. A great number of these charters have been collected in three volumes (see additional references for this chapter), and from them the local historian can derive a good deal of information about the purely physical side of the growth of many towns. The lord of the town often had it laid out on a new site adjoining the original village. Thus the town of Stratford-upon-Avon was laid out by the Bishop of Worcester on his demesne land about the year 1196. It was in the form of six streets, three running parallel with

---

* Henry Manship's *History of Great Yarmouth*, published in 1619, is one of the most useful of our town histories. It was compiled from the town records, many of which have since been lost. Some of the early seventeenth-century houses in the Rows have been described in detail by the late St John O'Neil in *Archaeologia* (vol. xcv, 1953), but so far as I am aware no one has considered the genesis of the unique plan of the whole town as shown in Swinden's map of 1738, for example, and how this was brought about.

the river Avon and three running roughly at right angles to it. On these streets he caused to be laid out plots of land of uniform size for the houses and gardens of the new burgesses. Immediately to the west of this newly planned area we find the ancient parish church of Holy Trinity, situated in a district which was already being called *Old Town* as early as the thirteenth century. This, beyond any doubt, represents the site of the original Saxon village of Stratford.

In the new town of Salisbury, created by the Bishop of Salisbury in 1225, the streets were laid out in a regular gridiron pattern, crossing each other at right angles, and we are told that the house-plots there were of a uniform size, seven perches long by three perches wide. It should be possible for the local historian to recover the boundaries of these original tenements of the early thirteenth century and to restore them to the map. These house-plots, or burgages, to give them their proper name, were not always of uniform size. At Sherborne (Dorset) the charter of Richard Poore, Bishop of Salisbury, granted in 1227–28, shows that there were three different sizes for burgage tenements: the first part was on the southern side of the way, from the chapel of St Thomas to the Castle, where the full burgage contained in length twenty perches and in breadth four perches. The second part was on the northern side of the aforesaid way, where the full burgage contained in length twenty-four perches and in breadth four perches. The third part was that extending from the chapel of St Thomas to the bishop's barn, where the full burgage was only two perches in length and two in breadth. Here we have zoning of houses according to size. The rents of the smallest tenements were 8d a year and of the largest 18d. Here again it might be possible for the local historian to rediscover the original layout dictated by Bishop Poore more than seven centuries ago.

In addition to laying out the site for a town, the lord in many cases also supplied the building materials. When Abbot Wulsin founded the town of St Albans at his abbey gates about the middle of the tenth century we are told that he provided the timber for the building of the houses. At Preston (Lancs) in 1188–89 the charter of John, Count of Mortain, goes on to say 'and of the said forest as much timber as they need for building their town, under the supervision of my foresters'. At Berkeley (Glos) the charter of Thomas de Berkeley in 1235–36 says: 'I have also granted to [the burgesses] for two marks of silver the timber which I have caused to be piled up in the new market place of Berkeley, for building or carrying away as it shall please them.' Several other borough charters refer in similar fashion to the provision of building materials. At Portsmouth we learn from another record that some houses were built of stone.

The magnate anxious to see a town grow up on his land, in order to provide himself with more ready money, sometimes also imposed penalties on burgesses who had not put up their houses within a year from the granting of the site. At Egremont (Cumberland) a penalty of twelve pence was imposed on burgesses who had not built within a year, and similarly at Okehampton (Devon).

The next question the historian of a town should ask himself, especially of a town created in this way, is where did the first inhabitants come from and what kind of people were they? Some new towns were stillborn either because they were badly sited, and not even the lord of the manor could overcome the facts of geography, or because it was difficult in some places to attract rural people into a town. Many of the inland Cornish towns in the early Middle Ages were largely populated by non-Cornish people. This is suggested by the lists of names in the early fourteenth-century tax assessments.

On the other hand, it is clear from the earliest records of Plymouth (Devon) that the new seaport which was growing up here from about the year 1200 onwards drew to a considerable extent on Cornish people for its early population. At Dartmouth (Devon), the earliest borough records (especially property deeds) show that the population in the first generation or so of the life of the town consisted to a large extent of the sons of free peasants from the surrounding countryside, and of the younger sons of gentry for whom there were few prospects at home. There were also some Scotsmen, a merchant from Winchelsea (who had perhaps set up a sort of branch office in Dartmouth), and a few aliens. The local historian should therefore have something to say about the composition of the urban population in the early generations of his town, based upon a close examination of all the surnames in the borough records, and, above all, the earliest property deeds and the earliest tax assessments, both local and national.

Though a number of speculations of this kind by rural magnates failed for one reason or another, the majority were successful to a varying extent. The foundation of the town of Stratford-upon-Avon in 1196 has already been referred to. Here the building plots were twelve perches long by three and a half perches wide. Each plot was roughly about a quarter of an acre. We know there were a hundred and nine acres within the burghal area since this area remained unaltered down to 1879. Allowing some space for roadways,

6.4 Boston, Lincolnshire

Boston Stump is one of England's famous church towers, a land and sea mark for miles around. Built of Barnack stone, it was begun in 1309 and took two hundred years to complete. The splendour of the church reflects the medieval wealth of the town. Its fairs were known throughout Europe, and corn, lead, and especially wool for the Hanseatic League were exported to the Rhineland and Flanders. Inland, the River Witham was navigable as far as Lincoln, and from there the Roman Foss Dyke provided access to the Trent.

The church is dedicated to St Botolph, an Anglo-Saxon monk from East Anglia, who has eighty churches in his honour. Domesday Book records a church but no urban development. 'Botolph's town' was created soon afterwards by the Breton lord who was responsible for similar developments alongside his castle at Richmond in Yorkshire. A narrow band of territory, which curved for half a mile along the east bank of the river, was taken from the marshland parish of Skirbeck, and a large triangular market place was laid out close to the church. The photograph shows how the original space has been encroached upon by permanent buildings, successors to the medieval stalls. Boston was one of the most successful new towns of the Middle Ages.

this means that the town of Stratford-upon-Avon was designed to take about four hundred houses, shops, etc. A survey of the town made in 1252 tells us that there were then about two hundred and forty burgage tenements, plus various shops and stalls, and about fifty plots of land apparently not built on. It would be fair to conclude from this information that the town of Stratford had got off to a flying start and that it filled up fairly quickly from the beginning.

THE EXTENSION OF TOWNS

There are many examples of towns which were so successful from the start that they were obliged to take in new land for further building or to absorb suburbs which had grown up immediately outside the original burghal area. At Bristol, for example, the lords of Berkeley encouraged the growth of the town of Redcliffe just across the river from Bristol. Redcliffe grew so rapidly as to rival Bristol itself. We hear of a church here as early as 1158—the present magnificent church of St Mary—although nothing of the existing church is older than about 1190. When in 1210 King John demanded a special aid, the men of Redcliffe were assessed to pay a thousand marks, exactly the same sum as Bristol. It was not until 1373 that Bristol succeeded in absorbing, and then only after a protracted struggle, this large and opulent suburb.

At King's Lynn, on the shores of the Wash, a new town—originally known as Bishop's Lynn—took form in the closing years of the eleventh century. The Lin was the name of a great shining inlet of the Wash—the Welsh word *llyn* means lake or pool—a rippling expanse of shallow water three or four miles across into which the Great Ouse and the Nar emptied themselves. Twice a day the yellow sands were left uncovered and traders from Norfolk crossed into the marshland on the other side and headed for Lincolnshire or the Midlands. Here where the Lin was narrowest—only a mile or so across to the estuary bar at Clenchwarton—a few traders made a permanent home on the eastern bank, on marshland belonging to the Bishop of Norwich, as part of his great rural manor of Gaywood. And here Herbert Losinga, first builder of Norwich Cathedral, began to build a church in the last years of the eleventh century. The church, now St Margaret's, he gave together with all the profits of the Saturday market beside it, to the Benedictine monks of Norwich about the year 1095. This was the original town of Lynn, confined between the two streams of Purfleet and Millfleet

6.5 The early growth of King's Lynn

The original borough of the late eleventh century lay between the Purfleet and the Millfleet, with a small extension along the waterfront of the Ouse which may well represent the site of the earliest merchant-settlement before the creation of the borough. In the third quarter of the twelfth century there was a large northward extension over the bishop's 'new land'. About the same date a large southward extension took place beyond the Millfleet, as far as the river Nar, to form the suburb of South Lynn.

and built upon a peninsula of reclaimed marshland thrust forward towards Clenchwarton bar on the further shore.

The new town flourished. The small peninsula was soon covered with streets and houses, and the waterfront lined with wharves. So rapid was the growth that the third Bishop of Norwich—William de Turbe, who reigned from 1146 to 1174—was obliged to extend the limits of the town by granting a large tract of newly reclaimed land lying on the north side of the Purfleet for further building. On this —'our new land' as he calls it—he built the church of St Nicholas and obtained the right from the Crown to have a second weekly market—the Tuesday market. The first market, that held on Saturdays, had been granted to the monks of Norwich, the second was not. It remained outside the jurisdiction of the monks and was laid out separately in the new part of the town. Hence we have two market-places in one town with a great church standing beside each: one in the old town of the late eleventh century, the other on the new land, the twelfth-century extension of the town. Each market-place and church represents a distinct phase in the physical growth of Lynn. There seems also to have been a great extension southwards from the original burghal area, beyond the Millfleet (see Map, p. 95). This extension was known as South Lynn. The appearance of the name North Lynn in a fine of 1199 suggests that South Lynn was already in being, and that it originated in all probability during the second half of the twelfth century. It grew rapidly, for by the early fourteenth century its tax quota was rather more than a third of that of Bishop's Lynn.*

Other towns which we know to have been extended in area to provide new land for building, or to have absorbed existing suburbs, were Scarborough, Burton-on-Trent, and Newcastle, and many smaller places. Often one finds that suburbs grew up outside walled towns at quite an early date and that these were occupied mainly, if not entirely, by the labouring class. This is a point which the local historian might well pursue through later centuries with the aid of tax assessments and rate books, which throw light on the comparative wealth or poverty of urban parishes inside and outside the walls and upon their social standing.

There is much else one could say about the topography of towns. Some of this topographical information will come from borough records of one kind or another, but much of it may come from the skilled examination of large-scale plans of streets and buildings. The late W. H. Stevenson was able to determine the exact limits of the original Saxon borough of Nottingham, and hence the limits of the later French borough which was added to it on the west and north after the Norman Conquest. He started with the fact that a railway cutting in 1890 disclosed a filled ditch and from this he traced the course of the embankment that it once stood inside. He found

---

* The parish church of South Lynn (All Saints) shows a certain amount of twelfth-century work in the chancel—additional proof of the existence of this part of the town well before 1200.

further clues in the peculiar arrangement of certain streets, and in the names originally borne by other streets. Eventually he was able to show that the original borough of Nottingham had been contained within a rectangular space of about thirty-nine acres. Three sides were formed by an earthen rampart and the fourth by a cliff overlooking the Trent. At Northampton the late Alderman Lee was able to demonstrate, again by means of a skilled dissection of the town plan, where the original tenth-century borough of Northampton lay and where 'the new town' was added to it after the Norman Conquest.

SOME REMARKS ON STREETS

There are innumerable topographical problems of this kind awaiting solution all over England. Not only were there more 'double boroughs' like Nottingham and Northampton than Domesday Book reveals to us (for example, Stamford in Lincolnshire) but the layout of the streets in many towns, if looked at with a fresh eye, suggests all sorts of puzzling questions. A series of kinks in a number of streets running roughly parallel with each other would suggest, for example, that at the point where all the streets make this bend there must have been some considerable obstacle which has now disappeared. The same remark applies to inexplicable bends on many roads or lanes today. Where there is no obvious physical reason for such an abrupt change in direction today the answer must be that when the road or lane or street was first trampled out there must have been some obstacle in the way which forced people to go round it.

It has been suggested, for example, in certain towns of Roman origin where the Saxon or early medieval streets do not lie exactly on the line of the Roman streets, that these must represent the

6.6 Stonegate, York

York's principal streets acquired names when *Jorvik* was the Viking capital of the north, so the Scandinavian word *gata* was commonly used. Stonegate was a paved street, the final section of the Roman road from Tadcaster into the heart of the legionary fortress of *Eboracum*. It linked the fortress (which had been established between AD 71 and 74) with the *colonia* or civilian settlement across the River Ouse. After the withdrawal of the Romans, York Minster was built on the site of the fortress, and the northern section of Stonegate was taken within the liberty of the dean and chapter.
Stonegate possesses many historic houses, including the remains of a Norman stone building. Mulberry Hall is an attractive timber-framed house of the fifteenth-century, with gables, a jetty and a pleasant row of oriel windows on the first floor.

irregular tracks trampled out in Saxon times by people who were forced to walk around the ruins of tumbled Roman buildings. Those of us who remember the appearance of a badly bombed town during and just after the recent war have seen this historic process in action for themselves. Where a large built-up area had been flattened by fire or bombing the inhabitants who remained to carry on their daily life and their shopping tramped out entirely new paths, taking short cuts across the flattened area, deviating where necessary around the rubble of some large building which had fallen into the direct line. The topographical development of an old town becomes clear to us if we not only use all the documents that are relevant for the purpose, but also observe how people behave today, for it will throw light upon the way in which they behaved in the past; and nowhere is this more true than in the way in which streets took their shape and direction in our early towns. Apart from the central street, the line of which may have been dictated by some physical fact such as an ancient ford or an early bridge, many of the side streets must have grown up in a rather haphazard and accidental way.

Other questions arise from the close examination of the original street-names in an old town. We all know that such towns usually contain a number of streets named after leading occupations, and the farther back we go into the town records, the more of this type of street-name will come to light. At Nottingham, for example, we still have Wheeler Gate, Fletcher Gate, Bridlesmith Gate, and so on. Many streets which were once called after a particular occupation have changed their names in the course of time, perhaps because that occupation ceased to be carried on there, and a new name grew up which supplanted the older one.

It was natural for people carrying on the same craft or trade to congregate together in the same part of the town. They did not fear competition any more than the adjoining stall-holders in a fish market or a meat market do today; and it was a great convenience for everyone that customers should know exactly where they were to be found. Hence sellers of milk or cheese, or the makers of luxury articles like goldsmiths, or useful people like blacksmiths, established themselves together in a row. In Birmingham to this day the gunsmiths and the jewellers still occupy distinct quarters of this kind.

We must envisage in the very early days of a growing town that most of the burghal area, even of a walled Roman town, consisted of open, empty spaces. Traders in a particular commodity would find themselves assembling and putting up stalls on some empty piece of land and probably more or less in a row. At first these stalls might be removable, but the next stage would come when they became a fixture on the site. Finally, the stalls would give way to small shops with dwelling houses above, and the rough trodden pathway in front of the stalls would be dignified by the name of street. John Stow in his wonderful *Survey of London*, published in the year 1598, tells us that this is what happened in London. Thus he says of Old Fish Street:

> These houses, now possessed by fishmongers, were at the first but moveable boards, or stalls, set out on market days, to show their fish there to be sold; but procuring licence to set up sheds, they grew to shops, and by little and little to tall houses, of three or four stories in height, and are now called Fish Street.

Of another street, formerly called Mountgodard Street, he tells us:

> stall boards were of old time set up by the butchers to show and sell their flesh meat upon, over the which stall boards they first built sheds to keep off the weather; but since then, encroaching by little and little, they have made their stall boards and sheds fair houses, meet for the principal shambles.

Some towns have a Milk Street. Such a street is recorded in the city of London about 1140, and in the city of Exeter some time in the reign of Henry II. The name means not only the street where milk was sold but probably the street where milk was produced also. In other words, when there was ample space in the early days, the cows were actually kept on the spot and milked there. The cowsheds must have occupied a not inconsiderable space and it leads one therefore to search the large-scale town plan to see whether the property boundaries (which are almost invariably ancient) suggest the former existence of an open space in the vicinity of the 'milk street'. That such an open place formerly existed in Exeter is suggested by the fact that the tenth-century church of St George (now demolished) had a blocked west door. The west end of the church was completely built up against at a comparatively early date, but the existence of this blocked doorway is clear evidence that at some date it opened into a space, and this space in turn opened out towards what is now Milk Street. Here, in all probability, stood the cowsheds of the twelfth century and earlier.

These examples of what can be done with old street-names, combined with a close reading of large-scale town plans, are given merely to suggest to students of other towns the interesting possibilities that may lie before them. At Stamford the Great North Road, where it passes through the town, makes two complete right-angled bends within a few yards, and a further abrupt bend shortly afterwards. It is almost incredible that such a narrow road, with such acute bends, should be carrying the heavy lorry traffic of the A1 today. These bends must obviously have an historical explanation, for they cannot have existed originally. The borough records do not help us at all in this enquiry since they were all destroyed by the Lancastrian army in 1461. They now date from 1462 onwards, long after the Great North Road had assumed this curious line. I was therefore driven, in the absence of local documentary evidence, to examine the large-scale plan of the town in the light of such information as could be gleaned from the public records. Even this was not conclusive until walking down Scotgate one day I noticed that the tower and spire of St Mary's, the mother-church of the town, lay straight ahead in a line which suggested at once that the original main road (now A1) had gone directly across what is now a closely built-up area to St Mary's church, and so down the hill to the ford over the river. Beginning with this basic clue, it was possible to evolve a plausible theory for the deviation of the original road from this straight and obvious course. The deviations were to be associated with the building of the castle on the western side of the town in the last quarter of the eleventh century, and with the establishment of the large market-place outside the castle walls. The theory is best illustrated by means of sketch maps (see below). It could never have been evolved without walking along the streets and noticing suddenly a particular alignment; and one can go on walking around the streets of a familiar town year after year and still make discoveries of this kind.

In some towns we may obtain clues about the early street-plan from the mention in Domesday Book of specific churches. If we plot the churches so recorded on a map we may well see that the basic street plan had been fixed by the eleventh century, although away from the main streets there were wide open spaces still occupied only by stallholders, or perhaps not at all. At Exeter, again, the boundaries of the nineteen urban parishes were fixed for the first time in the year 1222. Nearly all the churches of the city were in existence well before this date, but it was not until then that their specific territories or parishes were marked out definitively. Now this tells us among other things that wherever the parish boundary follows a particular street or lane in Exeter that street or lane was in existence before 1222. In other words, it enables us to fill in the very sketchy picture afforded by the Domesday evidence and to produce

6.7 Saxon Stamford, Lincolnshire

Possible limits of Saxon borough, centred on St Mary's Church, indicated by a heavy broken line.

6.8 Domesday Stamford, Lincolnshire

The map shows the development of the new borough to the west of the old, centred on the castle and market-place.

the much more elaborate street plan of the late twelfth century.

It would be interesting to know whether dates are known for the demarcation of parish boundaries in other old towns. Looking at the Exeter parish boundaries as they were set out in 1222, they give rise to questions which are at the moment unanswerable. The same questions must arise in other old towns even if we do not know the exact date at which the boundaries were drawn. I refer to the fact that although many of the parish boundaries run along the middle of a street or a lane, as one might expect for purposes of convenience, they also frequently dodge across the street and take in perhaps two or three tenements on the other side and then dodge back again. In the centre of the city, especially, the interlocking of parish boundaries in this way is most complicated, and it leads one to speculate why they should have been drawn in this extraordinary and apparently irrational fashion. Clearly the boundaries of 1222 were drawn in relation to particular properties, and the full explanation must lie ultimately in some unknown facts about property ownership going back into the twelfth century, if not earlier.

I know of only one other city or town where the approximate date of the parish boundaries is known, and this is Canterbury. Dr W. G. Urry's monumental study of *Canterbury under the Angevin kings* (Athlone Press, 1967) takes the demarcation of the twenty-two medieval parishes back to round about the middle of the twelfth century. Chapter ix, on the topography of the city at this period, should be essential reading for local historians working on medieval towns, though few towns if any have quite this wealth of record material.

SUBURBAN GROWTH AND IN-FILLING

Something has already been said about the early development of suburbs in the larger towns. It is for the local historian to decide why suburbs should appear in certain directions and not in others. Sometimes the early growth of a suburb is connected with industrial development depending on water power, and here we shall find the earlier suburbs towards and along a river. It is sometimes possible to arrive at an approximate idea of the degree of suburban growth by examining the tax assessments of 1524–25. If a suburb corresponds roughly with a parish or a particular quarter of the town which is separately distinguished in the assessments, one can see that by this date x per cent of the population were already living outside the walls. At Leicester, for example, it is possible to say that 45 per cent of the taxpayers were living, in the early sixteenth century, in the four suburban wards. Since many of the wage-earning class would have escaped even this comprehensive tax we could say with certainty that at Leicester the majority of the population were living outside the walled area by this date. One may arrive at another estimate of the degree of suburban growth by examining the Hearth Tax assessments for the third quarter of the seventeenth century. These will generally show a considerable increase in the extramural population over that of the sixteenth century. As the urban population continued to grow, however, there came a limit to the degree to which the town could grow outwards. In the complete absence of what we call 'transport facilities', it was not feasible for the working class to be housed too far from their work. At the same time there had grown up among the wealthier class in the town a desire to move outside the built-up area and to acquire or build a neat house on the outskirts. They vacated their large merchant houses in the main streets of the town and these were turned into tenements inhabited by a number of families. We find this happening in London as early as the sixteenth century; and it is apparent in some of the larger provincial cities during the second half of the seventeenth century, if not somewhat earlier.

In the eighteenth century, generally speaking, a further development took place. The large houses occupying medieval sites almost invariably had an extensive garden and possibly a courtyard as well. All this space became increasingly valuable as the town population grew. So we find the speculative builder acquiring such a site and building upon the garden or courtyard two rows of working-class cottages, facing each other across a narrow paved yard. These new properties were usually called 'courts' or 'buildings'. They were approached through what had been the side passage to the medieval and later house. Older people will remember this type of housing and its tunnel-like approach; but the great bulk of it was swept away in slum clearance schemes in the 1930s and afterwards, and it is now rarely to be seen. It was an interesting phase, however, of housing development. Medieval towns, and later towns down to the seventeenth century, contained considerable areas of open space and the increased population of the seventeenth and eighteenth centuries was housed mainly by filling in such of these spaces as were available. This was particularly true of towns in the Midlands and certain parts of the north of England which were surrounded by their own open fields. Where these fields remained unenclosed until a comparatively

6.9 Nottingham in 1820 (by H. Wild & T. H. Smith)

Sand Field and Clay Field, the two large common fields that lay to the north of the town, were not enclosed until 1845. Until then building development was restricted to the ancient limits of settlement. Nottingham was unable to cope with the population explosion, and the fine old city became infamous for its courtyard slums.

The street pattern shown on this 1820 plan was created in Anglo-Saxon and Norman times. A

32-acre Anglian burh in the east was served by the church of St Mary. The later churches of St Peter and St Nicholas were founded within the twelfth-century borough that lay alongside the Norman castle. By 1820 the large, triangular market-place of the Norman borough had been encroached upon by three blocks of properties, and the wide Parliament Street had replaced the northern section of the old town ditch and wall. Though the physical barriers had gone their restrictive influence remained.

late date, it was impossible for the town to grow outwards, in other words to develop suburbs, because the open fields always involved rights of common pasture after harvest over entire fields. No matter to whom particular strips belonged, they were subject always to the practice of common grazing. The owner of such strips could not sell any piece of his land in the open fields for building, however much he might have wished to take advantage of the pressure upon building sites, because by so doing he would have nullified the pasture rights of a great number of other people. They would have retaliated quickly (and legally) by destroying any fences or buildings that he might put up.

In such towns as this the 'in-filling' of every available bit of space within the burghal area began at a comparatively early date and by the early nineteenth century had produced the worst possible kind of slums. Nottingham was an outstanding example of the kind of town which was forced to go on building on every garden, orchard, or other open space, often quite unsuitable for building, because its open fields were not enclosed until the year 1845. The peculiar topographical development of Nottingham has been well described by the late Professor J. D. Chambers* and historians of open-field towns should refer to his work for guidance in this particular field. The interest of this type of town does not cease with the enclosure of its fields. Enclosure produced a great number of separate small allotments of land, most of which, if not all, became valuable immediately for 'development'. Hence we often get a number of building schemes rapidly developed quite independently of each other, and producing at times a most inconvenient arrangement of streets.

Not all housing development was of this disagreeable kind. In every growing town, land on the outskirts became increasingly valuable for building and owners were increasingly tempted to dispose of their property for this purpose. Some of these building developments for middle-class housing produced whole districts of a most attractive kind in the early nineteenth century or the late eighteenth. In Birmingham the sale of the New Hall estate and its development for building were sanctioned by a private Act of 1746. A part of the estate was kept for a time as a private park but the area nearer the town was laid out in broad straight streets, a well-planned develop-

---

* See *Modern Nottingham in the Making* (Nottingham, 1945) and *A Century of Nottingham History 1851–1951* (Nottingham, 1952). I have also discussed the three open-field towns of Nottingham, Leicester, and Stamford in my book *The Making of the English Landscape* (Hodder & Stoughton, 1955), pp. 216–24.

ment which can be clearly seen to this day to the north-west of Corporation Street.

In studying the physical growth of towns the local historian must keep in mind both the geographical factors (some of which have been touched on in this chapter) and also the historical factors, which are generally not so obvious. By the latter I mean principally the disposal or non-disposal of the property rights in a given area. The growth of a town in certain directions might be frustrated for generations, not only by the existence of open fields, but also by the existence on the outskirts of large enclosed estates which the owners either refused to sell or were debarred from selling by the law of entail. The expansion of Torquay to the west was delayed for many decades in the Victorian period by the refusal of the Mallock family, who owned the adjacent manor of Cockington, to grant any building leases, though it was clearly in their economic interest to do so. Similar examples of the influence of property rights can often be found elsewhere. Thus the local historian, while paying due attention to the geographical factors, must not overlook the influence of the concealed historical factors in his area.*

In the later period, too, the records of the Improvement Commissioners become of the greatest importance for the local historian. These Commissioners were special bodies created by statute and charged with the provision of certain public services such as paving, lighting, and cleansing the streets. The Improvement Commissioners were also to be found in many unincorporated towns. In their records we can often trace in detail the transition from the still largely medieval town to the town as we know it today, and we can trace, too, much of the detail of new building in the late eighteenth century and the early nineteenth.

HOUSES

From the streets of the town the local historian should now turn his attention to the particular houses. Something is said in Chapter 9 of the necessity for making a kind of building survey of one's chosen place. In a town this may be too large an undertaking and it might have to be limited to houses before a given date. There is also

---

* See especially Dyos, *Victorian Suburb* (Camberwell) for a wide treatment of these 'concealed' factors.

Scale *of* Chains

Priory Park

Sand Pits

6.10 Plan of Hitchin, Hertfordshire, in 1820 (detail)

The modern town-centre of Hitchin is immediately recognisable from this 1820 plan, and
many of the old timber-framed and Georgian buildings survive. Hitchin was founded as a
market town in the early Middle Ages and became prosperous through the wool trade. The
market-place was triangular in shape, tapering from Bancroft to the through road marked by
Bridge Street and Tile House Street. By the fifteenth century (and probably long before)

tradesmen's stalls and rows were permanently established in the market area, as at Middle Row, Stevenage and French Row, St Albans. A triangular wedge between Bancroft and the Market Place and a rectangular block between Bucklersbury and Sun Street were encroached upon in this way, as in many other English medieval market towns. The Market Place now forms a car park and is only a fraction of its former size, and the splendid Perpendicular church of St Mary's appears rather tucked away from the old commercial centre.

the need to describe the housing of past centuries as revealed by such documents as survive, coupled with the exploration of surviving buildings of different periods. Probate inventories are our best source for recovering information about the kind of houses our ancestors lived in. It is also worth while, if one lives in a cathedral city where the Bishop or the Dean and Chapter may have possessed much house property, to explore the archives of these bodies, above all, of course, the leases (and occasionally conveyances) of such house property to citizens. Some medieval leases and conveyances give a brief description of the house, telling us often what rooms it contained; and some later leases may contain long and rather elaborate descriptions, occasionally with a ground-plan, of houses of seventeenth- or eighteenth-century date. In general such records relate to what we may call middle-class housing, but we may also have a smattering of inventories and leases relating to the homes of small craftsmen and tradesmen. The records of the Court of Orphans at Exeter contain several hundred inventories for the period 1560 to 1643. These relate not only to a considerable number of houses belonging to merchants, great and small, but also to the houses of bakers, butchers, weavers, saddlers, fullers, blacksmiths, and numerous other trades. They also contain a number of inventories of inn-holders and hence give us some sort of picture of inns in the city in the early seventeenth century. Several English towns possessed such Courts of Orphans, which were set up in order to safeguard the interests of children who were left orphans at an early age, and their records should not be overlooked for our immediate purpose. Derek Portman's book on *Exeter Houses 1400–1700* (Exeter University, 1966) used these and other records to good effect.

The record material for houses in the eighteenth century is generally very scanty. Newspaper advertisements of houses to be sold or let are a valuable source.* With the eighteenth century and the early nineteenth we arrive at a period for which many typical houses of all classes still survive. The local historian should examine a number of these, making a plan and giving a description of them, since they are likely to perish in the course of time.

Even houses of the late Victorian period are by no means devoid of value for the local historian. In the Midlands and the north of England especially, where towns were growing rapidly in this period, the custom of dating new houses and whole terraces as they were

* For a fuller discussion of the documentary sources available for the history and development of vernacular building, see Chapter 9, pp. 182–90.

built tells the historian a good deal about the physical expansion of the town decade by decade. Much of this information could doubtless be derived from rate-books also, but there is everything to be said for the local historian walking his streets and recording all these dates directly on a large-scale map while there is yet time. Already, too, these little brick-built and stone-built roads and streets have acquired their own melancholy charm, with their gas-lamps and often their cobbled surfaces, and the historian who walks along them, rather than reads about them in a rate-book, will absorb unconsciously a feeling for his chosen place, even in its dimmer parts, that will eventually reveal itself in the warmth of his writing.

7 TOWNS: SOCIAL AND ECONOMIC HISTORY

Most of the social and economic history which appears in town histories is inclined to be scrappy and disconnected and to lack any major themes. This is probably because social history itself has until recently been treated as a sort of rag-bag into which one throws everything which is not clearly part of some other well-defined field of history. As for economic history, its treatment in town histories has suffered because local historians have not known what kinds of questions to ask in this field of enquiry and how to tackle them systematically. So we often get disconnected references to the wages paid in a town at a certain date in the fourteenth century, or to the prices paid for certain commodities at a particular date in the seventeenth century. This is simply antiquarianism and such facts have no real significance when presented in this way. I want, therefore, in this chapter to suggest some of the themes which I think are important in the study of social and economic history. I am aware that economic history has a forbidding sound and is calculated to leave many local historians stone cold. But this is a mistaken view: it merely means that one's interest in the subject has not been properly aroused.

We are all living economic and social history much more than we shall ever live, for example, military history or political history; and therefore this kind of history ought to interest us much more than the other kinds because we are intimately concerned with it every day of our lives, either as earners of money or as spenders of money. Our housekeeping bills are raw materials for the economic historian. The household accounts, if we still have them, of pre-war days already have a curiously historic flavour to those of us who read through them again today.

OCCUPATIONS

The local historian should, then, make a good deal in his history of a town of the ways in which his townspeople have got their livings in the past: in what kinds of trades and crafts, what their wages were and their general working conditions, the prices of the goods on which they spent their wages, and the kind of things they bought. We want to know also something of the ways in which they spent their lives outside their work: how they were educated, if at all, what kind of games they played or how they employed their leisure generally, what kind of health they enjoyed and so forth. It is not always easy for the local historian to write a systematic account of the occupations of his townspeople at different times, above all in the smaller towns, for which the records may be scanty. In large towns it is usually possible to build up a reasonably accurate picture of the way the townspeople earned their living by studying the register of freemen which sometimes gives the occupations of the men admitted to the freedom. By counting these and classifying them into groups we can obtain a fairly accurate picture of the occupational structure of the town.

We must remember, however, that there may have been certain trades in which it was not the custom to obtain the freedom or where perhaps the privilege was too costly for the majority of men in that trade to acquire it. Again, some towns were more selective than others in their admissions to the freedom; and we also find that the number of admissions in the same town may vary widely from time to time (possibly for political reasons). Even the fullest lists must therefore be used with care. Despite these qualifications, the lists of freemen convey to us a picture of the economic make-up of the town which no other kind of record can give us. We can supplement this to some extent by noting the occupations which are mentioned in other kinds of records, above all in Apprenticeship Books or loose indentures of which there may be a long series in some town archives. Transfers of property (conveyances, leases, etc.) may also bring to light the existence of a few trades which are not otherwise recorded. In default of early material, the existence of street-names derived from particular òccupations will provide us with a valuable clue to the dominant occupations of the town in the medieval period.

We can also obtain some significant information about the economic make-up of the town by noting the occupations of all those who were elected mayor. The mayor was almost invariably chosen from the wealthier class in any town, and if we find that the mayors tend to be drawn from two or three particular trades or crafts, we may be sure that these are the dominant occupations in the town from one point of view. They may not employ the most people, but they clearly produce the bigger incomes. At Leicester, for example, an analysis of the occupations of mayors during the sixteenth century shows that mercers and merchants are represented more times than any other occupation, nineteen times in all. But they occur thirteen times before 1550 and only six times between 1550 and 1603. In other words, mercers and merchants were clearly becoming less important in the economic structure of the town. On the other hand, in the eighty years from 1485 to 1564 the tanners produced only two mayors, while in the thirty years from 1565 to

7.1 The medieval guildhall, Leicester

The guildhall was built for the Corpus Christi guild, which was founded in 1343 and dissolved in 1547. Three eastern bays date from the fourteenth century and two western ones were added about 1450. Base-crucks, that is cruck blades which reach from the ground to a tie-beam but which do not continue to the ridge, were used in the earliest bays. The hall was the largest of a group of buildings that were arranged around a courtyard.

The mayor and corporation met originally in the Common Hall or Mayor's Hall in Blue Boar Lane, but they had begun to meet here instead by the end of the fifteenth century. They purchased the property in 1563 and continued to use it until 1876.

1595 they produced no fewer than ten. Clearly, tanning was a much more important industry in Leicester from the second half of the sixteenth century onwards, and this is confirmed by the number of butchers who became mayor in the same period. From 1485 to 1550 the butchers produced only one mayor, but in the thirty-three years between 1559 and 1592 they filled the mayoral chair seven times. This kind of elementary analysis over different periods produces information not only about the economic structure of the town at a particular time, but also about changes in the relative importance of different trades and occupations which we should perhaps not otherwise discover. One might conceivably extend the analysis of the occupations to the town council, or whatever the governing body was. This should reveal on an even wider scale the dominant trades and crafts in the town.

The urban historian who wishes to see what can be done in this field of enquiry is referred to my article in the *Transactions of the Royal Historical Society* (1956) on 'English provincial towns in the early sixteenth century', where he will find, for example, a comparative table of the leading occupations in three midland towns, Coventry, Northampton, and Leicester.* Each of these towns specialised to some considerable degree—Coventry was primarily a textile town, and Northampton and Leicester were already specialising in the leather trades. But what is interesting is to discover that in all three towns there is a basic similarity of economic make-up. The clothing trades provided work for 14 to 15 per cent of the occupied population; the food and drink trades for 15 to 21 per cent; and the building trades for 4 to $7\frac{1}{2}$ per cent. If we take these three fundamental groups of trades, we see that in any English provincial town it is likely that they gave employment to something like 35 to 40 per cent of the occupied population. We tend to over-simplify when we talk about the occupations of towns. Our local historians are obsessed with cloth and wool to the exclusion of almost everything else. There was a great variety of trades even in a predominantly textile town. At Coventry in the early sixteenth century there were about ninety distinct occupations, and in Elizabethan Bristol there were over a hundred trades for apprentices to choose from. Northampton and Leicester were smaller towns at this time but even they had sixty or more distinct occupations. The local historian must not content himself, therefore, with vague remarks about wool merchants or cloth merchants, and the woollen industry generally. He

* Reprinted in my *Provincial England*, pp. 68–85.

could almost certainly make much more of this side of his town than this.

Such lists and analyses of occupations are valuable in another way. If they are sufficiently detailed, for example if we have annual lists of freemen which also give occupations, we can trace exactly the beginnings of new trades and we can also ascertain sometimes how new occupations came into existence. It is well known that glass was made for churches and for rich men's houses throughout the middle ages, but that the houses of ordinary people did not achieve glass windows until the closing years of the sixteenth century when new methods of production brought the price of glass within the reach of the middle class. At Leicester we have one or two glaziers in the late fifteenth century, but with the cessation of church building their trade dried up and not a single glazier was admitted to the freedom of the town between 1496 and 1573. By the early 1590s there were four or five glaziers at work again in the town of Leicester, and from this we may deduce that the practice of putting glass in the windows of middle-class houses was now growing rapidly. If we look into the detailed history of individual glaziers we see that two of them at least had started their working lives as 'rough masons'. From this occupation it was an easy transition to the fitting of glass windows. In the same way, in the records of freemen admitted in the eighteenth century we can trace the rise of the profession of architect. Looking back through the records one may discover that a man who is described as architect in 1800 had begun his working life as a joiner. The uses to which these occupational records may be put are almost endless in their variety and they give us information about townspeople which is not otherwise recorded because it is so everyday and commonplace. It is the commonplace things that never get written down because we take them so much for granted in our own lives.

WAGES AND PRICES

So far, we have considered only the occupational make-up of the town and the kind of records that help us to ascertain it. We also want to know what wages people earned in different trades, and something about their working conditions. These are not easy questions to deal with, especially again in small towns which have no elaborate records, but in the larger towns we should turn first of all to the borough accounts, called variously in different towns the

Receiver's accounts, or the Chamberlain's accounts, or the Steward's accounts. These not only reveal the income and expenditure of the town, but they often give details of wages paid for particular kinds of work, and of the prices paid for various materials and commodities. This is particularly true if we turn from the annual accounts themselves to the vouchers behind them; that is, the individual bills and statements rendered to the Receiver or Chamberlain, or whatever he was called, for particular jobs. Here we get basic facts about wages and prices at a given time.

At Exeter, apart from a solitary account for 1306–07, the Receiver's account rolls and books run in an almost unbroken series of annual statements from 1339 to 1835. From 1836 onwards they are continued by the printed accounts of the Treasurer down to the present day. We have, therefore, in this city the materials for a continuous financial history for over six hundred years, and probably for a comprehensive history of wages and prices over the same long period. The Receiver's Vouchers have not been preserved over so long a period. They run from 1562 to 1834, with some gaps in the late sixteenth century. The Vouchers for 1835–36 are missing, probably lost in the great change-over from the unreformed Corporation to the new Corporation. From 1836 onwards the Treasurer's Vouchers carry on the series.

At King's Lynn in Norfolk the Chamberlain's Accounts begin in 1327–28 and form a splendid series down to 1835. At Bristol, the main series of financial records are known as Audits. The great and little audits run from 1532 to 1785, and the Vouchers survive from 1696 onwards. There are numerous other financial records among the city archives, all of which help to fill out the picture, most notably the journals which cover the period 1777 to 1926. The city records of Norwich include an almost complete series of Chamberlain's or Treasurer's Accounts from 1293 to 1835, followed by the City Treasurer's Account Books from 1836 to the present day. Again there are other financial records to fill in the details, including cash ledgers of various committees from 1721 to 1835.

Apart from the great mass of topographical information contained in such accounts and the corresponding vouchers, and the mass of information about wages and prices, the accounts may also be used by the local historian for their proper purpose—that is, to write a history of the town finances showing the income of the town and its various sources, and on the other side the expenditure. As far as I know, no town history has attempted to produce a picture of this kind. It would clearly be a most valuable addition to urban history if we could get it. It might conceivably be treated as a special enquiry on its own by a retired accountant or someone else especially interested in financial questions, without attempting to write a comprehensive history of every aspect of the town. *

ECONOMIC GROWTH AND CHANGE

The local historian of a town more than any other kind of local historian must see all around his chosen subject. He must know, in other words, what is happening in the other towns in his own county or region, whether they are growing relatively in relation to his own, whether his own town is keeping pace with the general rate of growth for the region, or whether it is stagnating or even declining at certain periods. This may most conveniently be done by comparing the tax yield of the various towns within a county for the years 1334, 1524, and (say) 1660, or one of the subsequent poll taxes. All the necessary records are to be found in the Public Record Office. Thus in Devon the historian of the little town of Totnes, which badly needs a competent history, would find that it stood a poor sixth in wealth among the Devonshire towns of 1334, a strong second in 1524, and had sunk to ninth in the poll tax of 1667. Facts such as these are the basic data for the historian of Totnes between the fourteenth century and the seventeenth. There must be similar towns and similar problems of economic and social change in almost every other part of England.

For the larger towns, which were of some importance in the national economy, it is necessary that he should know how his town is faring in terms of wealth and population in relation to comparable towns and cities. As the centuries go by his town may be emerging from comparative obscurity into the front rank of the towns of the kingdom. At a later date it may become clear that it is losing ground rapidly to towns of a similar character in other parts of England. Once he is able to perceive basic facts about economic growth and change as revealed by a comparative table of the ranking of towns, he is in a position to ask himself more fundamental and significant questions than he could possibly have asked if he had confined himself solely to the records of his own community.

It is not easy for the local historian to obtain such comparative

---

* The Bristol accounts were studied by D. M. Livock in the *Journal of Accounting Research* vol. iii, no. 1 (1965).

ideas about his town and others. For this reason I have given in an appendix a table showing the ranking of the leading provincial towns in this country between 1334 and 1861. This table is based partly upon tax assessments which show the taxable capacity of the various towns, partly upon population figures, and partly upon the Hearth Tax Assessments which are a rough and ready guide to the size of towns in the third quarter of the seventeenth century. The historian who wishes to obtain the comparative material for an earlier period will find the appendices in Stephenson's *Borough and Town* (Cambridge, Mass., Medieval Academy of America, 1933) a handy source for the ranking of towns between 1086 and the end of the twelfth century. No comparative material of this kind seems to exist in handy form for the thirteenth century.

Within this broad framework the urban historian is in a position to study the facts of economic growth and change in his own community. He will know before he begins his detailed enquiries into the relevant local records that there are certain broad changes which he is called upon to explain. It is an enormous help, especially when one is handling what may be a very large collection of records, to know beforehand what kind of information one is looking for and to be able to reject masses of facts which may be interesting in themselves but which one strongly suspects will lead nowhere. One may in fact come across a great deal of interesting material which ought not to be rejected out of hand. It would be unwise to clutter up a book with such detail if one is attempting to deal with major themes of social and economic history. But the byway information may well be worked up into an interesting short note or article for the *Proceedings* or *Transactions* of the local historical society.

A great deal of material for the economic history of towns which have been of some importance in the national economy (especially, of course, towns which have had overseas trade connections) will be found in the Public Record Office and to a lesser extent in some of the special collections in the British Library. This is a large subject, for which there is no short and handy guide. The local historian who is venturing into this field would do well to consult someone else's town history, written in the modern period, and to note carefully what kind of sources he has used in the national collections. One learns a great deal about the sources of local history from reading other people's footnote references. The standard *Guide to the Contents of the Public Record Office* (3 vols, 1963–68) is supplemented by *Current Guides* which record material acquired since 1966. The Public Record Office is now divided between two sites, one at

Chancery Lane and the other at Kew. Another invaluable guide is
that of *Maps and Plans in the Public Record Office*. Volume i (1967)
covers the British Isles from *c*. 1410 to 1860, region by region and
county by county. This is full of remarkable treasures, and the local
historian will ignore it at his peril. For the British Library the best
introduction is T. C. Skeat, *The Catalogues of the Manuscript
Collections* (revised edn, 1962). There are also the excellent little
Students' Guide to the Manuscripts of the British Museum, by Julius
P. Gilson (SPCK Helps for Students of History, 1920), and M. A.
E. Nickson, *The British Library: Guide to the Catalogues and
Indexes of the Department of Manuscripts* (1978).

The historian of a town will also find much valuable economic
and social information in the probate inventories, which have already
been referred to in another connection. They are especially rich and
detailed for the sixteenth and seventeenth centuries. The immense
collection of inventories at Lincoln will serve as an example:

> There are the multifarious tradesmen, the glovers, tanners, cord-
> wainers, tailors, bricklayers, joiners, potters, weavers, and glue makers
> whose stock in trade and debts are set forth in some detail, making
> possible a survey of the location and organisation of their trades. It
> is interesting and important to note, for example, that a Gainsborough
> joiner in 1697 had among his stock furniture ready made up, French
> beds, tester beds, and livery cupboards, and that a Brigg bridler had
> sold his manufactures in Lincoln, Howden, and Grantham. The organ-
> isation of retail trade is also well represented with the extraordinary
> mixture of stocks carried by mercers and apothecaries (a Stamford
> mercer of 1606 stocked among other things ribbons, salad oil, treacle,
> tobacco, frankincense, and knitting pins) and by the recurrence of
> chapmen and badgers serving small areas. A wealthy inhabitant of
> Folkingham, with no stock of goods, had stalls in Folkingham market
> and Stow Green fair in 1697. In Spalding it appears from an inventory
> of 1606 that trade in such goods as wheat, oats, faggots, and butter
> was to some extent in the hands of watermen, who seem to have gone
> as far afield as St Ives. The fishing industry is unexpectedly illuminated
> by a Grimsby fishmonger's goods (1607) which included sea green cod,
> colesea fish, Holland ling, staple ling, Iceland cod, and Scottish cod.
> The importance of the Trent as a trading route can be seen in the
> numbers of persons owning shares in Stockwith and Gainsborough
> vessels and holding bills of sale for places as far away as Whitby (1696).*

The inventories of Newcastle merchants printed by the Surtees
Society (especially vols. 2 and 38) are valuable not only for the descriptions of their houses, furniture, and plate, but also for the

---

* Lincolnshire Archives Committee: Archivists' Report for 1957–58, p. 51.

detailed lists of the contents of cellars and warehouses. These show the remarkable range of commodities that entered into Newcastle trade in Elizabethan times. Coal still played a comparatively minor part. The inventories supplement admirably the more general information that can be gathered from the Port Books and Custom Accounts in the Public Record Office, and tell us much besides about the range of a merchant's internal trade. Lists of debts are particularly valuable for this purpose. At Exeter, for example, the inventory of Harry Maunder, merchant, made in 1564, catalogues the contents of the warehouse, shop, and cellar, and ends with a list of 'Dettes dewe unto the sayd Harrye Maunder as appereth by hys Shoppe booke'. No fewer than a hundred and twelve customers, of all social classes, are named, with the goods they owe for, and the amount owing. The amounts vary from one penny to £18 9s 8d.

It need hardly be said that a good local historian will also read all the wills made by the inhabitants of his town (or rural parish). So far as merchants and traders are concerned, these contain a good deal of incidental economic information. The whereabouts of the wills and inventories for a given place is occasionally a matter of some obscurity. They may not be all in one place, or they may be in an unexpected place. The standard guides to this important subject are *Wills and their Whereabouts* by A. J. Camp (Society of Genealogists, 1974) and J. S. W. Gibson, *Wills and where to find them* (Phillimore, 1974), with details of many changes in the location of wills in recent years. Even if the enquirer believes that the wills for his town lie in the local probate registry or have been transferred from there to the local record office, he will find a great number of townsmen's wills also in the Prerogative Court of Canterbury in the Public Record Office. Broadly speaking, the will of the wealthier classes—those who held personal property in more than one ecclesiastical jurisdiction—will be found in this immense collection. The historian of such little towns, for example, as Totnes (Devon) or Stamford (Lincs), both of which have had an important industrial and commercial history in their day, will find a considerable number of their merchants' wills at the P.R.O., and he could not profess to write an adequate history of these towns, and many like them, without making this search. Thus from 1489 to 1629, roughly the heyday of Totnes industry and trade, there are no fewer than a hundred and twelve Totnes wills at the P.R.O., the majority of them those of substantial merchants. There are fifty wills for the Elizabethan period alone.

The wills in the Prerogative Court of Canterbury have been

indexed by the British Record Society from 1383, when they begin, down to 1700, except for the period 1630–52 which has been covered by the *Year Books of Probates*, edited by John and George Matthews in several volumes. They contain an enormous mass of information of all kinds about the upper minority of the population and no adequate local history can be written without this knowledge.

SOCIAL STRUCTURE

Something has already been said about the materials for composing a picture of the occupational structure of a town and of the methods involved in this kind of enquiry. It is also desirable that the local historian, if he is to present his material in a form useful to other historians, should try to build up a picture of the social structure of the town. This is perhaps not practicable for the smaller towns, but for the more important towns, which have their own considerable collections of records and also figure largely in the public records, it is possible to present such a picture at one or two periods of time. For this purpose, we are dependent upon tax assessments of one kind and another. It need hardly be said that the tax assessments of the past were not intended to be used in this way and the historian who uses them is faced with some formidable difficulties. Basically, these are two. The first is: Are we sure that the greater part of the population is accounted for in the assessment, and if not is there any means of finding out how many people escaped the record? The second question is: Assuming that the assessment is a comprehensive one or that we know at any rate how many are excluded, how near the truth are the particular assessments of a man's real or personal property? The majority of tax assessments to be found in the Public Record Office are quite useless for the serious study of the distribution of wealth in a given community. They are only of value as listing the principal inhabitants at a given date and therefore of some slight value to students of genealogy. But some are worth a close study.

The first tax assessment we can use with any confidence is the lay subsidy for 1524–25. This record exists, or should exist, for all towns and villages in the country except certain places which were specifically exempted from it.* This great assessment reveals two basic facts about the social structure of the time: (*a*) that there was already a great inequality in the distribution of worldly goods, and (*b*) that there was already a considerable class of wage labour.

Before using this record for himself the local historian should refer to the admirable article 'Wealth and trade in Leicester in the early sixteenth century', by Derek Charman, published in the *Transactions of the Leicestershire Archaeological Society* for 1949. This article will show him some of the deficiencies of the record, and also that valuable information can be extracted from it nevertheless. He should also consult *Desolation of a City* by Charles Phythian-Adams (Cambridge University Press, 1979) which uses these assessments together with other records to provide a unique portrait of a late-medieval city in decline.

It is likely that even in this comprehensive assessment a considerable number of townspeople escaped the assessor because they were too poor. At Coventry, for example, comparison with a fuller list of 1522 made ostensibly for another purpose, shows that about 37 per cent of the population escaped the 1524–25 assessment. At Exeter, a town of roughly comparable size, possibly one-third escaped assessment on the grounds of poverty. At Leicester, Mr Charman's article suggests again that about one-third of the town population are not recorded in the assessment. If we look at those who are assessed in the subsidy we can arrive at some important conclusions even if the individual assessments are lower than the true personal wealth of the people concerned. We can assume that if there is under-valuation it will be approximately the same for everybody or there would have been serious friction in the town. As an example of the kind of information we can extract from this record, then, we find that at Leicester the total taxable property amounted to £2,639 in 1524. Of this sum, one important merchant family, the Wigstons, owned rather more than one-quarter, and the top six families owned one-third of the taxable wealth in the town. The majority of taxpayers owned very little property indeed: the bottom half of the population owned only about one-seventh of the property between them. The Suffolk cloth towns of Lavenham and Long Melford show an even greater degree of inequality. In these two towns together the leading thirteen taxpayers, probably all rich cloth merchants, owned nearly two-thirds of the personal property.

* The Act of 1523 (text in *Statutes of the Realm*, iii, pp. 230–41) which authorised the collection of the subsidy exempted the following: Catherine, Queen of England, and the inhabitants of Ireland, Wales, Calais, Guernsey and Jersey; the English inhabitants of the Cinque Ports and the members thereof; the counties of Northumberland, Cumberland, Westmorland, and Cheshire; the bishop of Durham; the towns of Brighton and Westbourne; the wardens of Rochester Bridge; and the town of Ludlow.

In the countryside the degree of inequality, as we might expect, is considerably less but is still very marked. It can be calculated in exactly the same way as for towns.

One can also ascertain in many places the size of the wage-earning class. The assessment of 1524–25 was made on lands, personal property ('goods'), or wages. No man was assessed on all three, but on whichever category produced the most revenue for the exchequer. In the case of wage-earners, they are usually assessed on 'wages' but not always. At Exeter 47 per cent of the names on the 1524 assessment are those of wage-earners. There is also a small class ($3\frac{1}{2}$ per cent) of people assessed on 'goods' to the value of one pound, whom we may well suspect of being wage-earners. We can say then that at least one-half of the taxable population of the city in 1524 belonged to the wage-earning class. If we bring in the large class who escaped the assessment altogether (many of whom would be poor widows), the size of the wage-earning class rises to something like 60 to 70 per cent. An examination of the assessments for comparable towns suggests that the wage-earning class in these was about the same size, that is about two persons in every three. The record is not always as clear on this point as we should like. It looks as though the assessors in some towns classified the wage-earners under 'goods': that is, on their meagre personal estate which was reckoned to bring in the same revenue to the exchequer as if they were assessed on wages. Where then we have a town with very few people assessed on 'wages' and a great number assessed on 'goods' to the value of one pound we must regard the latter class as being really wage-earners and must count them accordingly.

In some parts of the country the assessments of the mid-1540s give more information than those of the 1520s, but as the sixteenth century went on the lay subsidies became less and less valuable. That collected in 1546 is the last that is really worth looking at from this point of view. After that date the subsidies roped in fewer and fewer people, and of those who were roped in the assessments became increasingly unreal. A commissioner of taxes in the 1590s declared that nobody was assessed at more than a tenth of his true wealth, and some at only a twentieth or even a thirtieth. An examination of this statement in the town of Leicester (comparing a man's subsidy assessment with the size of his personal estate at death as revealed in his probate inventory) shows this view to be correct. Direct taxation had become almost nonsensical for the time being.

The next records which we can use for the purpose of reconstructing the social hierarchy are the Hearth Tax assessments. For this purpose it is necessary to choose an assessment which includes the names of those who were exempt on grounds of poverty. Not all the assessments give this information. The fullest assessment from this point of view is generally the assessment of 1662 or 1664, although in my experience the assessments of 1670 and 1674 are valuable also.* If we assume that the size of a man's house, as measured by the number of hearths it contained, is a rough index to his wealth and position in local society, we can classify the town population by categories according to the house sizes. Those who are interested in following up this method of approach to the social structure of a town are referred to my *Industry, Trade and People in Exeter, 1688 to 1800*, pp. 111–22. A similar analysis has been made for the town of Leicester in 1670 (*V.C.H. Leics*, iv, p. 159).

It is easy to criticise this type of analysis on the grounds of deficiencies in the records and of an inevitable arbitrariness in the categories, but with care one can arrive at a fair picture of the social and economic structure of a town for the first quarter of the sixteenth century and the third quarter of the seventeenth. If we are not prepared to use these records in this way we leave ourselves completely in the dark on this important subject. They represent the best sources we have.

One could produce a similar picture to some extent by a painstaking analysis of the census schedules of 1841 to 1881 which give the occupations of the whole population, town by town and parish by parish. It is true that the printed census reports for these years give a rough classification by occupations, but this is too crude for our particular purpose. We must go back to the original schedules and build up our own picture. In a way it will be even more defective than the picture we obtain for the 1520s or the 1660s since we obtain no idea from the census schedules of the comparative wealth of the people enumerated. There is no means of ascertaining this at any time during the nineteenth century. But at least we shall obtain a picture of the size of the wage-earning class, of the professional class, and so on. It is the best we can do and it is worth having with all its faults.

* By far the best discussion of the various Hearth Tax assessments is contained in C. A. F. Meekings, *Dorset Hearth Tax Assessments, 1662–1664* (Dorset County Museum, Dorchester, 1951). See Appendix III especially. This also gives valuable summaries of the 1662 assessment for all the counties of England and Wales, and of the principal towns in each country. Every local historian should consult this volume before embarking on the actual assessments.

The foregoing remarks far from exhaust the study of social and economic history in a town. They are only intended to supply a firm skeleton, as it were, which the local historian will then proceed to clothe with living flesh, with the *details* of past life which alone make history come alive. And economic history, more than most kinds of history, needs this covering of human detail to make it presentable. I have said a good deal about the great subsidy of 1524–25, and the uses to which it may be put: on the face of it an arid kind of record. But when one reads under 'Southwark' that the tax-collector even extracted money from 'the 12 bawds of the Bank', this inhuman record comes alive in a flash and we catch a fleeting glimpse of some of the real people behind the columns of figures. We get the same feeling in reading the inventory of Robert Thorne, the merchant tailor of London who died in 1532, when the record suddenly lists among his possessions in Spain 'a house and slaves in Sevyle' worth £94.

One can all too easily criticise the average local historian for his remorseless and undiscriminating collection of details; but it is detail, rightly selected, that finally illuminates the generalisations, all the talk about taxable wealth and social classes, wage levels, and price movements. One must never forget that history is about *people*; and the local historian least of all should need this reminder.

8 FIELDWORK: THE LANDSCAPE

Many local histories, even the best, have one remarkable failing, and that is their complete neglect of what may be called the visual evidence of the past. You may ransack every source you can think of, printed and manuscript, in all the conceivable record offices in England and in your own district: but this is by no means the end of the story. There is scarcely a parish or a town history that sets out to tell us in one self-contained chapter what the place looks like. Even some of the best local historians think that all history is to be found in documents of one sort or another. They completely overlook the visible evidence all around them, the evidence of their own eyes. The prehistorian who is dealing with a period before there are any written documents, or the Romano-British archaeologist who has very few documents to help him, is forced to use this visual evidence. He digs for it, or finds it in the local museum, and whatever he finds he examines minutely; and he treats every fragment as a piece of evidence. But the historian dealing with periods of time when, generally speaking, there are abundant documents, completely forgets this valuable visual evidence and falls into the delusion that all history can be found in books and documents. Another delusion is that unless some piece of visual evidence can be confirmed or supported by some document it is not worthy of serious consideration. Let me give one illustration of what I mean. There is a first-class history by R. P. Chope of the large parish of Hartland in North Devon. This book was the fruit of a lifetime of research in the local records and among the records in the British Library and the Public Record Office in London. All this was well put together and the book is crammed with information. It so happens that this parish is full of the most interesting farmhouses dating in the main from the sixteenth and seventeenth centuries, though I suspect that some of them are in part medieval if only one explored them systematically. Several of these interesting houses stand on sites which are recorded as far back as Domesday Book. There surely should have been a whole chapter devoted to these fascinating houses: but there is nothing. They are as much historical evidence as anything written on paper, more valuable in fact than much that we get from documents because they cannot tell lies. They tell us facts about the past life of the parish that no written record ever set out to do, Mainly, of course, because the facts were too commonplace at the time to be considered worthy of record. People took their houses, their rooms, and the way they were furnished, completely for granted without reflecting about them in any way, in precisely the same way that we do our own houses. This is only one example of the kind of evidence that ought to go into every good local history.

I would say that every local history ought to begin with a chapter entitled 'The Face of the Parish' or 'The Face of the Town' as the case may be. Such a chapter might possibly come at the end of a local history as a kind of summing-up, but in the main I am inclined to put it first in the book for two reasons. It would give you, as the author, a kind of all-round picture of the place you were going to write about, clearing your mind of all the inessentials and giving you a few guiding lines throughout the subsequent chapters. Secondly, it would be an admirable introduction to the reader who might not know your town or parish. You give him this general picture of what it looks like today, a sort of conducted tour with a map on which you mark the interesting and significant things, so that his

8.1 Town End Farm, Cumbria

The best known of all the Cumbrian 'statesman' houses, Town End Farm was built by George Browne shortly after his marriage in 1623 and remained the family's property until 1944. It is now owned by the National Trust.

Troutbeck parish straggled for about a mile from Town Head to Town End. The Brownes were the most important local family and one of the wealthiest for miles around. George Browne was described as a yeoman of Troutbeck in 1525. The family moved up the social scale in 1623 when another George Browne (1596–1689) married Susannah Rawlinson of Grizedale Hall in High Furness. In the marriage settlement George agreed to build an entirely new house. It is likely that the previous building was timber-framed in the cruck tradition.

The new house consisted of a 'firehouse' separated by a cross-passage from the 'downhouse' or kitchen, with upstairs chambers. Later, a parlour range, dairy and bower were erected at each end and to the rear. When George and Susannah's son inherited the property his neighbours described him as a gentleman rather than a yeoman.

appetite is whetted and his curiosity aroused at the start. The reader is not likely to get excited if you give him to start with the rather cryptic entry from Domesday Book, followed by a forest of details about the manorial descent of the medieval period. Let the first chapter be 'The Face of the Parish'. It might even be the best chapter in the book.

I begin with an elementary suggestion, though I doubt whether one local historian in ten has ever carried it out. It is this: you should walk around and describe the boundaries of the ancient ecclesiastical parish or the boundaries of whatever is your chosen territory. (Towns, of course, present a special problem in this respect and they are dealt with separately in Chapter 6.) The boundaries of the ancient ecclesiastical parish are not always easy to discover. Those boundaries marked on the modern Ordnance Survey maps are the boundaries of the civil parish which may or may not coincide with the boundaries of the ancient ecclesiastical parish. Many civil parish boundaries are relatively modern, the result of nineteenth-century administrative changes, and therefore of no particular significance. The boundaries of the ancient parish can be found on the tithe map, which has already been referred to. Occasionally a tithe map may be slightly tattered and some of the boundary obscured, but if you then get hold of the tithe map of the adjacent parish you will recover the information you want about your own parish. Having ascertained the ancient parish boundaries in this way, you then perambulate them (which may take some time), noting if they have any special features, for example an unusually large bank and ditch or occasionally a boundary stone, or it may be a cross or the remains of a cross. You may make some archaeological discoveries by walking around the ancient boundaries; but even if you do not at least you will get the feeling of your chosen territory in a way that nothing else can give.

Inside the parish itself there are probably many visible marks on the landscape which call for inspection and recording. You may not be able to explain some of the things you see, for example a prominent earthen bank running for some distance along some fields or down the edge of a wood; but even if you cannot explain the significance of what you see it should be photographed and described as carefully as possible so that someone coming after you, perhaps a hundred years hence, may recognise what it is you once saw.

An indispensable handbook for the local historian engaged in field work is *Field Archaeology: Some Notes for Beginners*, issued by the Ordnance Survey (fourth edn, 1963). This handbook contains a great deal of valuable information about the minor features of the countryside which I cannot repeat or condense here. Every local historian should possess his own copy of this guide.

I am not concerned in this book with prehistoric sites, which are too big and specialised a subject to be covered in a cursory fashion. There are plenty of books on this subject for the guidance of the local historian. Even in the historic period, however, there may be archaeological sites, the meaning of which can be completely ascertained only by some kind of excavation. I do not wish to say anything which will encourage untrained amateurs, however enthusiastic they may be, to engage in excavation of any kind. It is something which requires skilled training, and unskilled excavation is likely to ruin a site completely for anyone coming afterwards. Nor will the amateur excavator, except in rare cases, really appreciate what he is uncovering or know how to record it properly. If, therefore, you think or suspect that you have in your parish a site which is interesting for your local history, you should not (unless of course you are trained as an archaeologist) attempt any work on it yourself. The best thing to do is to take advice from the nearest competent archaeologist, either at your local museum or elsewhere.

There is, however, a great deal of field work which can be done by the local historian without digging into and spoiling sites of archaeological interest, and I want to suggest in the remainder of the chapter some of the things which can and ought to be done.*

THE ROMAN PERIOD

In the Roman period there are undoubtedly a great number of roads still waiting to be discovered. The Ordnance Survey publishes a map of Roman Britain on the scale of sixteen miles to the inch (third edn, 1956) which marks all the Roman roads so far known. No road is marked unless its authenticity has been established beyond doubt. You will find on this map, however, many stretches of Roman road of which the exact course is still uncertain, and you may find that some of this uncertain course runs through your parish or district. Here is a problem which only a local historian can solve. In addition to these uncertain stretches of road there are probably

---

* For much fuller information about fieldwork methods and problems, see my book, *Fieldwork in Local History* (Faber, 1967).

thousands of miles of local Roman roads which have not yet reached a map at all, and here too the local historian can make his own discoveries. The clues for this kind of work are set out best in I. D. Margary's book *Roman Ways in the Weald* (Phoenix House, 1948) and also in his two volumes *Roman Roads in Britain* (Phoenix House, 1955, 1957).

There are also many Roman villas or country houses still awaiting discovery. These present a more difficult problem than the discovery of the roads since they are likely to be buried and to offer no visible evidence above ground. You should, of course, search minutely the air photographs of your chosen territory (if they are available) for any signs of buried buildings, enclosures, ditches, and so on. The interpretation of air photographs is not as simple as it might seem and it would be advisable again to seek the advice of your local archaeologist for this purpose.

It is possible also to discover a Roman villa from traces on the ground. I remember walking in Leicestershire to show a friend the site of the deserted medieval village of Hamilton. As we came over the brow of the hill and looked across a small shallow valley near the village site, we saw in the middle of a grass field a considerable whitish patch shining in the sun. We deviated from the medieval village site in order to find out what this patch could be. It turned out to be a considerable scattering of tesserae from the floor of a buried Roman villa which had been cut through by the farmer a few days earlier in making a land-drain across the field. The floor, which was composed of tiny cubes of the local white limestone, had been broken and thrown up to the surface and it was this which had attracted our attention. We walked up and down the line of the drain, which had been covered in, and picked up some handfuls of Romano-British pottery. Although this site has never been excavated there is unquestionably a villa buried at that point. One is

8.2 Silchester, Hampshire

The principal Roman road from London to the west of England was aligned directly on the east gate of *Calleva Atrebatum*, the town known in later times as Silchester. The metalling of the last half-mile of the road has gone, but the straight course can be followed on the ground. Silchester was the focal point of roads coming from Dorchester on Thames, Gloucester and Bath, Exeter and Old Sarum, and Winchester and Chichester.

The grid pattern of the Roman town is preserved by crop marks, and the boundaries by hedgebanks and some of the old flint-rubble walls. Excavations have located the forum and basilica and a nearby fourth-century building which has all the characteristics of an early Christian church. The present church of St Mary's stands by the farm at the former east gate and has architectural features dating from the early thirteenth century.

not often likely to make a discovery like this, but the moral of the tale is that you should always keep your eyes open when farmers or others are disturbing the surface of fields and roads.

The most common and telling indication of a Roman site is a scatter of Roman pottery on the surface of the ground. Anyone who walks over a ploughed field and examines the surface carefully, furrow by furrow, will be able to collect several pounds weight of fragments of pottery. Much of it may have found its way there casually, in loads of manure from a farmyard, and it may be of any age down to yesterday. But if there has ever been a dwelling in the field, the pottery will be very plentiful, and will, to the eye of an expert, immediately reveal the period of the dwelling. The vast majority of the sites marked on the Ordnance Survey map of Roman Britain were first found in just this way.

Other Roman sites which may come to light by systematic field-work will be found listed in *Field Archaeology*. They include small military sites, Romano-British hamlets and their associated fields, industrial sites, signal stations, and mining and smelting sites.

THE SAXON PERIOD

In the Saxon period one may discover linear earthworks, some of which at least are boundary banks. Here again much valuable advice is given in *Field Archaeology* which I do not wish to repeat. I want here to concentrate on Anglo-Saxon land charters.* There exist many hundreds, possibly thousands, of Saxon land charters relating to gifts of land made by the King or some magnate to religious houses or to other magnates. A great number of these charters give more or less detailed boundaries of the estate, especially from the eighth century onwards, and it is one of the most fruitful kinds of fieldwork open to the local historian to work out these boundaries precisely on the ground. Very few of these charters have been worked out in this way. Dr G. B. Grundy of Oxford worked out a great number of the charters for several counties, including Somerset, Oxfordshire, and Gloucestershire. But a good deal of his work, valuable though it is, is vitiated by the fact that he worked mostly from documents and maps in his study. He did not get out into the field and attempt to trace the visible remains of the boundaries. The result is that at times his working out of the boundaries goes astray, and occasionally

* See also Chapter 12, pp. 238–39.

whole charters are wrongly elucidated. Here more than anywhere it is essential to go out and get one's feet wet.

Having found the text of the local charter and having had it translated by some competent person, the next step is to start identifying the boundary points on the map. It is useless to plunge into the countryside without this preparation at home. The best map for this purpose is generally the $2\frac{1}{2}$-inch map (1:25,000) of the Ordnance Survey, though the time will come when one will have to use also the 6-inch map (1:10,560/1:10,000) and possibly even the 25-inch map (1:2,500). But for the preliminary working out the $2\frac{1}{2}$-inch map is probably the most useful scale. It is an almost invariable rule that the boundary points in the charter run in a clockwise direction. It is very rare to find them running anticlockwise, though this possibility must be borne in mind if all else fails.

Some of the boundary points given in an Anglo-Saxon charter (for example 'the alder tree' or 'the broken stump') will have disappeared long ago and it would be useless to look for them now; but many of the boundary points still survive and can be located by an assiduous searcher. Another general clue in reconstructing these lost boundaries is that they often follow, for considerable distances at least, ancient parish boundaries. One should know where these boundaries run as they may give just the clue that is needed. This, however, must not be regarded as a rule to be slavishly followed because parish boundaries are often later in date than these estate boundaries and deviate from them; but there is nevertheless a remarkable continuity at times between the Saxon estate and the ecclesiastical parish, and their boundaries may well coincide for a very long way.

Where a monastic estate is involved, one may be fortunate enough to find a later survey which will help enormously with doubtful points and clinch the argument. Thus a charter of King Athelstan granting an estate at *Lym* (Uplyme) to Glastonbury Abbey in 938 describes in detail the boundary of the estate. Nearly six hundred years later (in 1516) the abbey had a grand survey made of its properties, now among the Egerton MSS in the British Library. Dr Fox has shown that almost all the boundary points of 938 recur in the document of 1516, and so was able to establish the boundaries of the original estate on the ground.*

When one has taken the map-work as far as possible at home, the time has come to explore the ground on foot. Here one will

---

* H. S. A. Fox, 'The boundary of Uplyme', *Trans. Devon Assn.*, vol. cii (1970).

start from any point on the boundary of which the identification is absolutely certain. It does not matter where one starts, provided it is a *certain* point, because one is going to complete in the end a circuit. For this fieldwork one needs, of course, the 2½-inch map, a list of the boundary points in the charter, a notebook to record any special features along the boundary, and a camera in order to record any photographable piece of boundary, as for example a high bank or a conspicuous ditch. It may be said in passing that the photography of features of this kind is not at all easy. Unless one is an expert photographer the results are likely to be disappointing and it may be necessary to ask a more expert friend to make this side of the record. There is much more one could say about the fieldwork of Anglo-Saxon land-charters but space is short. One ought to say perhaps that the working out of the boundaries of one such estate may well take several days. Not only is the estate likely to be several miles around, but the pace will be slow because of frequent uncer-

8.3 Stanage Pole

Stanage Pole served a dual purpose as a landmark for travellers crossing the bleak Pennine moors and as a boundary point. It stood on the border between Yorkshire and Derbyshire and divided the lordships of Hallamshire and Hathersage. When the boundaries of Hallamshire were perambulated in 1574, the party proceeded 'to Stanage, which is a meere betweene the said lordshipps'. The parishes of Hathersage, Ecclesfield and Sheffield also met at this point. Graffiti on the stone base dates back to the seventeenth century.
Stanage is the 'stone-edge', a gritstone escarpment where millstones were quarried.

tainties as to the whereabouts of the next boundary point. Nevertheless, once this has been done the result will be the restoration to the map of a piece of Saxon topography that has long been lost.

THE MEDIEVAL PERIOD

The method of studying boundaries recorded in Anglo-Saxon land charters can also be used to trace medieval parish boundaries which were perambulated at Rogationtide and occasionally set down in writing. A great number of features in the landscape survive from the medieval period. Most of these are described in *Field Archaeology*, already referred to, and clues are given for their identification. Here I shall add only a few notes to what is said in that guide.

A number of the smaller castles still remain to be discovered, especially the so-called adulterine castles thrown up hastily in the reign of Stephen (1135–54). In some parts of England, especially perhaps the Midlands, these adulterine castle mounds with their accompanying baileys are fairly numerous and many have still to be recognised. They never had any stone buildings on the mound or in the bailey so that nothing survives except the flat-topped mound and the remains of the embanked bailey. The mound is sometimes wrongly described on the map as 'tumulus', but a closer inspection of it and the surrounding features should establish its true significance. Care should be taken not to mistake a large windmill mound for the motte of an adulterine castle.

Moated homestead sites are extremely common, especially in lowland areas and in clayey country. A great number are still unrecognised. In some parts of England, as in Essex and Suffolk and perhaps in the Midlands as well, nearly every parish contains a site of a moated homestead. In eastern England there may be several within one parish. Most of these sites are now deserted. The majority were made in the thirteenth and fourteenth centuries and they seem to have been abandoned generally by the sixteenth century when the invention of gunpowder and the establishment of a more stable central government made the moated site (which must have been very unhealthy and damp) unnecessary. Occasionally these sites have been put under the plough and many evidences of domestic occupation turned up to the surface; for example, broken pottery, glassware, roof tiles, etc. Until recently the presence of buried foundations was an insuperable barrier to ploughing-up, but

8.4 Little Moreton Hall, Cheshire

The most lovable of all England's timber-framed buildings, Little Moreton Hall is the product of three generations of the Moreton family, whose ancestors had lived at this place since the thirteenth century. The moat is probably much older than the house.

In Henry VII's reign William de Moreton built a typical H-plan house centred upon a great hall. His son and namesake employed Richard Dale, a local carpenter, to add a range in the courtyard with a new dining parlour lit by a large bay window. A similar window was inserted in the hall, and an inscription was carved above to read 'God is Al in Al thing: This windous whire made by William Moreton in the yeare of Oure Lorde MDLIX. Richard Dale Carpenter made thies windous by the grac of god'. William Moreton died in 1563, but his son John carried out his plans to build a gatehouse range with a long gallery along the second floor. When this gallery was completed about 1570 it would have appeared remarkably advanced for the home of a minor Cheshire gentleman. In later centuries the Moretons were rarely resident and made only small alterations to the Tudor house.

the bulldozer has altered all that. As a consequence some deeply buried sites have been brought to light; and some have probably been unknowingly destroyed. Fishponds and a number of embanked enclosures often appear near the site of moated homesteads.

In some parts of England there are a great number of sites of deserted villages and hamlets. These are most common in the Midlands where some counties have over a hundred of these sites; but even as far north as Northumberland there are a great number awaiting discovery and recording. Deserted village sites are discussed in *Field Archaeology* and have been dealt with at length by Beresford and Hurst, in *Deserted Medieval Villages* (Lutterworth Press, 1971). Reference should also be made to the Deserted Medieval Village Research Group, the Secretary of which is Mr J. G. Hurst, 67 Gloucester Crescent, London, N.W.1. Local historians can not only obtain from him information about any site in their own locality but they may be able to assist the Group by making their own discoveries in the field and notifying them for inclusion in the appropriate county list.

These sites of deserted villages and hamlets are naturally commoner in the Lowland Zone of Britain where the nucleated village was the most typical form of human settlement. In the Highland Zone, where the village is less common and the more characteristic forms of settlement are the hamlet and the isolated farmstead, the deserted village is obviously rarer and also much more difficult to locate. There is no doubt that there are deserted hamlets awaiting discovery in the hilly parts of western England, as was shown by Mr Jope's discovery of the medieval settlement at Great Beare (Devon). This was a small settlement in poor, ill-drained country, probably made in the early thirteenth century and probably abandoned at the time of the Black Death. All the pottery found was of thirteenth-century date. So far as is known, there were only two houses, and corn-drying ovens. At Trewortha (Cornwall) a purely pastoral settlement was discovered in the late nineteenth century about nine hundred feet up on the north-east side of Bodmin Moor. It was a compact cluster of about eight houses, probably first settled in the twelfth century. There are no signs of corn-growing or of tin-working, but it was clearly a permanent settlement and not a seasonal upland pastoral colony. The date of its abandonment is still unknown because the amateur excavators in the late nineteenth century dated the crude pottery as mostly 'British' and had no idea that they were really unearthing an early medieval settlement.

In the Highland Zone, therefore, the local historian may well find that there were hamlets or single farmsteads in his parish which are recorded in early documents and which can no longer be found. It will be his task in such cases to discover these sites on the ground, and Professor Beresford's *Lost Villages of England* will supply him with most of the clues for this purpose. Nor should it be supposed that the abandonment of farmsteads and hamlets is a purely medieval phenomenon. In some parts of England one will find many small mining villages and hamlets which were abandoned during

8.5 Deserted medieval village, Holworth, Dorset

The ground plan of the medieval village is immediately apparent from this splendid aerial photograph. The village street is preserved as a well-defined holloway, the slightly-raised square mounds of the house plots lie adjacent to it, and to the rear stretch the rectangular crofts or gardens.

Holworth was an Anglo-Saxon settlement on the Dorset chalklands, in the parish of Chaldon Herring. Like most deserted villages it was never large and its decline cannot be dated accurately. It was probably abandoned during the fifteenth century. Dorset deserted medieval villages are nearly all on the chalklands, and it may be significant that they are near Melcombe Regis, where the Black Death was introduced into England in June 1348. Villages were rarely wiped out at a single visitation, however, and many English settlements that were weakened in the fourteenth century did not disappear for another two or three hundred years. One of the plots was excavated in 1958 and revealed the foundations of a long-house or a farm with buildings arranged in one alignment.

the nineteenth century; and one can occasionally come across purely agricultural hamlets which have been abandoned within more recent times. All this should be recorded and plans made of the site and of the individual houses (see the next chapter) since they will gradually fall into ruin and will eventually be lost entirely.

Within five miles of the city of Exeter, there is a loose cluster of farmsteads called Nettacott. When I first saw it in the 1950s, the three farmsteads were empty and two were falling into ruin. Their lands had been taken into the large farm adjoining them on the west. This little settlement is first recorded by name in 1254 but is probably much older than that. It is a well-watered site with fertile red soil, and its name suggests that it started as a small pastoral settlement. In the course of time it seems to have developed into four farmhouses. One of these was a fine example of the house of a franklin of the fifteenth century, another was the house of an Elizabethan yeoman, and the third (now destroyed) the smaller house of a seventeenth-century husbandman. There was possibly a fourth house of which only some banks in an orchard remain. Here was a hamlet of three or four farmsteads visibly decaying in the middle of the twentieth century, and it illustrates exactly what was happening in many parts of England in the fifteenth and sixteenth centuries. History is not something which is dead and finished with. The good local historian will see it at work all around him.

MEDIEVAL PARKS

One tends to think of a park today as a tidy green undulating space dotted with groups of trees, around a more or less handsome house. But the word originally meant simply an area fenced off for the purpose of hunting, in a wild state. The earliest parks of this kind were royal. Some of them date from before the Norman Conquest, as for example Woodstock Park (now Blenheim) in Oxfordshire. Any subject who wished to make a park or hunting preserve was obliged to obtain a licence from the Crown and to pay stiffly for the privilege. Many such private parks were created in the twelfth century and above all in the thirteenth and fourteenth centuries. A great number of these have since disappeared completely from the landscape. Not quite completely, because the assiduous local historian will be able to recover the boundaries of these lost parks if he uses his eyes. The late O. G. S. Crawford devoted a chapter in

8.6 Bradgate Park, Leicestershire

A public recreational area since 1928, Bradgate is one of England's best preserved medieval deer parks. It was never landscaped in later times, for the house was abandoned in 1739, and red and fallow deer still browse among the rocks and bracken. The park was enclosed from the edge of Charnwood Forest sometime before 1274 when Roger de Somery granted it to the Earl of Winchester 'with the deer-leaps then made in it'. Boundary ditches can be followed alongside the outer walls and across the middle of the present 828-acre park. This park was greatly enlarged about 1500 when Thomas Grey, the first Marquis of Dorset, built a new brick house (one of the first in the country to have no pretence at fortification), two miles north of his old manor house at Groby. The village of Bradgate was removed when the park was enlarged.

Lady Jane Grey, the daughter of the third marquis, was born at Bradgate in 1537. At the age of sixteen she was proclaimed queen of England in preference to Mary Tudor, but her 'reign' lasted only nine days and she was beheaded.

Archaeology in the Field (Phoenix House, 1953) to medieval castle mounds and parks, to which the reader should refer for clues in this particular kind of fieldwork.

These medieval parks were usually surrounded by a massive earthen bank and ditch. Sometimes they were paled around and occasionally we hear of some being surrounded by a stone wall. If one knows that there was a park of this kind in one's own parish or district, it is a nice piece of fieldwork to trace the boundaries of that park which will, of course, date from the time of the original licence of the enclosure. Thus in Somerset we are told in the *Calendar of Inquisitions Miscellaneous* (vol. i, p. 36) in an inquisition dated 1251:

> How the park of Brewham belonging to Sir Robert de Mucegros was held enclosed with a hedge in the time of Richard and in the time of King John. In the time of King Richard the lord of the manor of Brewham was Richard, son of John, and he kept the park enclosed with a ditch and hedge and had deer in it all that reign. And when the said Richard, son of John, died . . . the wardship of his heirs . . . remained in the hands of the King until William de Montacute purchased it from King John and he kept the park enclosed with a ditch and hedge and had deer in it until King John, being angered against the said William de Montacute for a trespass done by him, took from him by way of ransom five hundred marks so that under the weight of this ransom the said William let the ditch and hedge of the park fall into decay and the deer go. Yet the park is still so enclosed that cattle cannot enter it . . . and the metes [boundaries] of the said park during the time of its enclosure were as under: from the ford of Wodessned towards Kingsettle along the old ditch to the house of Iweyn and thence southward around the croft of Iweyn to the house of Alexander Heyrun and thence along the old ditch to the house of Robert le Siviere, so that the house and croft of Robert are within the enclosure, and thence along the old ditch to the ford of Wodessned again; and all this enclosure and the beasts in it existed during the reigns of King Richard and King John.

Although the houses referred to in these boundaries have long ago perished, it should be possible for the local historian to recover the boundaries of this ancient park at Brewham. Similarly, in Hampshire we read in 1254 of the making of a park at Freemantle. We are told that this park was 1,136 perches round, each perch being twenty feet, making a total circumference of rather more than four miles. Part of it had already been enclosed with a ditch and hedged bank, and the remainder was in the process of being enclosed in 1254. It should be possible to trace some at least of the boundaries of this park also.

At Staple Fitzpaine in Somerset the Close Rolls (in which most of these licences to make private parks will be found) record that in 1233 Robert de Briwes and his heirs were given free warren (that is, liberty to hunt) in their demesne lands for hare, fox, and wildcat. Presumably this park was surrounded by a high bank and ditch from the beginning. In 1595 it was paled around and the payment for the pales at a penny a foot reveals that its total circumference was 5,120 yards. This park was disparked about 1800 but a local historian was able to discover its original boundaries. These took the form of a broad bank, ditched on both sides, with a double hedge at the top and a path between. In many places this bank was still conspicuous. O. G. S. Crawford also gives several examples of the recovery of the boundaries of lost medieval parks in his book, and Professor Beresford has a chapter on parks in his *History on the Ground* (Lutterworth Press, 1957).

INDUSTRIAL SITES

In *Field Archaeology* will be found clues for identifying sites of medieval and early modern industrial activities. These include kilns for pottery and tiles; traces of mining for iron, coal, lead, and silver; glass furnaces and salt-making. The Lincolnshire coast from Boston as far north as Grimsby is particularly rich in sites of former salt-making from Iron Age times onwards. On Dartmoor and the Cornish moors will be found considerable traces of tin-working at various periods. In Cornwall this activity dates back to prehistoric times, but on Dartmoor there is nothing earlier than the middle of the twelfth century. Those who live in these districts will learn to recognise the traces of old tin-works quite easily. Shaft-mining for tin probably first developed towards the end of the fifteenth century and became very active during the sixteenth, but no one has yet discovered, or at least recognised, these early mines, and it may now be impossible to do so.

The old lead-mining districts of Derbyshire are also a profitable subject for fieldwork. We hear of lead-workings being leased at Wirksworth as early as the ninth century, and the workings at Bakewell, Ashford, and Hope were important in the middle of the eleventh century and throughout medieval times. Mining continued actively down to the nineteenth century, and on the mountain-limestone plateau there are abundant traces of former buildings and workings.

8.7 Tideslow Rake, Derbyshire

The commonest form of lead mine in Derbyshire was the long, straight rake. Sometimes these rakes were open to the sky and now resemble deep gorges, but more commonly miners went below the surface as far as the water table. Their rakes are now covered with grassy hillocks and hollows formed by the uneven dumping of waste. Some rakes have been re-worked for fluorspar in modern times, a mineral that was of no use to the old miner.

Tideslow Rake takes its name from an ancient tumulus, Tidi's burial-mound, the final resting place of the Anglo-Saxon who gave Tideswell its name, a mile or so away. It dates back to Neolithic times, and is the largest surviving round barrow in the Peak District. To the west and north lie Great and Little Hucklow, named after Hucca's burial-mound. The rectangular fields of the parliamentary enclosure era reach up to either side of the rake. In the days when it was mined the place would have been even more bleak and lonely than it appears today.

Pottery sites of medieval and submedieval date are also a rewarding field of enquiry. That at Brill (Oxon) is now well known, but the kilns at Ticknall in south Derbyshire still await discovery (the pottery is already in museums). A number of good pottery sites have been located in Herefordshire; and there is no doubt a great number of kilns remain to be located in many parts of England. The effect on the landscape of some medieval industries is well illustrated in M. W. Beresford and J. K. St Joseph, *Medieval England: An Aerial Survey* (Cambridge University Press, second edn, 1979).

MISCELLANEOUS FEATURES

In some parts of England the local historian will discover in his parish clear traces of terracing of hillsides for vineyards. A number of vineyards are recorded in Domesday Book, especially on the western side of England, and traces of medieval vineyards are not uncommon in suitable terrain elsewhere, but they must not be confused with lynchets, which have long been known.

Before the war, large areas of the Midlands, especially, were covered with a very marked pattern of ridge-and-furrow. This has been the subject recently of controversy among some economic historians. In the main, however, there can be no doubt that it represents the pattern of open-field farming, which has been fossilised at some time by being laid under grass. Most of this pattern is therefore medieval and some of it may be even older. A little of it may be as late as the nineteenth century in date, especially on high ground brought into cultivation during the Napoleonic Wars. Much of this pattern of ridge-and-furrow was superficially destroyed by the extensive ploughing-up campaign in the war of 1939–45, but it survives nevertheless on air photographs, and these can be used to replace the lost evidence on the ground. Even if we do not know its precise significance yet—for example, how many ridges made up a typical strip in the open field?—or the precise date of parts of it, a detailed record of this remarkable pattern will be most valuable. Every ridge should be plotted for a given parish on the 6-inch map, within the framework of the modern field-system.

From the air we can detect not only the individual ridges, but also the existence of small units of cultivation ('furlongs') within the large open field. These are groups of strips, often surrounded by a low boundary-bank or balk which shows up clearly from the air (see Plate 7). We can also pick out other features of the medieval agrarian pattern such as 'common balks' or occupation roads across the fields, and headlands. The whole medieval pattern could probably be recovered, in some parishes at least.

Manorial boundaries can sometimes be seen as conspicuous features in the landscape. The exact boundaries of manors have not often been recorded, but where they have been (in 'perambulations' or on old estate maps) the local historian should walk the boundaries and record any special features they may present. In the Midlands, too, many villages had a boundary bank around their perimeter in medieval times, which can best be seen on deserted village sites.

Once the local historian learns to use his eyes in the local landscape, all manner of things come to light even in a countryside he may have thought he knew like the back of his hand. He will be able to explain many of them; others will be baffling. These baffling features can only be recorded exactly as the historian sees them, in the hope that one day their significance will be recognised.

DROVE ROADS

There has existed for centuries a considerable trade in cattle from Wales and Scotland across the borders into England. These cattle were driven over into England for fattening on richer pastures and ultimately for slaughter in English markets. They moved usually by special byways and over long distances. I touched on this aspect of local fieldwork in my *Fieldwork in Local History* (pp. 144–45). Books on the drove roads of Scotland and Wales appeared some years ago, but it was only recently that the English trade was written up by K. J. Bonser in *The Drovers* (Macmillan, 1970). His book is an admirable introduction to the economics and history of the trade, and furnishes many clues for the rediscovery of these lost lanes and byways. It is strongest on the North of England drove roads, and much more local work remains to be done on the Midlands and the rest of the country. Richard Colyer, *The Welsh Cattle Drovers* (University of Wales Press, 1976) follows the long routes out of Wales to the rich pastures of midland and southern England and shows how the trade was organised.

In the Midlands, too, the salt-ways have been studied in a rather spasmodic fashion, salt being a valuable commodity in medieval times for the preserving of meat and fish. There must be a host of local salt-ways awaiting rediscovery by the field-worker, pursuing various clues in documents and minor place-names on the ordnance map. David Hey has traced some in *Packmen, Carriers and Packhorse Roads* (Leicester University Press, 1980), a study of trade and communications in North Derbyshire and South Yorkshire which combines visual and documentary evidence, but in other parts of the country there is still a tremendous amount to work out on the directions and objectives of these ancient routes.

8.8 An ancient saltway

The Cheshire 'wiches'—Northwich, Middlewich and Nantwich—were a major source of salt from very early times, and a distinctive set of names can be traced alongside routes heading out of Cheshire to the medieval market towns of midland and northern England. The route shown here emerges from the Longdendale valley on its way across the Pennines to Rotherham, Barnsley, Doncaster and Wakefield. The stream (foreground) that formed the ancient county boundary between Cheshire and Yorkshire bears the name Saltersbrook. A few miles further on are Salter Hill, Salter Close, Salter Croft, Saltergate, etc.

This ancient route was not confined to the salt trade, but the salters were the most distinctive carriers in early times. The Cheshire portion (as far as the bridge) was turnpiked in 1732 and the Yorkshire section in 1741. It remained a moorland turnpike road until a diversion and new bridge were completed about 1830.

9 FIELDWORK: BUILDINGS

Every local historian should study all the buildings of his chosen territory closely. Even in the most unpromising village, apparently ruined by industrialism in the nineteenth century, he will probably find that there are houses of four or five different centuries, dating from the fifteenth or sixteenth centuries onwards; but he will not know this until he has made a thorough exploration of all the houses, both inside and out. A great deal of the antiquity of the house is hidden from the outside view: above all it lies in the interior of the roof.

Buildings of all kinds are the most revealing evidence for the local historian. I am sure some local historians realise this and feel they should do something about it, but they feel they have not the necessary technical knowledge of architecture, especially the kind of architecture, or rather building, which they are likely to be dealing with. It is difficult to date such buildings, and to know what are the significant things to look for.

To make an accurate and comprehensive study of your old buildings (say before 1850) will produce facts about the past history of your chosen place which no written record could have given you. Why is it, for example, that in parish after parish one finds so much evidence that farmhouses were rebuilt or much enlarged in the two or three generations from about 1570 to 1640? When the local historian comes across evidence of this kind, which is nowhere set down in contemporary records, he is compelled to ask himself what had been happening in local farming in the preceding decades to enable so many farmers to rebuild their houses, or at least to improve them substantially. In the north of England, above all in the four most northerly counties and in the dales of West Yorkshire, the great period for rebuilding seems to be from about 1650 onwards. But whatever the local period (or periods) of rebuilding may be, the local historian will have a problem on his hands to be solved. He must try to relate all this building activity to the farming (or local industrial) prosperity of the time.

I should like to see every parish history finish with a sort of building survey, a more or less detailed description of the parish or village as it is today, covering all the buildings, both domestic and industrial, that are (say) more than a hundred years old.

An excellent example of this is *Domesday to Dormitory: the history of the landscape of Great Shelford*, which was prepared by an adult education class at Shelford (near Cambridge) and concludes with such a survey. If you are dealing with a town you might have to confine yourself for reasons of time to surveying the buildings dating from before 1850 so as to make your task a manageable one. In a small country town you might well make your finishing date 1900, though this is not to say that nothing important was built after that date. The parish church and manor house, if there is one, are buildings which obviously call for description. Few, if any, local histories fail to include these. But what about the local railway station, which may still be a nice piece of early Victorian station architecture, or the remains of eighteenth- or nineteenth-century mine buildings, which may have no architectural quality but are nevertheless worthy of record as part of the industrial history of a parish?

As for farmhouses and cottages, and the small domestic dwellings which make up the bulk of our towns, there was little in print when I first wrote on the subject. Now there is an extensive list of books and articles and one can only make a rather invidious choice here. But of particular value are Brunskill, *Illustrated Handbook of Vernacular Architecture* (Faber, 1970) and Vanessa Parker, *The English House in the Nineteenth Century* (Historical Association, 1970).

The Council for British Archaeology has produced two most valuable little guides on this subject. Research Report II, entitled *The Recording of Architecture and its Publication*, is concerned with the large buildings in the main. Research Report III is perhaps more valuable to the local historian. It is entitled *The Investigation of Smaller Domestic Buildings*. This is another book which should be on every local historian's table. These reports are obtainable from the Council for British Archaeology, at 4 St Andrew's Place,

London, N.W.1. The latter report does not assume any previous architectural knowledge. It simply tells one in plain language what are the things one should notice and record about the outside and inside of ordinary domestic buildings and how to set about making a plan of an old house. Many people may feel that to make such a plan of an old house is quite beyond their capacity. Yet it is perfectly simple to do and all local historians should learn to do it. Some plans will be better than others, but any record is better than none, especially as we are dealing with buildings that are in constant danger of being pulled down or altered beyond recognition. It is important to record this perishable evidence before it is too late; and we all know how quickly a house or some other old building can disappear nowadays.

MAKING A PLAN

The equipment required to make a record of the smaller buildings of a parish is very simple. The most important item is a good tape-measure, preferably a proper surveyor's tape 66 feet long. You will need a friend to hold one end of the tape while you make the necessary measurements. You also want a block of squared paper so that you can record your measurements on a rough plan as you go. This rough plan should be redrawn accurately at home, as soon as possible after the actual visit, so that details are fresh in your mind. It is very important to note on your plan the *functions* of the various rooms, both present and original (where there has been a change, as has often happened).

You should put into the same notebook all the necessary notes about the materials of which the house is built, and any other information that cannot be recorded on the plan. If you are good at sketching, some drawings of the house and certain features like old doorways or mouldings or windows are a valuable addition to the record. Photographs are essential. Even a poor photograph is better than none and most of us can manage to take a reasonably good photograph nowadays. Photograph the building back and front, together with any particular features (inside or out) which seem worth recording in detail.

To revert to *The Investigation of Smaller Domestic Buildings*, there are two points one might add to the valuable information and advice contained therein. We are told quite rightly that one must pay particular attention to the thickness of walls, because marked

9.1 Netherfold farmhouse, Yorkshire

Several examples of this type of construction have been identified in South Yorkshire and the Vale of York and dated from the fifteenth to the seventeenth centuries. Netherfold has recently been given a dendrochronological (tree ring) date of 1495. A timber-framed barn to the rear of the property may be contemporary.

Originally the central hall was open to the rafters, but the other two bays had chambers. A parlour joined the hall on the west, and in the east a kitchen wing was separated from the hall by a passage running right through the house, behind the chimney stack.

All eight principal posts still stand on their stone blocks, and the wall-plates and tie-beams are well preserved, but the timber-framed walls have been replaced by stone and brick. The hipped common-rafter roof does not have a ridge piece; instead each pair of rafters is tied by a collar beam. Plans and elevations accompany an exemplary survey in P. F. Ryder, *Timber Framed Buildings in South Yorkshire* (S.Y. County Council, 1979).

variations of thickness in different parts of a house usually mean considerable differences in date. To this I would add that one should pay attention to differences of level inside a house, because in my experience marked differences of level on the same floor, so to speak, probably also indicate where additions have been made to an older structure.

There is one small point of criticism I would make about the pamphlet. In its last paragraph we are told that before 1600 it

was rare for a house to include a kitchen, 'before which it was normally a detached building. Not until after 1700 did it become normal
to incorporate a kitchen in the house'. I believe this to be too
sweeping a statement, and to be misleading in the West of England,
and perhaps other regions. I do not know how common the detached
kitchen may have been elsewhere in England, but in the West of
England one certainly finds kitchens as an integral part of the house
from the middle of the sixteenth century onwards, and I believe
that this may be true generally of farmhouses in the East Midlands.
On the other hand, the surveys of the manors of Lord Pembroke
show a considerable number of detached kitchens in Wiltshire in
1631–32, and they are undoubtedly to be found in other regions.

One or two other words of practical advice: in examining a
house, particularly if it is a detached one, one should walk around
the outside of the building first and notice its general shape and any
revealing features (for example, blocked doorways or blocked
windows, or broken-off masonry indicating where something has
been taken away). This is not only necessary from the historical point
of view, so to speak, but is also the best approach to the problem of
getting into somebody else's house. It is obviously not always easy
for someone who may be a total stranger to approach a house and
expect to roam all over it. One should always, of course, knock
at the front door and ask permission to look even at the outside of
the house and this permission is usually readily given. If, after this,
one is able to produce some information about the house which is
of interest to the owner or occupier the task of getting inside is
greatly eased. Men usually find it much easier than women to get
inside a house as they are rightly reckoned not to notice that the
house has not been polished and dusted for a day or two.

There are all sorts of practical considerations involved which no
one who lives in the country will need to be told about. Some times
of the day and some seasons of the year are more convenient for the
farmer or his wife than others. If you already know something about
the house, possibly the earliest possible recorded reference to it or
the meaning of its name if it is a farm with a separate name, this
kind of information will show that you are not an idle enquirer or
general busybody. Even so, in my experience, it is easier to do this
kind of fieldwork in some parts of England than in others. I find
that in the West of England country people, especially, have a surprising degree of historic sense and they are very ready to cooperate
in work of this kind if they are told something about the history of
their house. I believe this may be true also of the north of England

generally. Of the Midlands I am not so sure. The local historian is likely, however, to be in a specially favoured position. He or she will presumably be an inhabitant of the parish in question and will be known to most other people. It should not be at all difficult in such circumstances for the parish historian to arrange to see the interior of all the houses he or she wishes to inspect.

It is often impossible to tell the true age of a house merely by looking at the outside. Even what appears to be a most obvious and straightforward kind of house may conceal something quite surprising. I have never forgotten, some years ago, being asked to look at a house in the suburbs of Leicester which was said to have something vaguely described as 'a church roof'. When I arrived at the house it appeared to be a complete red-brick Georgian house,

9.2 Oakwell Hall, Yorkshire

Oakwell Hall has many of the characteristics of an Elizabethan and Stuart residence of a West Riding gentleman or clothier. The date 1583 is carved over the front entrance, suggesting that the house was built by John Batt. Seventeenth-century improvements include the great window, divided into thirty sections. From inside the house, however, it is clear that Batt encased an earlier timber-framed building. The great window lights a two-storeyed medieval hall, and the porch leads into a traditional screens passage with the service rooms on the right of the photograph. On the left, beyond the hall, a great parlour, the principal chamber, and several smaller rooms form a cross-wing.

Oakwell Hall was the inspiration for 'Fieldhead' in Charlotte Brontë's novel, *Shirley*, and is now a museum. The panelling in the hall has been unfastened in places to expose the earlier timber-frame and to show some of the carpenters' marks.

with the date 1789 over the doorway. All the doorways and windows
suggested that this was a house entirely built or rebuilt in that year.
I suspected that the 'church roof' would turn out to be some carved
Victorian woodwork which is often mistaken by the amateur for
something of antiquity. However, it was nothing of the sort. In
one of the attics there was a magnificent cusped principal rafter of
early fourteenth-century date, and when we crawled into the roof-
space there was a complete roof of this construction hung with bats
but in perfect condition, every moulding as sharp as on the day that
it was carved. In other words, this was really a medieval house,
with its original roof dating from about 1300–30, which had been
cased around with brick in 1789 and given new doorways and
windows at the same time.

In the same way in the west of England it is not at all uncommon
to look at a farmhouse from the outside and to see nothing which
indicates a date earlier than about 1800; but inside there may well be
rooms, doorways, and fireplaces of the sixteenth century, and upstairs there may be a complete roof dating from the fifteenth century.
Even if a house has a date on it somewhere, and it may be in a variety
of places, this is not necessarily the date of the complete building
and one must not be deceived by it. A great number of old houses
are not the product of just one period of building but of two or more
periods, and the date on the door or on the wall outside may be the
year in which some major reconstruction was carried out. It may
not mean even that. I remember a farmhouse in a Midland village
with a date and initials over the principal doorway which did not
tally with any of the visible features of the house. It turned out to
be the year in which a newly-married couple (as I found from the
parish register) took up their residence there. Thus the date on a
house must be treated as a bit of evidence, like any other, requiring
some independent check, and the best check is to explore the interior
of the house from the cellar, if there is one, up to the roof-timbers.
Nor should you be unduly put off by the owner or occupier telling
you that there is nothing of interest upstairs. Some occupiers of
houses exaggerate the antiquity of their houses considerably; but
it is surprising, on the other hand, how many occupiers who have
lived in a house for years have never noticed features which to the
trained eye are a clear indication of considerable age. The golden
rule is to try to see everything for oneself, and not to take anyone
else's word for anything in the building, least of all perhaps the
owner's word.

Where a house has been considerably altered in the course of centuries, your first inspection of the interior may be rather baffling, perhaps as baffling as looking at the interior of a rather complicated church for the first time. Often it is not possible to decide what the building history of the house is until you have got its plan down on paper and you can study it at leisure. There is, for example, a house in east Devon which at first sight was quite baffling, even to the most expert eye. Massive internal walls seemed to turn up in the most unexpected places but when everything had been measured and the plan put on paper it became clear immediately that these thick walls, which in the modern arrangement of the rooms appeared to have no rhyme or reason, represented a square tower house of the fifteenth century which had been completely embedded in later additions and alterations. Basically the house had started as a kind of square fortress put up by a local gentleman at the time of the Wars of the Roses when the countryside was being ravaged by the private armies of local magnates.

You may well find that a house, even a farmhouse or cottage, requires more than one visit to elucidate its structural history and plan fully. There are nearly always some points which one would wish to check later; and when one looks at the preliminary plan on paper it may suggest a theory about the house that makes one desire to go back and look at it with fresh eyes. Even if you never succeed in elucidating the structural history of a house, or rather in dating it approximately, your notes, drawings, and photographs will still form a valuable record for someone coming after you who may be able to supply the final answers. It is impossible to give specific guidance about the dating of this kind of building, partly because there were great differences in building styles and materials from region to region, and we have not studied these in sufficient detail to be able to reduce them to general rules as in church building; and partly because some materials in many parts of England are by their nature almost undatable and only long experience of that particular kind of material will enable one to suggest an approximate date for the building in such cases. Moreover, we have to take the element of conservatism into account. This is especially true of vernacular building, in which architects were rarely employed. Such building was the work of masons or bricklayers or carpenters, as the case might be, and the same styles and details of workmanship might go on for two hundred years almost unchanged. In the south Somerset region, for example, where Ham Hill stone was almost universally employed, it is not at all easy to detect any differences

First-floor plan

Ground plan

Section of
Beams
in Hall

Scale in Feet

0   5   15   25

9.3 Plan of early sixteenth-century farmhouse, Boycombe, Devon (after a drawing
by Maurice Barley)

This farmhouse at Farway, in east Devon, survives almost unaltered. It is fairly typical of
those owned and occupied by the lesser Devonshire gentry of the period. Note the two
garderobes (G) on the plan. Indoor sanitation like this was not found in the lesser farmhouses
of the yeoman and husbandmen. Fireplaces are indicated as F.

of detail or style between the late sixteenth century and the mid-eighteenth. Many other regions show a similar conservatism.

Again, the internal plans of vernacular houses vary from one social class to another—from the labourer's cottage up to the franklin's house in the country, or from the poor weaver's cottage in the town up to the house of the rich merchant: and they also vary from one region to another according to the predominant type of farming.

There are few books to help us date the vernacular buildings of the various regions. All dated houses should therefore be particularly noted (bearing in mind the qualifications expressed above about such dates) since they give us the best clue for the dating of similar houses in the district. Sometimes in a house of better class there may be a coat of arms over a fireplace bearing a precise date; or the arms themselves may be approximately dated with a knowledge of heraldry and of family history. It must be remembered that internal features such as dated fireplaces may well refer to an internal reconstruction of the house and not to the date of the whole building. The local historian will, however, learn most about the dating of this type of building from long experience in examining such houses and comparing one with another. When the ground plan has been drawn it should be possible to identify the various rooms by name. One sometimes finds that some of the groundfloor rooms have changed their use since they were originally built. For example, the kitchen end of the house may have become the parlour and vice versa, or there may be more than one kitchen, which the probate inventories (see later) will refer to as 'the old kitchen' and 'the new kitchen'. Sometimes the house has been turned around to face the other way. Quite a few sixteenth- and seventeenth-century houses of the farmhouse type in the West Country were originally built to face north or north-east, with their backs to the rain; but in the eighteenth century or the nineteenth windows were put into the back wall so as to get the southern sun, a new front door built, and the house now faces south. The handsome porch of the fine door on the other side of the house tells one when this has happened.

ASPECTS OF PEASANT BUILDING

There are three aspects of peasant or vernacular building in the countryside. To some extent these remarks apply to town houses also:

1. *Aesthetic*—the use of local materials, the choice of site. On this subject there is a fine passage in Wordsworth's *Guide to the Lakes*, in which he says:

The dwelling-houses, and contiguous outhouses, are, in many instances, of the colour of the native rock, out of which they have been built; but, frequently the Dwelling or Fire-house, as it is ordinarily called, has been distinguished from the barn or byre by roughcast and whitewash, which, as the inhabitants are not hasty in renewing it, in a few years acquires, by the influence of the weather, a tint at once sober and variegated. As these houses have been, from father to son, inhabited by persons engaged in the same occupations, yet necessarily with changes in their circumstances, they have received without incongruity additions and accommodations adapted to the needs of each successive occupant, who, being for the most part proprietor, was at liberty to follow his own fancy: so that these humble dwellings remind the contemplative spectator of a production of Nature, and may (using a strong expression) rather be said to have grown than to have been erected;—to have risen, by an instinct of their own, out of the native rock—so little is there in them of formality, such is their wildness and beauty. Among the numerous recesses and projections in the walls and in the different stages of their roofs, are seen bold and harmonious effects of contrasted sunshine and shadow. It is a favourable circumstance, that the strong winds, which sweep down the valleys, induced the inhabitants, at a time when the materials for building were easily procured, to furnish many of these dwellings with substantial porches; and such as have not this defence, are seldom unprovided with a projection of two large slates over their thresholds. Nor will the singular beauty of the chimneys escape the eye of the attentive traveller. Sometimes a low chimney, almost upon a level with the roof, is overlaid with a slate, supported upon four slender pillars, to prevent the wind from driving the smoke down the chimney. Others are of a quadrangular shape, rising one or two feet above the roof; which low square is often surmounted by a tall cylinder, giving to the cottage chimney the most beautiful shape in which it is ever seen. Nor will it be too fanciful or refined to remark, that there is a pleasing harmony between a tall chimney of this circular form, and the living column of smoke, ascending from it through the still air. These dwellings, mostly built, as has been said, of rough unhewn stone, are roofed with slates, which were rudely taken from the quarry before the present art of splitting them was understood, and are, therefore, rough and uneven in their surface, so that both the coverings and sides of the houses have furnished places of rest for the seeds of lichens, mosses, ferns, and flowers. Hence buildings, which in their very form call to mind the processes of Nature, do thus, clothed in part with a vegetable garb, appear to be received into the bosom of the living principle of things, as it acts and exists among the woods and fields; and, by their colour and their shape, affectingly direct the thoughts to that tranquil course of Nature and simplicity, along which the humble-minded inhabitants have, through so many generations, been led. Add the little garden with its shed for bee-hives, its small bed of pot-herbs, and its borders and patches of flowers for Sunday posies, with sometimes a choice few too much prized to be plucked; an orchard of proportioned size; a cheese-press, often supported by some tree near the door; a cluster of embowering sycamores for summer shade; with a tall fir, through which the winds sing when other trees are leafless; the little rill or household spout murmuring in all seasons;—combine these incidents and images together, and you have the representative idea of a mountain cottage in this country so beautifully formed in itself, and so richly adorned by the hand of Nature.

2. *Cultural*—these houses reflect social and economic changes in the countryside and again to some extent in the towns. They are the memorials of a peasant culture which has now disappeared. They are its monuments, just as much as those which express the culture of prehistoric times, and they are equally eloquent of a history which is scarcely, if at all, written in documents.

3. *Constructional*—the structural development of vernacular building.

In studying such houses, especially farmhouses, cottages, and buildings in the country generally, one should begin by noting the details of the site. The kind of soil, the shelter afforded, and the whereabouts of the water supply are all elements in the choice of site. Even where farmhouses lie in the village streets and not isolated in their own fields, considerations of soil and shelter will still operate to some extent, and the water supply will be as important as anywhere. In other words, we have to ask ourselves why a house was built just there and not somewhere else. We should also note, in the case of farmhouses, the relationship of the dwelling-house to the rest of the farmstead. According to the French geographer Demangeon, the essential problem for the peasant in building his farmstead was to establish a relationship (though not, of course, consciously) between men, beasts, and goods. The peasant does not withdraw from his cattle: he wants to keep them near, under his eye, and to keep near him under one roof all that belongs to him. This gives us what the French call the *maison bloc* or in Britain the 'long house', which groups all the essential parts of the farmstead under one roof. This is the most simple and economical of all the forms of the peasant house. It is found in all regions of small-scale farming, above all perhaps in pastoral regions, but in England it is rare to find this primeval type of long house still surviving. It may, however, be seen in certain places around the edge of Dartmoor, though the cattle no longer inhabit the lower end of the house.

9.4 Labourer's cottage, Shropshire

Labourers' cottages do not normally survive from before the late-eighteenth century, but in some parts of the country examples can be found from the Elizabethan and Stuart era. The Oaks stood at the edge of Myddlewood, which had become a distinctive squatters' colony by the end of the seventeenth century. First recorded in a rental of 1588, it was built by John Hughes, a labourer and younger son of a local farming family. Hughes's cottage was only one bay in length and was open to the rafters. The arrangement of the timber panels shows how another bay was added (to the left of picture); then a brick chimney was inserted and upper chambers installed. This two-up, two-down cottage belonged to another labouring family, the Hanmers, for most of the seventeenth century. Ellis Hanmer had arrived in the parish in 1581 when he built a one-bay cottage nearby. Such meagre accommodation was, however, better than that of his neighbour, Thomas Chidlow, a labourer who lived in 'a poore pitifull hutt, built up to an old oake'.

The French geographers also distinguish types of courtyard-houses in the countryside. As the scale of farming increases—more grain, more animals, more buildings—several buildings are constructed around a central courtyard. There are two basic types of courtyard house:

(*a*) *Closed courtyard*: continuous buildings around a closed courtyard, with the dwelling-house at one side of the yard so that everything is under the eye of the master. There is usually one entrance in this fortress-like complex of building—a large gateway through the side which flanks the road and opposite the dwelling-house. This gateway can be closed if necessary and carts and wagons left inside at night. Stacks are not left in the fields; all is safely gathered in and ample space is needed. Some of these great farms have barns as big as churches, often bigger than the parish church. Such farmsteads are characteristic of large-scale arable farming.

(*b*) *Open courtyard*: separate buildings grouped more or less singly around the courtyard which is open at least on one side. This is characteristic of large-scale pastoral farming. There are often several entrances to the courtyard, so that the farmstead is the focus of tracks from all points of the compass, permitting the animals to circulate freely between farm and pastures.

The peasant house is a farming tool. It expresses the character of the local farming of rural society. These are really discursive remarks on the subject, which has been little studied in this country. I draw attention to it so that the local historian may learn to look at the farms and farmsteads of his parish in a new light, and so that he may attempt to classify them roughly for himself and hence make a contribution to this subject in England.

TOWN HOUSES

The study of houses in towns excludes some of the considerations involved in rural parishes, but introduces others in their place. In the main streets of old towns, space became valuable from the thirteenth century onwards. There was, therefore, a tendency to build houses in the main streets with their gable ends to the street. We find this in Scarborough as early as the twelfth century. Henry II's charter of 1155 to the burgesses says *inter alia*: 'they shall pay to me yearly, for each house in Scarborough whose gable is turned towards the street, four pence. . . .' The gable-end type gives a narrow frontage on the street but behind this the site goes back to a great depth. Not only this, but in order to get more room on such a restricted site, we find cellars being excavated below the street level at an early date (at Canterbury we even find one cellar excavated below another in order to get still more room) and the house itself piled up one floor upon another until by the late sixteenth century or early seventeenth such houses might have four or five stories.

9.5 Merchants' houses and warehouses at King's Lynn (after a drawing by W. A. Pantin)

Away from the main streets there was usually much open space, and here we find generally the houses of less important people, the lesser shopkeepers and craftsmen, for example; and in the lanes and smaller streets, we should have found the small houses of the artisan and labouring classes. In some old cities the labouring class was housed mainly in the suburbs outside the walls from quite an early date. Practically all these smaller houses have been swept away long ago with the expansion of our towns and it is difficult to find a single example of this class left. But there still remain a number of larger houses in some of our old cities, notably in such towns as Chester and York. They are diminishing in numbers year by year with the modern mania for street widening and for creating the concrete deserts known as car-parks. It is important, therefore, that the historian of a town should pay close attention to the houses within his purview, and should do his best to make a record of them before he does anything else, since they are in such extreme danger of destruction. In recent years there have been an increasing number of studies of town houses, the most important of which are listed in the Additional References to this chapter.

DOCUMENTARY SOURCES

So far, we have been concerned only with the buildings themselves. There are, however, a number of documentary sources which supplement the evidence of the actual buildings and are equally valuable for this purpose. Both methods of approach, fieldwork and documents, are equally important—in this as in other branches of local history. The principal documents are:

(*a*) Probate inventories
(*b*) Glebe terriers and Faculty papers
(*c*) Old photographs and drawings
(*d*) Manorial surveys
(*e*) Hearth tax assessments
(*f*) Maps and plans
(*g*) Newspaper advertisements (for town houses).

(*a*) *Probate Inventories* were made for the purpose of proving a man's will and administering the personal estate which he left. An excellent account of this class of record and of the kinds of information contained in it will be found in *Farm and Cottage Inventories of Mid-Essex 1635–1749*, edited by F. W. Steer (Phillimore, second edn, 1969). Those who wish to use probate inventories should read the introduction to this volume before beginning work, and should study the layout and contents of the documents as set out in this book. Such inventories were formerly ecclesiastical records, since wills were always proved in the ecclesiastical courts down to 1858. In that year the old wills and inventories were transferred to the probate registries which were set up in various provincial towns. These registries then took over the proving and administration of wills. In many places the old wills and inventories remain in the appropriate probate registry, where they are sometimes not easy to consult because of the lack of facilities in these offices for historical research. At Leicester, however, the wills and inventories dating from before 1858 have all been transferred from the local probate registry to the Leicester County Record Office where they may be consulted freely. At Gloucester they have been transferred to the

Gloucester city library. Similar transfers have taken place in other counties, and it is to be hoped that before long all the pre-1858 wills and inventories will be housed in record offices which have the facilities for preserving them and for making them easily available to students.

These inventories usually cover a period of about two hundred years, from the sixteenth century down to about the middle of the eighteenth. In some regions, notably in Leicester, they cover the whole of the sixteenth century also, rather thinly before 1550, but after that in considerable numbers. In the Lincolnshire Record Office there are nearly 58,000 inventories for the period 1504 to 1700, and a further large collection covering the period 1700–1831. About 5,000 inventories date from before 1550. However, in most parts of the diocese of York inventories drawn up before 1689 do not survive. As with several other kinds of records, the local historian may be fortunate in this respect or he may draw a blank, but where the inventories exist they are absolutely essential to the writing of both town and parish histories. In recent years volumes of inventories have been published for several counties, mostly, for a limited period, as the total collections are so vast.

Probate inventories do not set out to describe houses as such. They are concerned with listing in more or less detail the personal estate left behind by a man or his widow, and in order to do this the makers of the inventory (who were usually neighbours) proceeded from room to room noting and valuing everything they saw. Thus in the fullest of these records, we get a list of all the rooms in the house and of every item of household goods in each room. This applies both to houses in country parishes and in the town. We also get, in the case of farmers, lists of all their farm goods, crops, livestock, implements, and so forth. For craftsmen we often get a list of their tools and implements, and of their stock-in-trade. Most craftsmen were also small farmers, and we therefore usually get also a brief collection of farm goods. We also have in these records more or less complete catalogues of the stock-in-trade of shop-keepers of all kinds. It will be clear from all this that probate inventories are one of the most valuable classes of records which the local historian can hope to find. Since they are concerned with the possessions of what may be roughly called the middle and lower classes in town and country, we obtain from them a mass of information about the everyday life of the period, and we can trace all kinds of social changes if we go systematically through a series of these documents over a long period.

9.6 Bishops' House, Sheffield

When William Blythe of Norton Lees, yeoman, died in 1631 the family's ancient timber-framed house consisted of a central hall with adjoining kitchen and buttery, and a parlour in the west wing, with upstairs chambers. His ancestors had lived in this secluded corner of Norton parish since the reign of Edward III, but the present house dates from about 1500, with the wing remodelled half a century later. Blythe's inventory shows that he was a prosperous yeoman and organiser of the local scythe trade.

Another probate inventory survives for his son and namesake, who died in 1665. This second William Blythe had built a two-storeyed stone extension to the rear of the wing, with a cellar and a staircase; the 'new chamber' and 'little parlour' served as bedrooms. The furniture in the house was listed in detail, together with Blythe's farm stock and equipment and over 2,000 scythes which were sold in the market towns of north-eastern England. William Blythe was a parliamentary captain during the civil war and one of the two officers responsible for demolishing Sheffield castle.

Like any other kind of record, probate inventories have their deficiencies. They vary in the amount of detail they give about a house and its contents,* though if one reads a long series of them one gets a sufficient quantity of information in the end. So far as the special study of houses is concerned they do not, of course, tell us how the different rooms are related to each other. This can only be deduced from examining different types of houses of the same period on the ground. Again, one-roomed houses, which certainly

* I am told by Professor Barley that the probate inventories for Cumberland, Westmorland and Lancashire rarely list the rooms of the houses they deal with.

existed in the sixteenth and seventeenth centuries, present a special problem in the inventories. The mere absence of the names of different rooms does not necessarily mean there was only one room and therefore no need to differentiate. Nevertheless, with sufficient experience one learns to detect some at least of the one-roomed houses from the nature of the contents and the status of the dead man or his widow. Finally, we do not get any clear picture in these records of the layout of the farmstead, i.e. the relationship of barns, stables, shippens, etc., to the dwelling-house.

(b) *Glebe terriers:* these are records made for the purpose of recording more or less precisely the buildings, land if any, and tithes and other emoluments belonging to a particular rectory or vicarage. They are, therefore, ecclesiastical records and most of them probably still remain in the offices of the diocesan registrar where they may usually be consulted without much difficulty. In some counties, however, they have been transferred to the appropriate local record office and are still easier of access. The glebe terriers begin in the closing years of the sixteenth century and form an irregular series at long intervals of years throughout the seventeenth and eighteenth centuries. For our immediate purpose many of them give a more or less detailed description of the rectory house or the vicarage, often going more fully into the materials of which the house is built, and the way in which it is laid out, than any probate inventory would do. They are interesting not only because they give us an account of the parsonage house at certain dates, but also because (if they are rather poor vicarage houses or the rectories of poor livings) they are describing a type of house indistinguishable from that occupied by a typical husbandman at the same time in the same district. They therefore help us to understand more about the houses of the laity of the parish.

Here, for example, is a description of the rectory house at Honeychurch in mid-Devon in the year 1727. This was a very poor living, and the house it describes might well have been the house of a seventeenth-century husbandman:

> One dwelling house in length about nineteen foot the walls of it are of earth & covered with reed & contains one under room called the Hall the floor of it is made with stone. It is neither wainscoted nor ceiled. Another little room on the right hand of the entrance called the milk house the walls of earth & covered with reed, the floor of earth.
>
> One upper room called the Hall Chamber & only covered over with reed.
>
> The outhouses are two, viz. One Barn adjoining to the east end of the dwelling house in length about twenty-four foot the walls of

earth & covered with reed. One Stallhouse usually called the Shippin adjoining to the west end of the dwelling house twelve foot in length the walls of earth & covered with reed.

This house still stands (though no longer used as a rectory) and was evidently built some time in the first half of the seventeenth century.

At St Neot, on the southern edge of Bodmin Moor in Cornwall, we have described for us the vicarage as it was in the year 1613. It then consisted of a hall, a parlour, a kitchen and buttery, all on the ground floor; several rooms on the upper floor; a milk house and outhouses. We are also told the vicarage had a walled court between the hall and the kitchen which gives us a clue to the ground-plan of the building. It also had a barn, a stable with a loft, and another outhouse adjoining. The glebe terrier for the same parish in 1680 goes into much more detail about the vicarage and is worth quoting in full:

It is the humble desire of the present incumbent that it may be considered what a sad and ruinous condition this vicarage was in when he was thereinto inducted AD 1660. And tis very well known (that in the late times of rebellion) this vicarage lay under sequestration for many years and during the time of that usurpation there were divers intruders successively hired by the sequestrators (one of them living in this parish) at a very low rate and slender salary who instead of repairing anything that was decayed did (together with some other licentious people who are since brought to a piece of bread and some to the jaile for theft) endeavour to level both hedges and houses with the ground cutting down the apple trees and many flourishing ash and other trees, burning the rafters and other timber both of the dwelling and outhouses, taking away the glass and iron bars of the windows so that all was in the highway to a total devastation, and none of those spoilers found of ability to make the least satisfaction. So that the incumbent was necessitated to betake himself forthwith to the building if he would have any house to put his head in at the time of his induction. And first the side posts and lintel of the door leading into the entry leaned so much outward together with the side wall built thereon (having taken water) that the incumbent was enforced to take it down and setting the door upright he (to prevent the taking down of more on both sides) erected (as a buttress) from the ground a large porch (for there was none afore) and built a study over it well planched timbered and covered with tiling stones. Over the entry is a chamber, the walls repaired on both sides and the partition wall between this and the room over the buttery taken down (being ready to fall) and rebuilt to the top by the present incumbent, the roof well covered with tile. Above the entry the hall and over that a chamber well repaired and covered with tile. The hall is floored with earth and wainscotted at the upper end. Above the hall a parlour floored with earth a great part thereof ceiled with fir which ceiling was carried away and sold in the church town by some of the intruders but recovered and set up again in its place, the walls also in a great part rebuilt from the ground, the chamber over it now planched, the roof all new timbered and covered with tile by the present incumbent. On the east side of the parlour is a little dairy floored with slate stones, the roof now timbered and covered with tile by the present incumbent. Outbuildings—on the East side of the house is a walled court and on the east side thereof a kitchen covered with reed.

For a somewhat later period there are Faculty papers relating to structural changes in the church or the rectory or vicarage. These changes required official permission in the form of a *faculty*. The application was often accompanied by plans showing the proposed changes. These plans may be of the highest interest: for example, in the Devon record office there are plans for major alterations at Whitestone rectory, made in 1775. These show the original medieval rectory (as described in earlier glebe terriers) and the proposed changes, mainly the handsome Georgian south front we see today. Much of the original rectory remains at the back, and the plans show exactly what was destroyed.

(*c*) *Old photographs and drawings:* these are particularly valuable for they often illustrate buildings which have been pulled down or altered beyond recognition. One can only make enquiries locally about the existence of such drawings or old photographs, and the best place to start one's enquiries is the nearest large library. Photographs and drawings will not tell us all we would like to know about a building, but they will probably give us additional information which we should not otherwise have.

(*d*) *Manorial surveys:* these again do not set out to give descriptions of houses, but they may give us some incidental information which should not be overlooked. Indeed, most surveys of manors are not at all concerned with describing the houses and cottages and say nothing about them. The elaborate surveys made for the Earl of Pembroke, however, in 1631–32 give a considerable amount of detail about the farmhouses and cottages at that date on the Wiltshire estate of the Earl. Thus the farmhouse of Edward Barter at Fovant is described as 'a dwelling house of four ground rooms, two of them lofted over'. There was also 'a barn of three rooms', and a stable adjoining. Simple though this description is, it gives us some idea of the Barter farmhouse. When combined with similar descriptions of other houses on the Fovant estate we obtain a fairly clear picture of farmers' houses in a Wiltshire village in the early seventeenth century. Some of these houses, we learn, had detached kitchens. We also get brief descriptions of cottages: John Hannam

held 'a cottage newly erected of two rooms and a little garden and orchard adjoining' for an annual rent of sixpence. Henry Barter's cottage also contained two groundfloor rooms and nothing else. Few manorial surveys go into such detail as this, but there are probably more than we might suspect, if we make an intensive search.

(e) *Hearth tax assessments:* these records again were not made for the purpose of telling us what houses looked like in the second half of the seventeenth century, but we can derive a certain amount of information from them about the size of houses and the number of fireplaces in them. The great majority of people lived in houses with only one fireplace, but they must not be dismissed simply as the rural proletariat, as some writers have done. The use which can be made of hearth tax assessments in this respect can be seen in my own book *The Midland Peasant*, in the final pages on peasant houses and interiors (especially pp. 299–300). Obviously, the hearth tax assessments are of very limited value for the study of vernacular building in the seventeenth century and they must be used with great caution; but they should not be entirely ignored.

(f) *Surviving maps and plans:* these will give us only the ground plan of houses at a given period of time, but they are useful as showing the varying types of ground plan at a particular date (L-plan, T-plan, and others) and for indicating the plan of the whole complex of farmsteads at the same time. The tithe maps of the 1840s and the enclosure maps, mainly of the period 1750–1850, should all be consulted for this purpose. Private estate maps may well exist from the closing years of the sixteenth century onwards. The information given by maps is meagre but may be useful in showing the prevailing type of ground plan in a given village. Differences in the ground plan may well reflect changes which were taking place in the internal plan of some houses.

(g) *Newspaper advertisements:* for houses in towns the brief descrip-

9.7 Calendars, Burford

Old water-colours and drawings can be a vivid source of topographical information, particularly when the artist is of national repute like J. C. Buckler. Collections of Buckler's works are held in various national and local repositories. This portrait of Sheep Street, Burford, in 1821 is housed at the Bodleian Library, Oxford (MS. Top. Oxon. 65,a. no. 139). Calendars (the third house from the right) no longer has the gabled wing that projected so dramatically from its upper storey. This late-medieval house has two rooms fronting the street and a long rear wing. Burford was a small medieval borough whose properties were arranged along burgage plots, but these plots were not as narrow as in some larger towns and so the houses did not need to have their gable ends towards the street. Burford was at the height of its prosperity as a wool town in the late-fifteenth and early-sixteenth centuries.

tions given in eighteenth- and early nineteenth-century advertisements (of houses for sale or to be let) form a useful source of
information. Thus in *Brice's Weekly Journal*, an Exeter newspaper,
under 5 June 1730 we find:

> To be let—a new built house in Northgate Street, next the George
> Inn, wherein Dr Mawzey lived, containing Kitchen, large Parlour,
> two spences, eight Lodging Chambers [bedrooms], six large closets,
> cellars, Courts and a stable, two garden platts—the water brought to
> the house, with Sash-Windows fronting the garden.

Or, in the *Exeter Flying Post* for 2 June 1780 we have described:

> A new built dwelling house in Bridge Street, adjoining the steps to
> the Island, containing shop, parlour, kitchen, pantry, six good Lodging
> Rooms, two closets and two garrets, with a Water Closet and Pump.

This appears to be, incidentally, the first reference to a water-closet
in any house in Exeter. It was then a comparatively new invention.
A systematic study of all the houses described in newspaper
advertisements during the eighteenth century would give us a
pretty good picture of the middle-class houses of the period in this
city.

SOME GENERAL REMARKS

It is impossible to touch upon all the questions that arise when
one makes a detailed study of the houses in a given village or town.
What happened, for example, to the Midland farmhouses under
the revolution brought about by the parliamentary enclosure of the
open fields? Many farmers built themselves new houses out in the
fields, in the middle of the compact block of land which had been
allotted to them in lieu of a multitude of strips scattered throughout
the open fields. So we get in hundreds of Midland parishes, and in
the country to the north, more or less handsome Georgian farmhouses standing alone in the fields. The ancestral farmhouses on
the village street were generally abandoned as such, and we often
find them today subdivided into a number of cottages, especially
where the village has become industrialised. In spite of later
changes, however, once can still detect their original type and plan.

Going further back in time, what structural changes occurred in
a given locality during the Great Rebuilding of 1570–1640? Why
is there little or no evidence of this rebuilding in south Somerset,
but of a later rebuilding period from about 1670 to 1800? When did

the long-house type develop? Was it general throughout England, or was it confined to the pastoral Highland Zone? And when was the long-house type of building abandoned: in other words when were the cattle removed from the house itself and installed in a separate building in the yard? On Dartmoor, for example, this may be a comparatively recent development but no one seems to have recorded this profound social change.

It should be said that when one comes to study cottages, nothing seems to survive before the late seventeenth century. What the estate agent calls an Olde Worlde cottage, if it is genuine, is almost invariably in origin a husbandman's house and not a labourer's cottage at all. We know that a great number of true cottages for the labouring classes were being built in the last quarter of the sixteenth century. Contemporary records make that abundantly clear. But all these cottages seem to have perished. They were probably built in the cheapest and quickest way, and they probably had a life of a hundred to a hundred and fifty years, so that they decayed and were being replaced from the late seventeenth century onwards. Quite often they were rebuilt in brick, which was then a new building material in most parts of England so far as the smaller houses were concerned. We can therefore only study the English cottage, so far as surviving specimens are concerned, from about 1680 onwards. For earlier cottages we have to rely upon such information as the documents may give to us.

INDUSTRIAL BUILDINGS

In many parts of England there are the remains of industrial buildings of one sort and another, many of them relics of a long outmoded phase of industry. In their simplest form these may take the shape of framework-knitters' cottages (in the Midlands) or of weavers' cottages (in West Yorkshire), both of which were characterised by long upper windows in order to throw the maximum light on the frame or the loom. Such relics of the domestic system of industry are becoming rarer every year, and typical specimens should be photographed, planned, and fully described, before it is too late.

One may also find specimens of the next stage of industrial development—the small workshop, still operated by hand labour and not by power of any kind. This, too, usually has a characteristic plan and elevation, and should be recorded in detail. On a larger

9.8 Weavers' cottages, Yorkshire

Scattered farmsteads, cottages, and hamlets clustered into folds are an ancient and characteristic feature of the Pennines. During the Industrial Revolution scribbling and spinning mills attracted new settlements in the valley bottoms, but weaver-farmers continued to work at home in the hills, for their craft long remained at the domestic stage. As in this example at Bottoms in the parish of Almondbury, an upper range of windows extended all along the front to allow the maximum amount of light to fall on the weavers' looms. The house is built of local sandstone, with ashlar used for quoins, lintels and mullions; the weight of the slate stones forced the builders to design houses with the lowest pitch of any traditional building in England. The first edition 6-inch Ordnance Survey maps of the 1850s show that these West Riding houses normally had crofts with tenters for stretching woven pieces of cloth after their return from the fulling mill.

scale altogether, but also in danger of perishing without a proper record, we have in the north of England especially fine examples of early water-power mills in the remote valleys beneath the moors. In Derbyshire, particularly in the Derwent Valley, we have fine water-power mills of late eighteenth-century date at Cressbrook, Belper, and Milford, accompanied by contemporary housing for industrial workers.

Even more remote are the remains of the old lead-smelting industry of the Yorkshire dales. The lead-mills have been admirably recorded by Robert T. Clough in *The Lead Smelting Mills of the Yorkshire Dales* (Keighley, 1955), in a survey which is a model

9.9 Quarry Bank mill, Styal, Cheshire

In the early days of mechanisation cotton mills were worked by water power and were sited in rural areas. In 1783 Samuel Greg of Manchester decided to build a mill on the bank of the Bollin at Styal, a small farming community housed in thatched, timber-framed cottages. Greg had to attract outside labour in the two accepted ways of the age. First of all, he built Oak Cottages and other accommodation and provided a chapel and school in the manner of Richard Arkwright at Cromford, Jedediah Strutt at Belper and Robert Owen at New Lanark. Secondly, he built Apprentice House for up to 100 pauper children, who came not only from local villages but from places as far away as Chelsea and Hackney. Greg's venture was successful and the mill was soon extended with a steam engine and extra water wheels. The mill and the community are now owned by the National Trust.

of its kind. A similar survey is badly needed for the decaying buildings of the Cornish tin-mining industry, the gaunt roofless engine-houses which are a familiar part of the scene on the western moors. Nearly every region in England had industries of some kind, some of them peculiar to a particular district. The local historian should make himself responsible for recording the remains of any such past industry or trade, and especially the visible remains of any buildings there may be. In this connection the tithe maps of a hundred years ago or so are often of great value in locating vanished industrial sites, or in reconstructing sites which have partly perished. For larger industries, such as the ironstone industry of western Yorkshire, and many others in which local landowners were interested, there may be valuable topographical and other information in private estate papers or the records of old industrial concerns. The value of business records has become increasingly recognised in recent years, and the local historian should not overlook them in his search for material.

10 HEALTH, DISEASE, AND POPULATION

THE SELF-CONTAINED PARISH

The study of population changes is of fundamental importance in any local history. In non-urban communities especially it may be the master-key to the history of the community over several centuries. The great majority of English parishes were for many centuries more or less self-contained communities, producing nearly all their material requirements within their own boundaries. Thus the local schoolmaster who wrote the history of the parish of Warton in north Lancashire in the early eighteenth century says of his parish:

> The inhabitants of this parish may truly and with comfort, say, that they have, within their own limits, all those good things (wine and oil excepted) which Jesus the wise Son of Sirach reckons the chief and principal things for the whole Use of Man's life, viz. Water, Fire, Iron and Salt, and Bread; Flour and Wheat, Honey, Milk, and the Blood of the Grape, and Oil and Clothing and an House to cover Shame. In a word, they freely enjoyed all the four elements, Fire, Air, Water, and Earth, and have each of them very good.

Of the Midland parish of Wigston Magna I have written elsewhere in the following terms which might well apply to almost any parish in England:

> Wigston produced all its own food, clothing, light, power, and building materials, and nearly all its own heat, out of the most commonplace natural resources; for the parish was not specially endowed by Nature in any single respect beyond the fact that its clays, with constant hard labour, were capable of producing good crops. For its buildings—

houses, barns, and boundary walls—it had its own clay, used in the preparation of the long-lasting 'mud walls'. The boulders in the clay, of every size from pebbles upwards, provided the necessary footings for all these mud walls, and the mortar that bound them came from Wigston's own lime-pit. Wheat-straw or selected reeds from some special corner of the parish provided the material for thatching houses and copings for mud walls. The parish had its own sand-pits and gravel-pits, the latter especially valuable when the coming of turnpike roads in the eighteenth century made better surfaces necessary; and when the general use of bricks for domestic building came in in the last quarter of the seventeenth century good brick-earth was found right in the village.

The willows that fringed the streams of the parish provided wattles for sheep-hurdles and other temporary fences, besides the framework for 'wattle-and-daub' farmhouses, a more substantial construction than mud alone. The furze of the common pastures, though there was not much of it, was burnt in the bakehouses, brewhouses, and kitchen fires, as were the 'shreddings' or loppings off the hedgerows also.

As for its crops, the parish grew enough flax and hemp to meet its own needs for linen sheets, napkins, towels, and clothing; it produced enough wool from its own sheep to keep the five or six village tailors well supplied. Its barley, grown over several hundred acres every year, supplied food and drink; and its wheat, rye, oats, peas, and beans provided food for all men and beasts. Every cottage and farmhouse had its own poultry (chiefly geese, but ducks and hens were numerous), and most kept pigs and bees. All had herb-gardens and many had small orchards: so the village had meat, eggs, cheese, butter, milk, honey, apples, and herbs of all kinds. The parish generated its own power: for the wind did not blow to waste but was harnessed to two or three windmills: and the waters of the little river Sence were not allowed to flow unused across the parish boundary. Since the middle of the twelfth century they had turned the water-wheel at Crow Mill, and from time out of mind they had yielded a few precious fish, the only fishing water in the whole parish.

Wigston was not exceptional in practising this high economy of all its natural resources, nor was it by any means exceptionally endowed. It was, indeed, less fortunate than a great number of other parishes, for it lacked building stone, coal, a sufficiency of large timber for building purposes, iron for farm implements and gear, and the inevitable salt; and most of these things had to come from elsewhere, though usually not far.*

Country parishes lived off their own resources, using money for merely marginal purposes to purchase the few things they could not produce themselves. On the other hand, the natural resources of the great majority of parishes were more or less fixed in quantity. The area of land available, for example, could not be expanded once

* *The Midland Peasant*, pp. 190–92.

all the waste had been taken in and broken up. In the Midlands this had generally been accomplished by the end of the thirteenth century; but in the west and north of England, where there was much more upland waste, we find a good deal of land still being taken into cultivation during the seventeenth century. Thus the chronology of population changes and their effect on the rural economy will vary from one region to another in England, depending upon the opportunities for the expansion of the available natural resources.

So, in the absence of any discovery of minerals which might transform the economy of a parish and enable it to support a much larger population, or the introduction of some local industry which would have the same effect, we have to envisage the economic history of most country parishes as that of an increasing pressure of population upon limited natural resources.

Fortunately, the population of rural England did not rise without serious interruptions. By the early fourteenth century, for example, there had developed an acute pressure in the lowland half of England at least, amounting to a 'land hunger'. This might have become intolerable within the next century had not successive epidemics of bubonic plague wiped out a considerable proportion of the population everywhere and so relieved the pressure. In general terms these great losses were not made up again until towards the end of the sixteenth century; and in many parishes we can detect during the course of the seventeenth century the rising land hunger which had been characteristic of the thirteenth.

In the seventeenth century, too, the effect of the rising level of population was aggravated by the engrossing of farms; that is to say, the throwing together of a number of small tenements into one large one, farmed by one man. Thus when there were more young men looking for farms in which to start life, there were fewer farms available. The land hunger of the seventeenth century must have played a considerable part in the emigration movement from this country across the Atlantic.

All this is a highly simplified account of complicated changes over several centuries, and there will be important local variations from this simple version. But I have set out merely to show how important for the local historian is a study of population changes in his area.

MEDIEVAL POPULATION

It is difficult to arrive at reasonably accurate population figures
during the medieval period. Not only are the sources few, but they
are not easy to interpret with accuracy. For the majority of places
we have, of course, the population recorded in Domesday Book
(1086). This recorded population probably represents a complete
household in each case, except perhaps in the case of the slaves (*servi*)
who are to be reckoned as individuals. It is better to leave the total
population in the form of households, since we do not know the size
of the average household in the eleventh century. If, however, we
wish to translate households into people, the customary multiplier
of five is still probably the best. The American scholar J. C. Russell,
in his book, *British Medieval Population* (New Mexico, Albuquerque,
1948), thought a multiplier of 3·5 gave more accurate results, but
later work suggests that this figure is much too low.

For a detailed criticism of Russell's figure, see J. Krause, 'The
Medieval Household: Large or Small?' (*Econ. Hist. Review*, ix,
1957). Local historians will also find stimulating and valuable an
article by H. E. Hallam on 'Some Thirteenth-Century Censuses', in
the *Econ. Hist. Review*, x, 1958. This shows *inter alia* the profound
importance of the local customs of inheritance for the size, structure,
and mobility of rural populations. Dr Hallam finds that the average
household in three Fenland parishes in the thirteenth century
numbered 4·68 persons. Not the least interesting of his results is the
remarkably high population of these medieval parishes. Several
of them had 3,000 people or more. The custom of partible inheritance (equal division between sons) tended to produce a much
greater density of population than the custom of primogeniture,
which gave all or most to the eldest son. Partible inheritance
prevailed in various regions of England. There seems to be no
simple explanation for its geographical distribution.

The next important source for the local study of population is
the Hundred Rolls of 1279, but these survive in the necessary detail
only for a number of Midland counties and even then are not complete. The poll taxes of 1377–81 are much more comprehensive.
Again, the interpretation of these in terms of population presents
some difficulties. The reader is referred on this subject to an important article by M. W. Beresford on 'The Poll Taxes of 1377, 1379,
and 1381' in *The Amateur Historian* (vol. iii, no. 7). In addition
to all these records the local historian may be fortunate enough to
find detailed extents or surveys of the manor in which he is interested

for various dates in the thirteenth and fourteenth centuries. The figures given for the various kinds of tenants in these extents must be treated with some caution. We cannot necessarily add together the number of free tenants, customary tenants, cottagers, and others enumerated in the document in a given year, to arrive at the total tenant population. A free tenant might well hold some customary land, and to that extent there would be a certain amount of double counting in the record. Even so, the extents are useful for the student of population changes, especially if he is able to use them in conjunction with another type of record and can achieve some rough agreement between the two. For the whole of the fifteenth century we have virtually no information about local populations. The local and central records for this century are generally less informative, or more sparse, than those for the centuries which precede it and come after it.

POPULATION SOURCES, 1524 TO 1801

The first national census of population did not take place until 1801. Until that date we have to depend for our knowledge of population changes upon a variety of records, very few of which were designed specifically to produce this information. Let us begin with the local records that are available for the sixteenth century. The most important of these by far are the parish registers of baptisms, marriages, and burials. These should date, as every local historian knows, from the autumn of 1538, but it is rare to find a register which is complete from the beginning. In Leicestershire, for example, only about one parish in ten possesses such a complete run, and some counties are probably worse off than this. Many registers begin in 1558 because Elizabeth I, towards the end of her reign, enacted that the old registers should be copied into parchment books for their better preservation, and incumbents were instructed to begin their transcription with the first year of her reign. This explains, of course, why for forty years and more we may get the same handwriting in the parish register. It does not mean that the same parson was there all the time. Parish registers have, however, often been badly kept and a great number have perished. Many parishes have nothing to show before the eighteenth century.[*]

---

[*] Deficient registers can sometimes be remedied from the Bishops' Transcripts in the appropriate diocesan registry, but these are inclined to be patchy until the late seventeenth century.

Assuming, however, that the local historian is fortunate enough to possess registers from at least the second half of the sixteenth century, he can make effective use of them for the study of population changes in his parish and also for the study of public health over the last four hundred years. I shall come to this point later.

It is clear that if the registers were accurately kept, we should be able to arrive at some idea of the total population of the parish in a given decade. One can generally ascertain by inspection whether or not the record is likely to be complete. Assuming that it is, we can use the number of baptisms in a given decade to calculate the total population at that time. If we take the total baptisms over a period of ten years and hence find the average number of baptisms per year, and multiply this result by thirty, we shall arrive at a fairly close estimate of the total population.* It is necessary to take the average of a ten-year period and not a single year as the number of baptisms often fluctuates widely from year to year, sometimes for obvious reasons and sometimes not. At Plymouth, for example, the number of baptisms in the year 1589 was only 123, because most of the male population of the town had been away at sea for the greater part of the year before. But in 1590 the number of baptisms rose to 181, and in 1591 to no less than 239. From these figures we can estimate that the total population of Plymouth at the time of the Armada was about 5,500, and that it was rising rapidly in the last decade of the century. We should expect this in a booming 'war town' such as Plymouth was in the last quarter of the sixteenth century.

One sometimes sees it stated that one can arrive at the total population by using the burial entries and marriage entries in the registers, but both these are too dangerous to use for this purpose. The number of burials fluctuates so much from year to year, according to the incidence of plague and other epidemics, that it is quite unsafe to take even an annual average over a decade. As for marriages, some parishes appear to have been fashionable much as they are today, and the number of marriages in their registers does not reflect the population of the parish itself. Moreover, for rural parishes the number of marriages per annum is too small to give satisfactory results. Again, marriage-rates could and did change. Carew, the historian of Cornwall, remarked in the 1580s that people were marrying much younger than they used to. It was an

---

* See Tate, *The Parish Chest* (Cambridge University Press, 3rd edn, 1969) for a Note upon Registers and Population Statistics, for various cautionary remarks.

age of expansion, in general of good employment, and young men and women married earlier as a consequence. In times of a contracting economy and irregular employment they married later in life. All this makes any use of the marriage statistics for our purpose much too problematical.

It is true indeed that birth rates could also vary, even under natural conditions, for various reasons such as earlier marriages, and possibly a better diet and better living conditions generally. Nevertheless, the number of baptisms is the least unsatisfactory guide to the total population at any given time, especially if we can find another type of record to work upon which will produce a confirmatory result. By the early eighteenth century, more so in some parts of England than in others, the growth of nonconformity makes it increasingly difficult to use the parish register of baptisms as a basic source for population study. Although everybody except Jews and Quakers was obliged to be married in the Church of England, nonconformists of all kinds could be baptised and buried elsewhere. To arrive at a true estimate of population in, say, the eighteenth century, we have to know what proportion of the population were nonconformist, and to make allowances accordingly. There are certain records which enable us to arrive at this information. Nonconformist registers of baptisms and burials are now housed at St Catherine's House in London, where a complete list of them may be seen. They relate mostly to the latter part of the eighteenth century and the early nineteenth down to 1837.

There may be other local records that throw light upon the subject of population. One may find in the parish chest a copy of the population return called for under the Act of 1695, which imposed duties on births, marriages, and burials, as well as on bachelors and widowers. Returns under this Act are very rare but they occasionally come to light. The rate books of the churchwardens or the overseers of the poor sometimes give us a good idea of the total number of households in a parish, as well as giving us virtually a directory of all the ratepaying householders and the farms where they lived. If we have at the same time a list of the households too poor to pay the church rate or the poor rate, we are in a position to know the total number of families in the parish. Such detailed assessments for rates may be found from the late sixteenth century onwards.

Another type of record which may be used with effect is to be found in diocesan registries. Episcopal visitations of the diocese sometimes give the estimated population of the parish, such as the enquiry made by Bishop Wake in 1705 in the diocese of Lincoln. In the diocese of Exeter the bishop sent out a detailed list of questions in 1744 which asked, among other things, the number of families in each parish, so that we have in Cornwall and Devon a fairly good census in a particularly lean period. It is true that a number of parsons were too lazy to find out how many families there were in the parish and they return a suspiciously round number. But the majority of the answers return numbers which have all the appearance of truth.

In addition to the local records which can be used for the study of population, there is a wide range of records in the central archives which the local historian should consult. The assessments for the great subsidy of 1524–25 appear to be fairly comprehensive in rural parishes, and may be used as a rough test of the total number of households, though again with some caution. In those parts of England, for example, where it was customary for farm servants to live in and not to occupy separate cottages, it would probably be difficult to ascertain the number of separate households with any degree of confidence.* For many parts of England the chantry certificates of 1545 give a more or less accurate estimate of the number of communicants in the parish. These are described in the record as 'houseling people' and represent the number of inhabitants aged about fifteen and over. To take Plymouth as an example again, the chantry certificate states that there were 2,000 houseling people in the parish. Assuming that this figure is reasonably accurate, and on the further assumption that children under fifteen accounted for 40 per cent of the whole population at any given time (which is the best estimate we can yet make), this gives us a total population for Plymouth in 1545 of about 3,330. Some of these chantry certificates have been printed for particular counties but most remain unexamined in the Public Record Office.

In the year 1563 all the Bishops of England and Wales were asked by the Privy Council to make a return for their dioceses which was to include a statement of the number of families in each parish. Unfortunately, most of these returns are now missing. Those that survive are contained in Harleian Manuscripts 594 and 595, in the British Library. The surviving returns relate to the dioceses of Bangor, Canterbury, Carlisle, Chester, Coventry and Lichfield, Ely, Worcester, and St David's. There are incomplete returns for the

---

* For the deficiencies of the 1524–25 subsidies, even in rural areas, see McKinley, *Norfolk Surnames in the Sixteenth Century* (Leicester University Press, 1969).

dioceses of Durham, and Bath and Wells. Harleian Manuscript 618 contains the return for the whole of the vast diocese of Lincoln except the Archdeaconry of Stow, and Rawlinson ms. C790 in the Bodleian Library is the return for the diocese of Gloucester. There are also returns for the year 1603, which give the totals of communicants, nonconformists, and Catholic recusants. Harleian Manuscripts 594 and 595 cover the dioceses of Gloucester, Norwich, and Winchester, and the Lincolnshire record office has the return for the diocese of Lincoln.

Quite another class of record are the Muster Rolls and Books in the Public Record Office for various dates during the sixteenth century. These give the names of all the able-bodied men between the ages of sixteen and sixty able to serve in a military capacity, and usually what kind of weapon they should provide. There are numerous returns for the latter part of the reign of Henry VIII which may generally be tracked down through the printed volumes of *The Letters and Papers of Henry VIII*. Most of these appear to be Muster Lists for the period of about 1539–42. Under Elizabeth I there is a further long series of muster lists for the period 1558 to 1588. Those for 1558–60 are unsatisfactory to use: there was far too much evasion of the muster, and also in 1559 a great epidemic which falsified the returns. But the muster of 1569 is, for many counties, a very full one giving what is virtually a house-to-house enumeration of the male population of every parish. Those local historians who wish to use this class of record should consult first of all an article on 'The population of Elizabethan England', by E. E. Rich in the *Economic History Review* (1950). A table here gives county totals for all musters between 1560 and 1588, and will show the local historian which years are most profitable to consult for his own county. Thus for Cornwall and Devon, the muster totals are highest in 1569, for Lincolnshire in 1587, and Suffolk 1580. For Yorkshire the muster of 1573 shows the highest total. It is rather rash to attempt to form an estimate of the total population on the basis of the number of able-bodied men in a given parish, but in my limited experience of these figures a multiplier of six or seven will give a total somewhere near the true answer for the average parish.

In the seventeenth century there are a number of useful records for the study of population. Best of all perhaps are the Protestation Returns of 1642, which are now preserved in the library of the House of Lords, where they may readily be seen by students of local history. These give the names of all males of the age of eighteen and over in every parish who subscribed to the Oath of Protestation. A list of the surviving returns will be found in the appendix to the Fifth Report of the *Historical Manuscripts Commission* (1876), pp. 120–34. These returns also list the names of all those, who were very few, who refused to subscribe to the Oath. In this way, we discover the names and the number of recusants, though it is probable that many recusants signed for the sake of peace and quiet. In the parish of Colyton in East Devon, where 547 men signed and 27 did not, we read of a nice distinction—'John Carswell not obstinately refuseing, but scrupulously forbearing' to sign.

We could obviously use a return like this to form a fairly accurate estimate of the total population. We may assume that the number of females is roughly equal to the number of males in a given parish, so that if we double the number named in the Protestation Return, we obtain the total of the adult population. Assuming as before that about 40 per cent of the total population were below the age of fifteen to eighteen, we must multiply the adult population by $\frac{10}{6}$.

We may compare the results obtained from this source with the so-called Compton Return of 1676, partial copies of which survive in the William Salt Library at Stafford, Lambeth Palace, and the Bodleian Library. These are arranged on a parish basis and give the number of conformists, nonconformists, and Roman Catholics over the age of sixteen (both men and women). We have to adjust this result again so as to allow for the children in the population.

Two further classes of record in the central archives are valuable for the study of population-changes. In 1660 Parliament voted a tax, partly on social rank, partly on wealth, and partly a poll tax, which covered all persons above the age of sixteen years. Many of the detailed assessments for this tax survive in the Public Record Office, and in the case of the larger towns copies may survive among their local archives. Apart from the immense value of a comprehensive assessment of this kind for the genealogist and for the student of parish history, it is obvious that the record is invaluable as a source for computing the total population at this date. It is possible that if the assessment for 1660 does not survive for a given place, a later poll tax assessment may be available.

The other important class of record for this purpose, as well as for others, is the Hearth Tax assessments. The Hearth Tax was collected from Michaelmas 1662 to Lady Day 1689, but local assessments were returnable to the Exchequer only from Michaelmas 1662 to Lady Day 1666, and from Michaelmas 1669 to Lady Day 1674. Not all these returns survive in the central archives. In

10.1 Old Hall Farm, Youlgreave, Derbyshire

Mr Henry Fox was taxed on six hearths for this property at Michaelmas, 1670. The house was then forty years old. Local coursed limestone was used for the walls, with quoins, lintels, window dressings and a stone slate roof from the millstone grit measures. The house has gabled roofs and mullioned windows, and the ground floor windows also have transoms. The main block is one room deep, with 'house' and kitchen separated by an axial chimney stack and the entrance. The wing contains a parlour, with a rear buttery and staircase. All the rooms are chambered over, and a storage chamber above the kitchen was reached by an external stair. The L-shape plan is typical of many houses of yeomen or minor gentry in the north midlands during the first half of the seventeenth century.

general, the assessment for Lady Day 1664 seems to be the most comprehensive from the point of view of names, including as it does all persons both chargeable and non-chargeable to the tax. It occasionally happens that other assessments are fuller, so that the local historian should examine all assessments that survive for his chosen place and decide for himself which is the best for his purpose. The assessments relate to households rather than to separate houses. In a rural parish this distinction hardly matters, since in all probability we should have found only one family to each house at that date; but in the towns there was already a good deal of 'doubling-up' especially in the poorer parishes. The Hearth Tax assessments, being related to households, are not easy to use for the purpose of computing the total population, but it may be necessary to use them for this purpose where the poll tax assessments are missing.

This completes the list of records available during the seventeenth century for the study of population, except where detailed rate assessments survive locally. In the eighteenth century we have virtually no records that throw light upon population changes except those already mentioned above—notably returns of population made in answer to episcopal enquiries. This is a particularly unfortunate gap in our sources for two reasons. On the one hand, nonconformity was spreading rapidly in many parts of England so that the Church of England records become less and less reliable as a survey of the total population. And secondly, large areas of the country were being industrialised, especially during the second half of the eighteenth century, and there were dramatic population changes of which we still know far too little.

In 1801 we have the first national census, thereafter repeated at ten-yearly intervals (except in the year 1941). The printed reports for each census are available in all good libraries and it is easy to extract the totals decade by decade for one's town or parish. It need hardly be said that population changes during the nineteenth century and the early twentieth may be just as important as any changes in the distant past, and in many places much more so, and they should be given equal attention.

LOCAL POPULATION STUDIES

Since I first wrote this book, the study of population by local historians has made considerable advances. On the professional level, indeed, the subject is now called Historical Demography. In the autumn of 1968 a new journal appeared called *Local Population Studies*, published in association with the Nottingham University Department of Adult Education, and those local historians who wish to pursue this particular line of research would do well to acquire it. The contents of each issue are somewhat wider than the title might suggest. For example, there have been articles on perinatal mortality, the incidence of suicide, popular education and literacy, pre-1841 census enumerators' schedules, and a wide variety of other subjects of interest to local historians, whether they are accomplished mathematicians or not.

A few years ago L. Bradley published *A Glossary for Population Studies* (*Local Population Studies* Supplement, 1971) which, though somewhat mathematical in places, is invaluable and again covers a wider range of subjects than the title might indicate. The use of this glossary will save local historians from some elementary errors, even if they do not attempt the higher flights of the subject.

Some societies of local historians (for example, the Edmonton Hundred Historical Society in Middlesex) have formed small groups for population research in conjunction with the Cambridge Group for the History of Population and Social Structure. This Group's activities are reported at intervals in *Local Population Studies*.

EPIDEMICS AND DISEASE

It is astonishing how little we know about the health of the people of this country in past centuries, certainly before the nineteenth century. The standard work on the subject, Creighton's *History of Epidemics in Britain*, was published over seventy years ago. It contains valuable information, especially for the sixteenth and seventeenth centuries, but there is a great deal more to be discovered on this subject. Here the local historian who is medically inclined should be able to make a substantial contribution. For this purpose the burial registers of his town or his parish are the one and only source, except again in the larger towns, where there may be passing references to plagues and other epidemics in other records. Since parish registers begin only in 1538, and the local historian will be fortunate if he lives in a place where the registers are still complete, he can only expect to pursue this subject over the last four hundred years. Even so, there is a vast amount of material waiting to be extracted and analysed.

By examining the burial registers systematically for every year and counting the number of burials in each year, the local historian will be able to trace not only major outbreaks of bubonic plague and other epidemics, but he will also bring to light a number of lesser epidemics. He will discover that in any particular decade there is a 'normal' number of burials per annum. If this 'normal' number is markedly exceeded then there is some epidemic factor at work. He may then, by looking more closely at individual entries, detect that (whatever the epidemic may be) it breaks out at a certain time of the year and dies away a few weeks or a few months later. He may also observe that it hits chiefly people of a certain class. With this information, and with the help of a historically-minded medical friend, he may be able to suggest what the epidemic was—for example influenza, typhus, or bubonic plague. In the sixteenth century there was a mysterious and rapidly killing disease known as the 'Great Sweat'. The nature of this disease has never been properly explained. It is said to have been brought to this country by the army of Henry VII when they landed in west Wales in 1485. The periodic outbreaks of the disease in the sixteenth century are said to have caused the greatest mortality among the well-to-do, so much so that in some parts of England the disease, whatever it was, was sardonically called by the common people 'Stop gallant' and sometimes 'Stoop Knave and know thy Master'. Whether this disease was as selective among classes as the general populace appeared to believe is a matter for the local historian to settle for himself. The 'Great Sweat' is said to have appeared for the last time in 1551. There had been earlier outbreaks in 1508, 1517, and 1528.

The plague, more strictly the bubonic plague, entered this country for the first time in August 1348 and was known from the beginning as 'the Black Death'. It struck again and again during the second half of the fourteenth century as monastic chronicles and other contemporary records show. Although it continued to break out in the countryside in later centuries, it caused greater devastation in the towns. It was no longer a general epidemic over the whole country but became sporadic and localised. It is said to have become essentially the disease of the poor—those who were worst fed and worst housed, and those who could not escape into the country at a moment's notice. We now know that the 'Black Death' was carried by a particular sort of flea which inhabited the black rat. Since rats were probably much more common in the houses of the poor, and above all in the congested quarters of the larger towns, it is not surprising that the plague came to be regarded as the particular affliction of the poorer classes. It disappeared from England in 1666, its last outbreak being the great plague of 1665 in London in which nearly seventy thousand people perished.

The local historian can also, in pursuing this enquiry, notice the incidence of the plague within his town or parish and try to suggest the significance of it. At Hampton-on-Thames, Mr Garside discovered by analysing closely the 119 burials in the year 1603 that ninety-nine of these are noted as having died of plague. But the plague was not even general in Hampton-on-Thames. He notes that two-thirds of the deaths occurred in 20 per cent of the families, and that more than half of the families suffered no loss at all. Altogether, forty-six families were affected by the outbreak, and of these nine families lost four persons each, and five families lost three each. Mr Garside does not say whether in fact these are the poorer families, but it certainly looks as though they may have been. One notices the same concentration of the plague upon a limited number of families in country parishes and other parts of England, even on the remotest farms. The burial register of Bridford, a remote parish on the edge of Dartmoor, swept by bracing air all the year round, shows that no fewer than seven members of the Westcott family died in 1591 between 26 August and 15 October, though they all lived in isolated farmsteads.

One sometimes notices in the burial registers that when a parish suffered in one epidemic it seemed to escape the full impact of the next, which might be decimating a neighbouring parish, as though some immunity had been conferred on its population. This, too, is a subject which the local historian ought to explore. Again, since the impact of the plague on towns was so devastating, not only in the number of deaths but also in the total disruption of normal trading life, many towns instituted strict quarantine regulations with the object of keeping out of their streets anyone coming from an infected area. We do not know how effective these regulations may have been, but the local historian could ascertain this within a given county by examining the burial registers of towns and country parishes over a wide area. Occasionally, and especially from the eighteenth century onwards, parsons note in the burial register all deaths due to some exceptional epidemic, though mostly we are left to discover the nature of the visitation for ourselves.

For the nineteenth century local newspapers form a valuable source of information; and there are also certain important Parliamentary Papers, above all for the larger towns. Most notable are the report of the Select Committee on the Health of Towns with Minutes of Evidence (1840), the Report of the Poor Law Commissioners on the Sanitary Condition of the Labouring Population (1842), and the report of the Royal Commission on the State of Large Towns and Populous Districts with Minutes of Evidence and Appendices (1844–45). These, and other Parliamentary Papers bearing on the subject of public health, will be found listed in the *Select List of British Parliamentary Papers, 1833 to 1899*, edited by Professor and Mrs Ford, pp. 81–86. In the larger towns, too, there should be the annual reports of the Medical Officer of Health.

Just as the study of the financial history of a town has been recommended as a distinct branch of historical enquiry for a retired accountant, or someone else with a special interest in finance, so the study of the subject of public health, epidemics and diseases, may be commended to any historically-minded medical man. He would be in a far better position to tackle a subject of this kind than the layman, since his special knowledge would enable him to make sense of the data in a way not possible to others. Here again is a field of enquiry in which the local historian can make an important contribution to the history of England as a whole. Any new history of epidemics will necessarily have to be based upon a number of detailed regional studies. In this field these are much more likely to be carried out effectively by the amateur historian than by the professional.

11 THE HOMES OF FAMILY NAMES

MOBILITY OF POPULATION

One of the most deeply rooted and false ideas about English social history is that the majority of our population were rooted to the soil in one place until quite recent times. Those who have attempted to study the genealogy of a particular family, especially of the farming or labouring class, will know how false this notion is. It is rare to get a run of a hundred years in one parish for one family. There is good reason to believe that this mobility of both town and rural populations was marked as far back as the twelfth century. The numerous towns which grew up in that period must have recruited their early population largely from the surrounding countryside.

In the countryside itself there was a great deal of movement from parish to parish. In Leicestershire, for example, only one family in every ten listed in the poll tax assessments of 1377 remained in the same village by the early sixteenth century. We find only a hard core of persistent families who go on for century after century, usually those with a little land of their own which they cling to. Peyton found that the population of Nottinghamshire was highly mobile between 1568 and 1641, but though this was almost certainly true, he used the wrong sources to demonstrate it. He used the names listed in lay subsidies in that period, but as these subsidies are known to have been highly selective, and to have covered only a small proportion of the population, it is impossible to draw from them firm conclusions about the disappearance rate of families.

One can safely do this only by laboriously making a list of all the family names in the parish register over a given short period, and comparing it with another list for a similar period a century later. Even so, we must take account of names appearing in every other class of local record; for example, names of witnesses to all the wills in the chosen periods, names appearing in conveyances, leases, manorial records (court rolls and account rolls), and later on names appearing in nonconformist records. If we do this we discover how very mobile even the rural population was at all times. In Devon, for instance, even in the rural parishes, three families out of five disappear from their original villages within a hundred years. Most of these families seldom go very far. We find that we pick them up again within a radius of five to ten miles of the place from which they started. Many, however, moved into the towns during the sixteenth, seventeenth, and eighteenth centuries, especially the clothing towns, the seaports, and later on the growing industrial towns of the Midlands and the North. There are several fascinating aspects of mobility which local historians can pursue, either singly or as a small group. One of the most valuable is the detailed study of the distribution of family names in a given area. The remarks I have made above merely scratch the surface. Now let us plunge beneath it.

Most people are aware that there are surnames which seem peculiar to a single county, or perhaps to a neighbouring group of two or three counties. Thus the surnames of Yorkshire and Lancashire are quite distinctive, and also widely different from those, say, of Cornwall and Devon. The distribution of family names is, however, a much more complicated subject than this, and covers such an immense field that it is admirably suited for group study by local historians. The purpose of this chapter is chiefly to discuss the sources that are available, and also the numerous pitfalls—some of them by no means obvious.

Dr H. B. Guppy published as long ago as 1890 his book on *The Homes of Family Names* on a county-by-county basis. This was a pioneer work and for nearly eighty years it remained the only book in the field. It was a massive undertaking and like all pioneer work it has serious faults, as we discover in seeking to extend the range of knowledge. Dr P. H. Reaney's *Origins of British Surnames* (Routledge, 1967), is the best introduction so far available for surname studies. I should also mention three other books in a related field, that of the meanings of family names. These are C. W. Bardsley, *Dictionary of English and Welsh Surnames* (1901) and the same author's *English Surnames* (1873; reprinted David & Charles, 1969); C. L'Estrange Ewen, *A History of Surnames*

11.1 Blingsby and Blanksby

On the northern edge of the park that surrounds the Elizabethan Hardwick Hall is the minor place-name Blingsby Gate. Local farmers know the fields as the Blingsbys, and this is the name by which they were known in Bess of Hardwick's time. A map drawn by William Senior in 1610 marks 'Blingsbie' as the name of a field covering 38 acres 1 rood 20 perches. Blingsby is a small deserted medieval village, and the usual mounds and hollows that identify such sites can be seen in the field. This was Blanghesbi in Domesday Book, a Viking settlement named after a certain Blaeingr. The place-name has changed a little over the years, but the original pronunciation is preserved in the local surname, Blanksby, a name that is not often found more than twenty miles from the original village site.

(Kegan Paul, 1931); and P. H. Reaney, *Dictionary of British Surnames* (Routledge, 1958). All give a number of dated references (usually early) to a vast number of family names and are useful in this respect; but what I am concerned with here is the *distribution* of family names and not their meanings, which calls for a knowledge of linguistics. For this particular study we must collect *all* references to given surnames and not merely a rather haphazard selection designed for another purpose.

Guppy believed that despite the rapid extension of communications during his lifetime, certain classes of people remained pretty well fixed in or very near their ancient place of origin. But he chose his social class too carefully and narrowly: he regarded 'the Old English Yeomen' as the most stable section of the community, the least affected by foreign immigrants, the most bound to a locality through their land. He therefore limited his counting to the farmer class in nineteenth-century directories, and he produced some extremely interesting and at times valuable results.

Even the surnames of Smith and Jones are far from evenly spread. At the time Guppy was writing there were fifteen times as many Smiths in Worcestershire as in Somerset, taking the highest and lowest figures under this name.* Cornwall had only 32 Smiths per 10,000 of population, as compared with, say, 270 in Gloucestershire. The mighty tribe of Joneses shows an even wider spread, with Cornwall showing the lowest proportion (14 in 10,000) and Shropshire as high as 500. The name is basically of Welsh origin, so the highest density of Joneses is to be found along the Welsh border counties and of course in Wales itself. The uneven distribution of Smiths requires a more sophisticated historical explanation. Thus what might seem the simplest example of family distribution turns out to be more complicated than one would have thought.

Guppy's method and his sources were too selective. To count only the farming class and no other; to use only nineteenth-century directories and no other source: this is to invite results that are either rather obvious at times and at other times misleading. When we break this subject down into a single county, a single parish, or a single family, using the widest range of sources that are available in central and local records, we begin to see that the truth is infinitely more complicated than Guppy supposed, and that to examine the problem at only one period of time merely gives us a very limited and simplified picture. I want, then, to illustrate methods, sources,

---

* Guppy expressed his figures in terms of so many per 10,000, so eliminating differences of size and total population between different counties.

and pitfalls by selecting particular counties, particular parishes, and particular families, and looking at them in greater detail than Guppy could hope to do when attempting to cover the whole country. Even so, much of what I shall set down will be inconclusive, and doubtless will not uncover every pitfall. This is immaterial, for my main object is to stimulate further research in as many parts of England as possible into an almost inexhaustible field.

DEVON FAMILY NAMES

A preliminary enquiry into the distribution of Devon family names today, using only one source, produced some useful quick results, but they call for much further work. The easiest source to use is the telephone directory, in which names are listed alphabetically. It represents a sample of about one in three of the population. This is a large sample though it might well be objected that it does not represent a fair cross-section of the community. Telephone users are broadly what we may call the middle class, a far wider sample than Guppy's farmers. Though some names may escape notice altogether the objection that a whole social class is missed out is partly met by the fact that every family, in the course of several generations, has produced both 'successful' branches, and 'unsuccessful' branches who do not figure in the telephone directory. I am using these words merely as a convenient shorthand, and not implying that possessing a telephone is a criterion of status or 'success', whatever that may mean.

The point I am making is that the telephone directory probably does not miss as many different surnames as might be supposed. It is a far wider source than Guppy's directories, as we shall see a little later, and therefore more valuable as an index of present distribution; yet it clearly has its defects. The electoral register for every town and parish would be an even better sample of the whole population. It is slower for counting purposes, but a group project ought to use this source rather than the telephone book. The latter is valuable, however, as a starter, having taken care, if the geographical county is the field of study, that the full range of directories is used. Telephone directories do not necessarily coincide with county boundaries.

If we take a number of distinctive family names and trace their whereabouts today from the telephone directory we discover that though Guppy was incorrect in believing that the farming class as a whole remained relatively fixed to their original localities, many families do in fact reveal that they have moved only within a small radius over the centuries. We must, of course, exclude those members who have moved to London or to what used to be called the Empire, as all families can show examples of this movement during the nineteenth century. Ignoring this general trend, we find that often the range of movement is remarkably small.

Chugg is a peculiarly Devon family name. It is found in North Devon in a tax assessment of 1332; and today no fewer than thirty-three of the thirty-six Chuggs in the telephone directory are to be found in the same corner of Devon, heavily concentrated in one small area round Barnstaple and Braunton. We do not know the meaning of this name, but it occurs in the farm-name Chuggaton and so is of extreme antiquity.

Pugsley is another distinctive Devon family name, originating in one farm of that name in a North Devon parish. Today twenty-seven out of forty-three Pugsleys in the telephone book remain in North Devon. Moreover, the fact that there is only one farm of this name indicates that all the Pugsleys in Devon, or anywhere else, originated in a common ancestor some six or seven centuries ago. This has been found to be true in other parts of England. Even if a name is now widespread nationally, it frequently goes back to a single origin in a particular region. There must be many exceptions to this statement, and it remains for intensive local research to show how generally true it is. One could take a dozen Devon family names of this distinctive type and produce roughly the same results, but a final example must suffice: the surname Churchward occurs at Paignton as far back as the 1332 subsidy. Of the sixteen Churchwards in the telephone book today, no fewer than thirteen are still in that district.

A PARISH CASE STUDY: NEWTON ST CYRES (DEVON)

So far I have used a single source for surnames and arrived at what are apparently some simple results. If we take a single parish, in this case Newton St Cyres about four miles from Exeter but still truly rural, we begin to run into some unexpected difficulties and it is only fair to reveal these to the student of the subject. In the 1851 census the parish had a total of 1,139 inhabitants. The first astonishing fact is that an examination of the original enumerators' schedules in the Public Record Office shows that this one parish throws up no fewer than 242 different surnames. Of these, 75 occur only once, half of them the names of servants living in with the more well-to-do families. Twelve names occur 15 times or more, the maximum (Crump) being 38 times.

Pursuing this parochial enquiry in *White's Directory* for Devon in 1850, an almost contemporary source, we make the painful discovery that White includes only 27 of the different names in Newton St Cyres, i.e. only 11 per cent. Even if we exclude all the single-occurrence names, which is going to an extreme, we are left with the fact that the directory lists only one surname in every six. It must therefore be dismissed as a useful source, however promising it may have seemed at first sight. No doubt a sample in other counties would show a similar result. The Devon directory is so unrepresentative in this parish that of the twelve most common names in 1851, seven are not mentioned at all.

As to mobility, a comparison of the different family names between 1851 and 1970 (electoral register) shows that only 67 of the original 242 survive after 120 years. If we exclude the single-occurrence names, the proportion is 67 survivors out of 167. A hundred names have disappeared in four generations, roughly 60 per cent. It might be said that the proximity of a large town like Exeter could unduly influence the results in an age of better communications, but earlier centuries show just as great a mobility.

The Protestation Returns of 1642 have already been referred to (see pp. 203–5). These included the names of all males aged eighteen years and over. The omission of children probably does not matter, so far as surnames are concerned; but the list will obviously omit elderly widows and single women and so will not be a complete coverage of surnames, though possibly as full as an electoral register today. A count of the number of different names for Newton St Cyres in 1642 gives 101 names. But if we turn to the parish registers (which survive from 1554) and count all the different names (baptisms and burials only, since marriages could bring in 'outside' names) between 1630 and 1650 we get 133 different names in the baptismal register, and 55 others among the burials, a total of 188 names. This is nearly twice the number recorded at a single moment for the Protestation Return, and illustrates yet another difficulty when we confine ourselves to a single source. It also illustrates once again the continual mobility even of a rural population. At a given moment of time one is likely to obtain an incomplete picture of the names 'belonging' to one parish. A decade or two in the parish register is probably a better choice. This tentative study of one parish would seem to suggest that single parishes are not a good area of study. Names disappear more or less steadily at all periods, though most surnames do not stray far away. They remain concentrated within a relatively small territory, or so it seems in a great number of cases. But what is the ideal area of study? That is something the student or group must decide on the basis of trial and error.

FAMILY CASE STUDIES: 1. FINCHAM

The geographical county is an enormous but not impossible unit for the study of this subject, but is itself a somewhat arbitrary unit as family-names stray over county boundaries; and the parish is too small a unit for the best results though it may still be worth close attention. What happens if we take a distinctive surname and follow its distribution over a period of time? For this purpose I choose first

11.2 Distribution of Fincham surname in Norfolk and Suffolk, 1524 (tax lists)

late nineteenth century. He does not mention it under Norfolk, though the name clearly derives from the village of Fincham in west Norfolk and nowhere else. Though the Finchams held land in Fincham from before 1100, it does not follow that all who bear that name today can point to this particular ancestry. Any man who moved from Fincham to another town or village would be likely to derive a new surname from his old abode, though often, too, he might be known by the name of his trade. But locative surnames form a considerable proportion of all names* and it does not follow that all Finchams derive from a single ancestor. It *may* be so, and can sometimes be shown to be so for a few families, but it is an assumption that needs proof. Fincham is a very distinctive name and we might therefore think we can follow it around without much difficulty and with a good deal of certainty about our results. Yet this is not so. Even a preliminary study like this soon runs into what appear to be inexplicable difficulties.

Mr McKinley's massive study of Norfolk family names was limited to a short period in the 1520s, which was chosen for two principal reasons: first, that family names had become relatively fixed by that date and changes due to change of location or trade, for example, had practically ceased; and secondly, that the taxation and other records for the period 1522–25 were exceptionally full. His index for this short period runs to tens of thousands of names, yet there are only two Finchams among them, one of them in the ancestral village still. The neighbouring county of Suffolk, for which the lay subsidy returns of 1524–25 have been printed, show that there were four John Finchams, in four separate parishes, at that date—Thelnetham, Cowling, Saxham Magna, and Wickham. It might seem reasonable to deduce from these facts that the Finchams had mostly migrated from Norfolk to Suffolk by the early sixteenth century. Yet if we look in the modern telephone directories we find Finchams in eight places in Suffolk and in no fewer than thirteen different places in Norfolk. Anything could have happened in the 450 years between 1520 and 1970, but it is hard to imagine that all but two Finchams had in fact abandoned Norfolk by the early sixteenth century. It is clear that the distribution of the Finchams in Norfolk needs much further research, and a good intermediate point would

---

* By far the best discussion of this point, and of other factors affecting the development of surnames, is R. A. McKinley's *Norfolk Surnames in the Sixteenth Century* (Leicester University Press, 1969). This intensive study of one county over a very limited period should be read carefully as an example of the methods, sources, and pitfalls involved in county studies of this kind.

11.3 Distribution of Fincham surname in Suffolk, 1674 (Hearth tax)

the name Fincham, which Guppy noted as peculiar to Suffolk in the
be the hearth tax assessments of the period 1662–74. The Suffolk
hearth tax assessment for 1674, which fortunately has been printed,
shows that the four parishes inhabited by Finchams in the 1520s
had become eleven parishes 150 years later. Maps (pp. 218–21)
show this spread of the name in 1524, 1674, and 1970. It should be
said, too, that the subsidies of 1524 and 1525, comprehensive though
they were, missed a considerable number of the poorer people.
Mr McKinley collected a considerable number of names from the
so-called Military Survey of 1522 (which survives for only a few
counties) which do not appear in the tax assessments two and three
years later. The moral of all this is that one must gather surnames
from every conceivable source, and all feasible periods, before
making generalisations about the distribution of even apparently
straightforward family names.

11.4 Distribution of Fincham surname in Suffolk, 1970 (telephone directories)

FAMILY CASE STUDIES: 2. THIRSK

Once again, let us take a distinctive family name derived originally from a single place, the little town of Thirsk in the North Riding of Yorkshire.* Unlike the above brief case study of the Finchams, which drew on a number of sources, this examination of the Thirsks relies upon a single source; but it has the great merit of being the most comprehensive record one could hope to find. The state registration of births, marriages, and deaths began in 1837, and the records are lodged in the form of great indexes in St. Catherine's House. Marriages may be ignored for this purpose, as a certain proportion of people marry away from 'home' so that any count

---

* I owe my information about the distribution of the Thirsk family in the nineteenth and twentieth centuries to Mr J. W. Thirsk, to whom I am grateful for permission to publish his interesting results in summary form.

could be misleading. The same observation can, of course, apply to births and deaths, but to a very much smaller degree.

The Thirsks began moving from the North Riding into the East Riding at some unknown date, though some remained. A complete count of all Thirsk deaths from 1837 to 1947 shows that of 492 deaths, no fewer than 185 took place in Hull and Sculcoates (now part of Hull), and 128 in other places in the East Riding, including York. The West and North Ridings contributed only 62 deaths; Lancashire and Cheshire 71; and the remainder of England only 46. Thus the Thirsks remained remarkably concentrated over a period of 110 years, four generations which one commonly associates with increasing mobility. About 63 per cent lived and died in the East Riding, most of them in a much smaller area than this.

Turning to the registration of births, and taking only the period 1837–87, there were 361 Thirsk births of which 290—exactly 80 per cent—were in the East Riding. After 1887 there is much more dispersal, so that the period 1837–1947, which was used for deaths, is probably too long a time to give us a completely accurate picture. Ideally it should be broken down into at least two half-centuries to take account of growing mobility from the 1880s onwards.*

This complete search of the St. Catherine's House indexes for births and deaths from 1837 onwards is obviously a perfect coverage for the distribution of family names in England and Wales; but it can only be used for families with a rather uncommon surname as it is very time-consuming. Nor could it be used for anything larger than a particular name. Obviously, there are a great many more records which could be used to trace the distribution of Thirsks in the sixteenth to eighteenth centuries; but the purpose of this particular case-study has been to show how one class of record can be used for a limited class of names.

FAMILY CASE STUDIES: 3. MAUNDER

Maunder is a peculiarly Devon name, and Guppy lists it as such. It seems to be the same as Mander in other parts of the country. According to Bardsley's *Dictionary*, it is derived from the Middle English word, *maund*, a hand-basket, hence it means 'basket-maker'. The 1332 tax assessment for Devon, published by the

---

* Since this was written a breakdown of the deaths for the period 1837–87 shows 81 per cent in the East Riding, and again a much greater dispersal after 1887.

Devon and Cornwall Record Society, contains about 10,600 names but not a single Maunder. But this proves little in view of the deficiencies of this record, which are discussed later. We are therefore driven to locate the family in the sixteenth century, from parish registers, wills, and church rates. Even this coverage is not complete but is probably reasonably so. Guppy contents himself with one casual reference as late as 1684; but the Maunders can be found in ten parishes, in mid-Devon for the most part, during the sixteenth century. The earliest reference is at Cruwys Morchard, west of Tiverton, going back to a manor court roll for 1368. *Kelly's Directory of Devonshire* (1939: the last published for the county) shows them still in the parish at that date, and the electoral register for 1970 shows one Maunder household still there after six hundred years.

Between 1368 and the sixteenth century there is a great gap in the kind of records that serve our purpose. Then we come to the subsidy of 1524 and the early parish registers. Church rates and wills provide a couple of early references where the registers are incomplete. Thus the surviving registers of Morchard Bishop do not begin until 1660, but a solitary church rate for 1601 shows William Maunder paying 14d towards the maintenance of the church, and we can assume they were there at least in the closing years of the sixteenth century. Again, though the earliest Maunder will in the parish of Halberton is dated 1609, John Maunder refers to 'the monument or tomb of John Maunder my father, standing at the south side of the church in the churchyard'. Once again we can assume they were here by the late sixteenth century.

Kelly's *Directory of Devonshire* for 1939 shows Maunders farming in nineteen parishes, well scattered over the county in contrast to the sixteenth-century locations. Of the ten parishes where they lived before 1600, they farm in four to this day. The electoral registers would undoubtedly show an even wider spread and would have to be searched before one could produce a distribution map of the name today.

SOME GENERAL CONCLUSIONS

In recent years a completely new field of English history has been opened up by Mr Richard McKinley and Dr George Redmonds, who have made very detailed studies of the distribution of family names in Lancashire, Norfolk, Oxfordshire and the West Riding of Yorkshire. Financed by the Marc Fitch fund and based at the

Department of English Local History at the University of Leicester, the project is designed to eventually cover every English county. The earliest volumes have already offered useful pointers to local historians elsewhere in the country.*

In the West Riding, Dr Redmonds found a very high proportion of locative surnames (i.e. names drawn from places)—about 50 per cent, as against a national average of about 16 or 17 per cent. To speak of a 'national average' may well be a largely meaningless term, for we shall probably find as more of these detailed studies are made that regional differences will appear in many parts of England. The fact that locative surnames form a high proportion of the whole in the West Riding may be due to the dispersed nature of early settlement, giving the landscape a multitude of hamlets and separate farms, each with its own name. Similarly I would expect my own county of Devon, with its very dispersed settlement, to show a high proportion of locative surnames based on single farmsteads. That this is so in the West Riding is borne out by the fact that most locative surnames derive from small settlements in the Dales and the surrounding hills. Few come from the low-lying eastern part of the Riding, where the village is the more characteristic form of settlement.

One of Dr Redmonds's more interesting discoveries is that most locative surnames seem to have originated with a single family only, though this is rather difficult to prove conclusively. I think again the same may be true in Devon, where a surname such as Pugsley can only come from one farm of that name in the remote parish of Warkleigh. In Devon, again, the Reddaways, who were at the farm called Reddaway in 1242 and are still there, must have started here as a single family. Today, besides the remarkable survival of the aboriginal family (I use the word in its proper sense) most of the Reddaways still farm in the countryside round about, though they have also given rise to distinguished academic figures in both Cambridge and London universities.

Many locative surnames in the West Riding show a characteristic pattern of movement and ramification, beginning with one or two families in the fourteenth century, not spreading more than a few miles from their points of origin until the sixteenth century, then gradually spreading along their own dales and rarely from one dale to another. In the eighteenth century they spread into the new

* I am indebted to Dr Redmonds and Mr McKinley for permission to use their major conclusions here.

woollen towns; and in the nineteenth we see a great growth in numbers rather than a wider spread.

If one examines the telephone directories, it appears that most of the holders of West Riding locative surnames are still living in West Yorkshire. All the evidence seems to show that the population of West Yorkshire is very largely home-grown, even to the present day, with only moderate influxes from Lancashire and north-east England, and only moderate outward flows. This conclusion may not surprise staunch Yorkshiremen, but it is as well to have it proved statistically and not emotionally. Other counties may well show a different pattern over the past hundred years for historical reasons. When farming was depressed in West Yorkshire, or men had to find other work for various reasons, they found ample opportunities for employment in their own industrial towns and villages; but when the great farming depression hit Devon, or the labourers at last revolted against their intolerable wages and housing conditions, they had to leave their native county altogether. Many became policemen in the West Riding and in London.

Similarly, in Cornwall the massive slump in tin and copper mining led to a great exodus in the nineteenth century, not so much to other parts of England as to mining regions all over the world. The movements of population, and hence of family names, would therefore show a different pattern from that of West Yorkshire; yet even here we must be careful not to exaggerate, for both Cornwall and Devon retain a high proportion of characteristic surnames. Even to this day it is said to be difficult to get a true Cornish man or woman to leave Cornwall, even to come into Devon which is regarded as a foreign country.

Mr McKinley's conclusions about Norfolk family names are rather more difficult to summarise briefly, partly because his was a more limited study in time. His monograph should be read carefully by anyone undertaking a similarly detailed survey, not least his special study of one manor (Forncett) for which ample materials were available. Readers of this chapter will be accustomed by now to the surprises of the subject. In this one Norfolk manor, no fewer than 719 different surnames turn up between 1332 and 1565, of which as many as 439 occur only once. Even allowing for all possible qualifications to these numbers, such as the fact that some surnames may not have become stable hereditary names, the number of different surnames is surprisingly large, and even where they occur more than once they are found only for a short period. The land-market was evidently very active in the fifteenth and sixteenth

centuries, and the tenants of the manor were changing frequently. We tend to seize upon obvious examples of farming families that stayed in the same manor or village for generations or centuries, but these are the minority. Nor were the long-stayers at Forncett entirely the free population, what Guppy would have called 'the Old English yeomen'. If we take the 29 families who were there before 1400 and still there in the early sixteenth century, 20 were families of freemen and 9 were families of serfs. After 1400 there were only 19 unfree families in the manor, so that practically a half of them persisted for several more generations. The unfree families were a relatively stable element in the manorial population, like many of those with substantial land-holdings. Such detailed studies, besides being of great value to genealogists, are altering drastically our traditional picture of the medieval village.

The total number of different surnames in this country is almost impossible to calculate, even to estimate. For Norfolk alone, Mr McKinley carefully refrained from printing any total because of the obvious difficulty of defining what a separate surname is. Not only is there the question of variations in spelling the same name, but also the possibility that names with the same or similar spellings may have different origins. Subject to these reservations, the number of distinct surnames in Norfolk in Henry VIII's time could have been as high as about 12,400, though if all variant spellings were lumped together the number would be about 5,500. Even such approximate figures as these must be treated with caution, but they serve to show the immense scope of the study of the distribution of family names in this country.

Apart from Mr McKinley's special conclusions about Norfolk surnames in the 1520s, which are best read in his own monograph, he has arrived tentatively at some general conclusions which he allows me to quote. Again, we must regard these remarks as a purely general guide, subject to variations in different regions as the work goes forward. He writes:

11.5 Carnpessack, Cornwall

Built of cob and stone walls, 3 feet thick, this L-shaped farmstead occupies a site that was fortified in prehistoric times. The name was recorded as Karpesek in 1230, *car* or *ker* meaning a fort, and *pesek* meaning broken down. No trace of the fort remains, but Iron Age and Romano-British potsherds have been found nearby. The farm is a small dairy-holding of 56 acres, divided into seventeen fields.

Its owner in Henry VIII's reign was known as Carpyssack, so a Cornish surname (with a variety of spellings) was derived from the old farm name.

I am more and more inclined to think that many surnames go back to a single origin. Even if nationally a name is fairly widespread, it often has a single origin in each region, and this is perhaps especially true with occupational surnames. In the twelfth and thirteenth centuries there is a distinct class structure in surnames with a majority of landed families having locative surnames, occupational surnames being largely confined to artisans and traders (not many derived from agricultural pursuits), and many serfs having nicknames, often of a bizarre nature. By about 1500 this structure has vanished. All the evidence suggests a considerable mobility of the rural population from the thirteenth century onwards, evidence about earlier periods being lacking. Occupational surnames, even those derived from specialized crafts, are found just as frequently in rural areas as towns.

SOME SOURCES AND THEIR LIMITATIONS

Workers in this field of family names too often assume that an apparently 'full' tax assessment gives one a pretty complete coverage of the population at a particular date. Some tax assessments are obviously much fuller than others, and the experienced searcher learns which to use and which to ignore. But the fullest assessment may, on checking against some other records, turn out to cover only a minority of the population, or if not an absolute minority then to omit a painfully large section of the population at that date. For example, the earliest tax assessments in most parts of England are those for 1327 and 1332 (earlier assessments occasionally occur in certain areas, but the local historian will know of these in his own locality). Now the 1327 return for Devon contains about 11,390 names; that for 1332 some 10,600. The return for 1332 was chosen for publication* as being better preserved than the former, but the observations I am about to make are not affected to any noticeable degree by the slight difference in total numbers. Under the city of Exeter the 1332 return lists only 119 names, plus another 24 in two suburban areas—a total of 143 names. Yet a record in the city archives, which is a local assessment for the repair of the city gates, gives a list of 420 names in 1377. This was after several severe outbreaks of plague since 1348. The population in 1332 must have been appreciably higher than 420 households: in other words, the tax assessment covers only a small minority of the householders of the city, possibly as few as a third or a quarter.

At Leicester the 1327 subsidy lists 105 taxpayers, but local

* *Devon and Cornwall Record Society, New Series*, vol. xiv (1969).

tallage rolls list between 300 and 400 payers in the same period. Here again the national tax covers only a third or less of the population. Indeed, when one compares the 1332 subsidy list for Leicester and an almost contemporary tallage roll (1336) the disparity is even more alarming, both for the genealogist and the local historian. The number paying the subsidy in 1332 drops to 73, whereas the local tallage roped in no fewer than 445 names.

One can make similar checks for parts of rural Devon. Without going into great detail, a comparison of a 1292 extent (or survey) for Berry Pomeroy and the tax list of 1332 shows that the latter ropes in only one in every four or five householders. Not all parishes show such depressing results as this, but it is as well to know that everywhere even the fullest tax list is selective, sometimes highly so. This does not mean that we need give up these records in despair, only that they need using with great caution and, if possible, checking against other records that happen to survive. Thus in his close study of the Norfolk manor of Forncett, Mr McKinley was helped by a long series of manor court rolls and court books beginning in 1332, by manorial accounts, by a fine manorial survey of 1565, and by Ministers' Accounts in the Public Record Office.

The major population sources for the period 1524 to 1801 have been discussed in the preceding chapter. The same sources, except the census of 1801 (for which the original enumerators' schedules no longer survive),* can be used for the study of surname distribution; and to these we can add the original schedules for 1841 to 1881 which list all names. These schedules give as near a complete coverage as one could ever hope to get. The only difficulty is their sheer bulk if one is covering a large area like a county, and the expensive consideration that they are housed in London. In recent years, however, many record offices and libraries have obtained microfilms of census schedules for their county. The 1851 census was the first to require information about the exact birthplace of all persons, and hence is the starting-point for much genealogical research apart from all else.

The limited value of the nineteenth-century directories has already been touched upon. It is possible that later directories are somewhat wider in their coverage, but in my opinion they remain of dubious value for the study of surname distribution, though the later Kelly's county directories may give a first approximation along

---

* An odd return may survive here and there amid parish records. One such (1801) has been found in an Exeter parish and is now in the city record office.

the lines followed by Guppy, but with a wider range of social classes. This, however, is not good enough after eighty years. The current telephone directories, for all their deficiencies as a source, are infinitely better as a sample and are easy to use for counting. Even better are the electoral registers which have a coverage of at least ninety per cent, as against the one in two or three of the telephone directories.

It should be clear by now that the study of the 'Homes of Family Names' and their distribution and spread since the time of Henry VIII offers an immense field of study. I limit the extent of time advisedly, partly because medieval sources are not easy to use, and with few exceptions are far from even reasonable in their coverage; and also because a great number of surnames had not yet become fixed and hereditary. By the time of Henry VIII, however, we have two major sources to work upon—the comprehensive taxation records of the 1520s and the beginnings of parish registers of baptisms, marriages, and burials in 1538. Even these records have their shortcomings, but the perfect record does not exist.

The pioneer work of Guppy took a big step forward when in 1965 the Marc Fitch Fund set up at the University of Leicester a research fellow in the Department of English Local History to work exclusively upon the origins and distribution of British surnames. It was a munificent gesture, and marked the academic recognition of a new and important branch of English history of the greatest value not only to the genealogist but also to the social and economic historian.

Perhaps I might quote a little of what I said in introducing Mr McKinley's monograph on Norfolk names, the first fruit of the Fitch benefaction:

> We have seen since the early 1920s the study of English place-names grow into an impressive row of scholarly volumes indispensable to workers in a number of other historical fields. I am certain that the study of British surnames will grow in the same way within the next twenty or thirty years. . . . From regional studies of this kind historians will eventually learn a great deal about the migration of ordinary families at all periods from the thirteenth century onwards, what form these movements took, and how far people went in, say, the course of a century. Many other questions of general historical interest suggest themselves. We shall eventually see more studies of a socio-genealogical kind of ordinary families. That is, not just the bare bones of a family genealogy, but what I might call the social history of such a family, relating it to a background of English history in general. I have done this for my own family from the fourteenth century to the present day. The East Anglian family of Fitch has been studied in the same

way, the results of this investigation being briefly summarised in Sir Anthony Wagner's *English Genealogy* (Oxford University Press, 1960). A corpus of such studies would be of the greatest historical interest and value.

The fact that this study of the distribution of family names has been given an academic status should not, and need not, deter the amateur from playing a full part in this kind of research. Nor, I hope, will my insistence in this chapter on the pitfalls of the subject deter anyone from entering upon it. As I have said above, the perfect record nowhere exists; we must merely make full allowances for the imperfections of which we are aware. This study seems to me to offer particular attractions to adult education classes and to members of Women's Institutes. But do not forget to provide proper distribution maps of selected names. A good map says more than pages of text at times. And even a common surname may well be worth mapping and reveal something significant in its distribution. Let me close with one striking example. Even using Guppy's simple statistical method, the surname Williams is eighteen times as common in Cornwall as in Devon. The only English county that surpasses Cornwall in its proportion of Williamses is Herefordshire (for this purpose I count Monmouthshire as Welsh). Now the distribution of Williamses in Cornwall is far from a random one, as the maps show. The first map is based upon a count of the electoral registers for 1953 (when this work was begun)* and involved no fewer than about 20,000 different surnames. It should be said that Mr Richard Blewett, who began this great work at the age of seventy-three and completed it at the age of eighty-eight (local historians never die, they only fade away), adopted a method of counting which may not appeal to all statisticians. *All* adult voters, both men and women, were counted, not simply the head of the household. So a man-and-wife Williams were counted as two, not one, on the ground that each man who gave his surname to a woman on marriage would probably have a sister who would *lose* that surname on her own marriage. I am myself not completely happy about this argument, but the difficulty must be mentioned as all who use the electoral registers must decide for themselves on their technique of counting. In any event, such an assumption does not alter the picture of distribution, merely the total numbers involved.

---

* I am greatly indebted to Mr Richard Blewett of St Day in Cornwall for placing his researches so unreservedly at my disposal.

11.6 Distribution of Williams surname in Cornwall, 1953 (electoral register) (after a drawing by Richard R. Blewett)

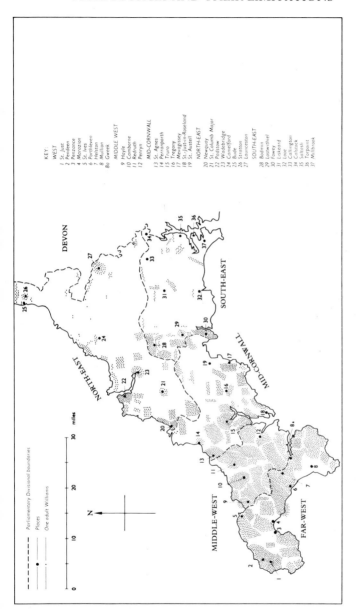

11.7 Distribution of Williams marriages in Cornwall, 1560–1812 (after a drawing by Richard R. Blewett)

Mr Blewett, having finished his counting, then transferred his results to maps. All surname groups with 180 or more examples were mapped, which produced an atlas for Cornish surnames of some 400 maps.

Taking the surname Williams, then, as our example, two important conclusions were reached. Though apparently a common enough name, the name falls most heavily in the far west of the county, and in the middle. Large parts of the county have few or none. Secondly, a count of all the Williams marriages between 1560 and 1812, from printed parish registers (here the old Phillimore series of Cornish Marriage Registers proved invaluable) shows that the surname group (it is perhaps incorrect to call them a *family*) has scarcely changed its distribution over the generations. Out of a total of 5,266 Williams marriages, no fewer than 3,153 took place in the far west and middle west of Cornwall, i.e. between Truro and Land's End. Again, the method is not a perfect one statistically as the period of counting is spread over a very long period (about 250 years). Ideally, one should make a separate count for say each century, so that minor shifts in distribution are brought out; but in this instance the pattern seems so heavily fixed that little error arises. Many other Cornish surname maps also show these peculiarities of distribution, for some of which a plausible historical explanation will be forthcoming. Every county in England will throw up such problems, and the construction of an atlas on what may be called the Blewett model for each would be a major enterprise of inestimable value.

FAMILY HISTORY

In the last few years there has been a phenomenal growth of interest in Family History, with local societies springing up all over the country. The subject was once the preserve of those who sought ancestors with manor houses and coats of arms, but its new devotees are content with what they find, knowing full well that most people must have had humble ancestors. My own family were generally nothing but farmers, but I was able to follow the family name back through the records to the early 1500s and in all probability to just before the year 1400, when William Hochekyns was born. In 1419 he and his wife Christina were living in Beaminster, and the family remained in Dorset until they moved across the county boundary

11.8 A family photograph

Family photographs rarely have names, dates or places attached to them, so identifying them is often a time-consuming but pleasurable task. Studio portraits can sometimes be dated approximately if the photographer's name can be identified in trade and commercial directories. The curtain backdrop places this photograph in the 1880s, a date which is confirmed by the style of dress.

The head of this family was Amos Garland (1839–92), a farm labourer from Thurlbear, near Taunton, who in middle age moved to the Sheffield area to find employment as a coke-drawer. His wife, Mary Knight (1838–1902), was a dressmaker. Both she and her husband signed marriage and birth certificates with a cross. Their children were Amos, junior, and Mary Ann. A great deal can be discovered about such ordinary families through census returns, parish registers and civil registration.

into Devon in 1584. Apart from the farmers in the pedigree, who remained in the border area, one generation moved into the city of Exeter, where they became bakers as a result of the deep depression in English farming in the 1820s. My father retired as a baker in 1950; the rest followed various professions. Ordinary families like my own can be traced back for several hundred years if one perseveres and has a certain amount of luck. By tracing their family tree many people have discovered the excitement of historical research and have widened their interests by finding out as much as they can about the local communities in which their ancestors lived. Family history need not be a narrow preoccupation with names and dates and relationships but can be an excellent introduction to the wider concerns of local history. One day we shall have a number of good family histories on our shelves which will make an immense contribution to our understanding of English social history.

12 SOME SPECIAL TASKS

I have already suggested to local historians that they need not always try to write a complete history of their chosen place from beginning to end. You might well decide to devote yourself to a close study of a limited period, especially perhaps the nineteenth century and early twentieth. The sources are abundant and they require no knowledge of Latin or of old handwriting. Moreover, the recent past contains so much that is preserved only in people's memories. It is in great danger of being completely forgotten unless some good local historian takes the trouble to record it.

The nineteenth and twentieth centuries are exceptionally interesting because there has been such a total transformation of life in almost every local community. They are worth studying if only for that reason. We must take care to avoid the 'antiquarian' trap—if one may call it that without disrespect to the antiquaries—of assuming that the older the events and things we are dealing with, the more interesting they necessarily are. Moreover, there are many places in England, especially in the industrial areas, which have practically no history before the nineteenth century. This applies also to certain seaside towns, such as Blackpool and Southport.

Or you may decide to devote your attention to a close study of your chosen place in another period which particularly appeals to you. Provided the period that is chosen has some coherence in itself there is no reason why such a limited study should not be both interesting to the author and valuable as a contribution to our knowledge of the local history of England.

There are, however, many other interesting possibilities open to the local historian and I propose to discuss some of these in this chapter. Not all of them will appeal to everybody. Your choice will depend much on whether you are primarily an outdoor worker in the field of local history or one who prefers to work indoors on documents. One cannot, of course, separate the two approaches as neatly as all this. Every good local historian must be a good bit of both, but your bias may be towards one or the other.

ROMAN AND SAXON FIELDWORK

I have already suggested in the first chapter on Fieldwork (chapter 8) that local students are often in the best position to add to our knowledge of Roman roads. The exact course of many of these roads is either uncertain, especially in the hillier regions of England, or still completely unknown. Prehistoric and other trackways also offer considerable possibilities, more in some parts of England than in others. At this point a warning must be issued against what O. G. S. Crawford has called 'one of the craziest books ever written about British Archaeology'. This was Watkins's *The Old Straight Track* (4th edn, 1949). The number of intelligent people (and others) who have been seduced by the arguments in this book is legion. Watkins's main thesis was that if you drew a straight line on a small-scale map it passed through a number of 'significant' objects on the ground, for example church-towers, ancient ponds, barrows, and so forth. These straight lines were supposed to represent alignments laid out by prehistoric man for his own purposes. In a country such as England, where antiquities of all kinds lie comparatively thick upon the ground, it is almost impossible to draw a straight line on the map without going through half a dozen of these antiquities. I once came across an advanced case of Watkinsmania in which the victim was drawing diamond-shaped patterns on the one-inch map of his district, each line passing through a number of what he called significant points. One can see dimly the reason for having a number of straight tracks in a piece of countryside, but why prehistoric man should have walked in parallelograms, finishing up where he started, is an unfathomable mystery. The principal argument against Watkins's thesis is, of course, that you can go on drawing straight lines until the map is covered with them. It is inconceivable that such a system of trackways was ever necessary or could ever have existed. It is better never to have read *The Old Straight Track*, but if you have read it, try to forget it.

The study of local trackways is full of pitfalls. In hilly country like Devon, with thousands of well-defined ridges in its topography, the great majority of which are followed by roads or tracks, it may be difficult to distinguish the significant trackways from the others, or to distinguish trackways of different periods. Those who wish to devote themselves to this branch of local topography should begin by reading chapters six and seven in Crawford's *Archaeology in the Field*. For those who are concentrating on filling up gaps in our knowledge of Roman roads in a given locality, reference has already been made to I. D. Margary's *Roman Ways in the Weald*.

I have already said something, too, in an earlier chapter about the working out of early estate boundaries from Anglo-Saxon charters. Some counties have a considerable number of charters which give more or less detailed boundaries, and the competent local student might very well concentrate on this aspect of local topography in his own district or even county. He or she may well find that it becomes a life work to elucidate satisfactorily the boundaries of perhaps fifty to a hundred charters in all parts of a given county; but it would constitute in the end a substantial addition to our knowledge of the topography of Anglo-Saxon England. There are many difficulties in this particular kind of work but the determined student need not be discouraged. One of the first difficulties is merely to discover what charters exist for a given county, since the texts of the charters are scattered in various books, and many are unpublished or have been published in obscure places. Professor H. P. R. Finberg performed a valuable service to local history and topography in the south-west of England in *The Early Charters of Devon and Cornwall* (University College of Leicester, 1953), in which he listed the seventy-two known charters for Devon and the twenty-nine known charters for Cornwall, giving the whereabouts of each text and bibliographical references to any discussion upon it. In the same handlist he has worked out in detail the boundaries of a Devon charter of 976, and has discussed its historical significance. Fieldworkers in this period should refer to his 'perambulation' as an example of how to do it, or alternatively to the perambulations of Saxon charters by Dr T. R. Thomson as published in the *Wiltshire Archaeological Magazine*. Dr Cyril Hart has performed a similar service for the county of Essex, listing seventy charters for the Anglo-Saxon period, and some fifty for the early Norman period.[*]
One would like to see detailed lists made in this fashion for every

---

[*] Professor Finberg and Dr Hart have added greatly to these earlier collections of charters since this was first written.

county which possesses such charters. Some counties, however, offer little or no scope in this branch of fieldwork. Thus Leicestershire has not a single charter giving estate boundaries, and Rutland possesses only one.

CHURCH SITES

I should very much like to see some good local historian make a study of all the sites of the ancient churches of his or her home county, or of a particular region. By 'ancient' I mean churches of medieval or earlier origin, as modern church sites rarely have any particular interest in themselves. What determined the exact site of these ancient churches? All sorts of theories are advanced but no one has studied this question at all fully. Most people know that in a great number of places it was the lord of the manor, or of the preceding Anglo-Saxon estate, who built the first church: and it is assumed that he built it close to his own house. There were indeed a great number of such 'private churches', but in the great majority of places much more obscure factors are involved. Even in a village, the reason for the particular site of the church may not be at all obvious. Or rather, there may be something peculiar about it: it may stand on a marked eminence dominating the whole of the village square as at Ugborough in South Devon. It may stand

12.1 St Martin's Church, Canterbury (view from the chancel into the nave)

When St Augustine arrived in Kent in 597 the Christian religion was already known at the royal court, for Ethelbert's wife was Bertha, a Frankish princess who had been allowed to practise her faith and have her own bishop, Liudhard. According to Bede, the queen worshipped on the east side of the city of Canterbury in 'an old church, built in honour of Saint Martin during the Roman occupation of Britain'. Here, Augustine's missionaries 'assembled to sing the psalms, to pray, to say Mass, to preach, and to baptize, until the king's own conversion to the Faith gave them greater freedom to preach and to build and restore churches everywhere'.

Remarkably, some of the ancient fabric of this church still stands at the western end of the present chancel. In the photograph the exposed band of brick walling under the windows on the left survives from the church that Bertha and Augustine knew. It is built in regular courses of Roman tiles, and is probably of sub-Roman date. The square-headed opening, now blocked, near the chancel arch led originally to a vanished porticus, or side chamber. The blocked arched doorway to the left is of slightly later date, probably of the early seventh century when the nave seems to have been built. The characteristic Anglo-Saxon rubble masonry of the latter, seen on the west wall, contrasts with the very different building technique of the earlier structure.

Here then is one of the most historic church sites in the land. It occupies a slight rise, alongside a Roman road, within the limits of one of the Roman extramural cemeteries. A famous medallion of Liudhard has been unearthed in the churchyard, amongst a deposit of Anglo-Saxon and Frankish gold.

upon a large circular mound as at Moreton (Dorset) or Taplow (Bucks.). It may stand at one end of the village in what one would think an inconvenient position, or right away from the village or town altogether. There must be an explanation for all these varia-tions. Where the church stands well away from the village or town it can often be shown that the settlement originally lay around or near the church. The village has moved away at some later date, usually down the hillside to a main road which became im-portant in the twelfth or thirteenth century, and attracted people to it. There are several examples of this kind of movement in various parts of England, leaving the parish church high and dry in the fields.

Where there is no village, but only a parish of scattered hamlets and farmsteads, what decided exactly where the parish church should be built? Was it a cross-roads convenient for people in most parts of the parish? Was it a holy well or spring? Or some pre-Christian site of religious significance? At Knowlton (Dorset) the ruined church, parts of which date from the twelfth century, stands in the middle of a circular earthwork. There is no village anywhere near: the church stands alone. There is in fact a small group of these circular earthworks in the vicinity, which have been shown to date from the Bronze Age and to have been used for religious cere-monies in the succeeding Iron Age. Possibly the earthwork in which the church now stands continued to be used for religious purposes right down into Christian times. It seems clear that the first Chris-tian church was deliberately built inside this earthwork because of its long association with earlier religions, the tradition of which was still clear in Christian times.

At Oldbury-on-Severn (Glos) the church similarly lies inside a circular earthwork which commands a magnificent view of the Severn estuary, and the village lies at the foot of the hill. Presumably

12.2 St Peter's Church, Conisbrough, Yorkshire

Conisbrough's place-name means 'the king's stronghold', for it was an important Northumbrian military centre on the banks of the River Don. Domesday Book reveals that it was still the headquarters of a major lordship in the late eleventh century, and a hundred years later an impressive castle was built here with a cylindrical keep. The church originally served the whole lordship and early in the twelfth century still had several scattered daughter churches in South Yorkshire. Late-medieval rebuilding has disguised the Anglo-Saxon design from outside, but the interior may be as early as the eighth century. Its proportions, blocked openings and massive side-alternate quoins are strongly reminiscent of such notable examples as Ledsham and Monkwearmouth further north. The architectural evidence supports inferences from documentary sources that St Peter's was the minster church for most of that part of Yorkshire which lay south of the Don.

the earthwork at Oldbury once had the same significance as that at Knowlton. At West Wycombe (Bucks) a church dedicated to St Lawrence stands inside a ringwork crowning a hill, a place of great strategic importance commanding three converging valleys. The entire inner area of the earthwork is occupied by the church and churchyard. At Cholesbury (Bucks) there is also a church dedicated to St Lawrence inside a roughly oval earthwork. Whether the dedication to St Lawrence in each case has any significance is not clear. It may be a coincidence. In Devon, the church at Brentor was built about the year 1140 on the very summit of a steep volcanic cone, lashed by every storm, and as difficult for the parishioners to get at as it could possibly be. It is surrounded by a churchyard in which there can be very little depth of soil and which is, therefore, extremely inconvenient for burials. There must have been some special reason for the choice of this difficult site. The base of the cone seems to be surrounded by a continuous rampart of earth, and it may be that here again this isolated and conspicuous hill was the scene of pagan worship long before the first Christian church was built upon it.

These are rather obvious examples to take. A detailed study of church sites would reveal, especially on the western side of England, any number of mysteries to be solved. Norfolk also presents many problems relating to the siting of its ancient churches. Not all its isolated churches by any means derive from the 'migration' of the original villages, though recent archaeological work suggests that in some places at least there was an original village (in Saxon and Norman times) round the church. A great deal of this particular enquiry would necessarily be based on the reading of maps indoors, but the time would come when the student would have to visit every site personally because all sorts of significant minor features are not recorded on even the large-scale maps. At each of these sites a talk with the parson, and above all, perhaps, with the gravedigger, might produce rewarding information.

There are two other lines of approach to this subject besides the intelligent use of large-scale maps. We should try to discover which are the mother-churches in a given district or county: that is, the primary churches in the district from which a number of daughter-churches were later founded. If we can ascertain in some way the identity of the mother-churches in a district they will almost certainly stand on sites with a special significance.

It is not easy in some parts of England to discover which are the mother-churches and which the daughters, but prolonged enquiry in various kinds of records will produce most of the answers. The grouping of parishes, chapelries, townships, and tithings in the early census reports is often of great value in locating the mother-churches of a particular county, especially in the north of England and the Midlands. In this connection students will find particularly useful the *Comparative Account of the Population of Great Britain in the years 1801, 1811, 1821, and 1831* (published as a parliamentary paper in 1831). The relationships shown in such nineteenth-century sources, however, are only those that survived into a late period. In Lancashire they may reflect the original organisation in its entirety, for the Lancashire parishes remained very large and very few until well into the nineteenth century; but elsewhere there were early relationships which had disappeared, or rather had been obliterated, long before the nineteenth century. The student must therefore pursue these in other records, notably the early ecclesiastical records such as the Bishops' Registers.

Place-names ending in 'minster' invariably indicate the existence of the mother-church of a district; and it is usually not difficult to compile a list of the daughter-churches which were founded from the central minster. Such daughter-churches were often known in later times as chapelries and are, of course, not to be confused with the modern use of the word chapel, which is generally confined to a place of nonconformist worship.

Place-names are of some help, then, but much can also be done by scrutinising a large-scale map showing the boundaries of ancient ecclesiastical parishes. One often notices in this way that certain parishes fit into each other like pieces of a jigsaw puzzle. This suggests that they once formed a single compact estate, and that they have been carved out of this estate to make separate parishes, leaving the mother-parish considerably reduced in size (see Map, p. 58). The mother-church would tend, I think, to have been sited somewhere near the middle of its large territory. Where we find a known mother-church close to the edge of its own parish we may be fairly certain that it has lost some territory on that side, that another parish has been created out of it. This kind of evidence, the fitting together of ancient parish boundaries into larger original areas, must, of course, be used with the utmost caution; but there is no doubt that it can be a most fruitful method of approach to this obscure subject and that it can yield information of which there is no other surviving record.

In addition to place-names, and the intensive reading of the map, there is also the evidence of church dedications. This is an even more dangerous kind of evidence to use, but it should not be ignored solely on that account. Old dedications have been forgotten or deliberately changed, or have been corrupted into something nearly unrecognisable. There are probably hundreds of known examples of a change of dedication, especially where a church was completely or largely rebuilt in the medieval period. Thus at Moreton (Dorset) the original dedication was to St Magnus the Martyr but by the order of the Bishop of Salisbury, dated 28 August 1410, the day of dedication was changed to the Sunday after the octave of the Assumption of the Virgin Mary. There must be hundreds more cases where the original dedication has been changed, but where no official record of the change now survives. The dedication of churches to Celtic saints is particularly full of pitfalls, especially dedications to a popular saint like St Petrock. It would be more than rash to assume that in plotting the dedications to St Petrock we were following in the footsteps of the saint as he missionised in South-West England. It is likely, however, that more or less unique dedications to rare saints represent actual foundations by the saint himself or herself, and therefore that this line of approach is much more profitable in Wales than in England.

If we are fairly certain, as certain as can be, that we are dealing with the original dedications of a group of churches, a possible clue to early history is afforded by the similarity of the dedication saint. Thus I once observed on the large-scale map of Devon that the parishes of Honeychurch and Exbourne had obviously been carved out of the large parish of Sampford Courtenay. It was almost certain from the map, too, that the parish of Belstone had originally been a part of the great estate centred upon Sampford. When I pursued this clue a little further, I discovered that all three churches, whose parishes had been carved out of Sampford, were dedicated to St Mary. This could hardly have been an accident, even though dedications to St. Mary are the commonest of all. It must be confessed that the present dedication of the mother-church of Sampford Courtenay is to St Andrew, and there is no record or suggestion that it was ever anything different. It looks, however, as if the three daughter-churches were founded as part of some episcopal plan at about the same period. Some churches were built by private persons, others (perhaps most) as a part of some central plan of organisation directed in all probability by a bishop. Both origins must be kept in mind by the student.

It would be interesting to know if other students of this subject elsewhere in England find the same common dedications among groups of daughter-churches, though one would hardly expect a common dedication unless they had all been founded at approximately the same time. It has been suggested, but the theory needs much more testing than it has yet received, that where we have a number of urban churches with the same dedication in the same town they have originated from a mother-church of that dedication. If this theory be true, it would provide a valuable clue to the topographical development of towns in a particularly obscure period.

It is clear that the siting of ancient churches is a subject full of interesting possibilities, above all in those parts of England where the village may hardly be said to exist and where the church stands isolated in its parish. It has always seemed to me, looking at the one-inch map of Herefordshire, that here is a county which offers material for a rewarding study along these lines. All over the map of this county one observes parish churches the sites of which, looking at the map alone, cry out for explanation; and the same is probably true of the adjacent county of Shropshire. There is much more one could say on this subject; but the student in various counties and regions of England will undoubtedly make a number of important discoveries for himself if he sets about the work systematically and takes the subject far beyond the limits suggested in these few pages.

STREET-NAMES

A complete study of the street-names of an old town, or of all the towns in a particular county, would also make a fascinating special task. Many readers will know E. Ekwall's book on *The Street-Names of the City of London* (Oxford University Press, 1954). Even if one does not know London well, or even care much about visiting it, this is one of those irresistible books in which one begins to dip at random and goes on reading. London, of course, is a very special case so far as the richness of this material is concerned, but cities like Bristol and Norwich and Exeter, and a number of others, could well be treated in this way.* The volumes on *The Place-Names of Devon* deal with the street-names of Exeter, Plymouth, Barnstaple,

---

* The street-names of York have been fully dealt with in the volume on *The Place-Names of the East Riding of Yorkshire* (English Place-names Society, pp. 280–300) and, even more extensively, in A. Raine, *Medieval York* (Murray, 1955).

and other towns, giving dated references to streets and elucidating their meanings. But even these towns have a great deal more to reveal on this subject than is yet in print, and most towns in England have not yet been tackled at all in this respect.

This, it must be confessed, is a task calling for some special training and knowledge. It means going through masses of medieval and later records, and a knowledge of both palaeography and Latin is therefore required. Furthermore, if one is to go beyond a mere collection of references to streets, lanes, etc., and attempt to elucidate the meanings of the names, one must have a sound philological training. A few names will have obvious meanings, for example, Goldsmith Street, or Church Street, but the majority are not so obvious and it would be rash to start guessing at their meanings. If you have no training in philology, it would be better to confine your study to a careful listing of all the references to the streets, lanes, and roads of your town, giving the date and the source of your information, and to leave the matter there. Such a collection will not only be of great interest to fellow townspeople but will also be of value to the editors of the English Place-Name Society when they come to cover your particular town.

FIELD-NAMES

It is not generally realised that every field in rural areas had its own name, and still has, though modern fields tend to have dull and prosaic names. Nevertheless, one of the major tasks of local historians—and this one is above all suited to Women's Institutes with their extensive rural coverage and numerous branches—is to make a survey of the presentday field-names, since change is now so rapid in some parts of the country. This involves asking every farmer in a given parish the name of his fields, listing them, and plotting them, if possible, on the six-inch Ordnance maps.

The Devon Federation of Women's Institutes started this task at my instigation in 1964, and brought it to a conclusion six years later. Doubtless other counties have done the same thing. But even if one does not attempt the whole county, which is the ideal project, the single local historian ought to do this for his or her own parish, as a record for posterity. Even the Devon W.I.s could not get a complete coverage, in a county with some 430 ancient parishes, and in which not every parish by a long way has a W.I. branch. Nevertheless, the results were impressive, and are now lodged with the county record office for consultation. One vast parish had more than two thousand fields, with their individual names. Others were far less formidable.

Curiously enough, even in anciently enclosed counties like Kent or Devon or Essex (and others) field-names do not necessarily remain constant. Farmers in some counties have a way of giving new names, especially if they have been throwing old fields together to form a larger one for their machinery. So, to complete this particular task, one ought to go back to the tithe maps and awards of the 1840s, where every field is named, and record these also. The local coverage of tithe maps varies enormously (see pp. 42–43) but wherever they exist one should put their field-names alongside the modern names for comparison. Even where names have not been deliberately changed, there may well have been a remarkable corruption in spelling and pronunciation over the last 140 years. The best guide on the subject is J. Field, *English Field Names: A Dictionary* (David and Charles, 1972).

Earlier field-names will be found recorded on old estate maps, and in old deeds and in glebe terriers (*q.v.*). All should be listed, with a dated reference. But if this advanced work is not feasible, the list of modern names should at least be done while there is yet time. I commend this task to adult education classes, to Women's Institutes, and to any local organisation with the facilities for group study.

CATALOGUES OF MAPS

Another useful specialised task for the local historian, if he is particularly fond of maps, is to compile a complete catalogue for a county of all the local maps that can be traced. There exist for a number of counties catalogues of the maps of the county itself, or of large areas within it, but I mean here, particularly, maps below the county level—parish maps, estate maps, and town plans. Such a catalogue, if properly compiled, would be of the greatest value to local historians in the county. Instead of searching rather blindly to see if anything of this kind existed for their chosen place, they could simply refer to the catalogue and discover what existed and where. Your catalogue should therefore embody sufficiently detailed descriptions of these maps to tell the enquirer whether they are likely to contain information that will be of use to him. The amount and kind of information that one should note may be ascertained by consulting, for example, other catalogues of maps which have been prepared by experts, such as *A Catalogue of Inclosure Maps in the Berkshire Record Office*, edited by Peter Walne (1953). One would naturally begin by going to one's local archivist, partly to see whether anyone else is doing the same work and therefore to avoid useless duplication, and partly to obtain expert advice on the amount of information which he or she thinks it is desirable to have recorded in the catalogue. The archivist will, of course, also be able to say where a great number of these maps are to be found. Some will be in his own care (enclosure maps, some estate maps, tithe maps, town plans) but many will be in other repositories and in private hands. For example, most counties include land which belongs or has belonged to colleges in Oxford or Cambridge, and these colleges may well have early estate maps for their properties. Many private landowners also possess collections of estate maps. So far as towns go, the local librarian should know the whereabouts of all the extant plans.

A good example of such a list for a town is that by K. Bonser and H. Nichols, published in the *Transactions* of the Thoresby Society (1958). This covers all printed maps and plans for Leeds from 1711 to 1900. There are no fewer than 374 entries, which include maps published in connection with schemes for waterworks, sewerage, tramways, canals, railways, public health (e.g. a 'cholera map' for 1833), and private estate plans for housing and street development.

Such a catalogue of local maps is clearly a large task, something to keep one ticking over steadily in retirement for about five years; and it is also something which, when completed, will cause future generations of local historians to rise up and bless your name.

INDEXING OLD NEWSPAPERS

The value of old newspapers to the local historian has already been mentioned (see pp. 36–39). One of the greatest obstacles to their use is the lack of any index to their contents, and to search them blindly is a formidable task. Occasionally one finds a manuscript index compiled by private enterprise, but in general one must face a massive pile of newspaper files without any such aid. Some local historians, therefore, who have no particular desire to write a connected history of their town might well consider making an index to their local newspaper as a lasting benefit to others, besides being a fascinating task in itself. It is most important that such an index should follow some consistent plan, and not the private whims of the compiler. It is tempting to omit particular items or kinds of information on the grounds that no one is likely to be interested in such a subject, but nothing is more certain than that the very things one has decided to omit are the major interest of someone else. The fuller the index, the better it will be.

The index recently made by a Local History Group in the University of Hull to the contents of *The Hull Advertiser and Exchange Gazette* may serve as an example of what can be done.* The newspaper ran from 1794 to 1867. So far it has been indexed from its beginning in July 1794 to December 1825. Regular repetitive material such as market and agricultural reports, details of current fashion in dress, and similar matters, had necessarily to be omitted. Details of theatre advertisements, unless they appeared to be of unusual importance, were also omitted. A list of master headings was compiled before work was started, designed to cover all that the local historian could reasonably expect to get from a Hull newspaper of this period. Such a list was valuable also in keeping the various members of the group on the same lines and in preventing those with special interests from ignoring or playing down references likely to be of interest to others. Since this list of master headings is the result of much discussion and long experience, I give it here for the guidance of students in other parts of England who might wish to undertake a similar task:

Agriculture	Antiquities
Amusements	Architecture, Domestic
Army	Music
Associations (Miscellaneous)	Navigation
Brewing and Inns	Navy
Bridges	Newspapers
Canals	Parliament
Charities	Personalities
Commerce	Police (and administration
Costume	of Justice)
Crime	Philanthropy and Poor
Docks	Population
Education	Postal Services
Electricity	Press Gang
Emigration	Prices
Enclosures	Printing and Publishing
Erosion	Property

* I am greatly indebted to Mr K. A. MacMahon, Staff Tutor in Local History in the Department of Adult Education, Hull University, for the details of how this work was carried out, and for permission to print the list of master headings evolved by his group.

Fairs	Public Health
Ferry	Publishing (*see* Printing)
Finance	Railways
Fishing	Recipes
Food	Religion
Freemasonry	Roads
Furniture	Shipping
Harbours	Slavery
Horticulture	Smuggling
Inns (*see* Brewing)	Sport
Inventions	Streets
Irrigation	Sunk Island
Justice (*see* Police)	Theatre
Libraries	Timber
Lighting	Trades
Literature	Travel
Local Government	Trinity House
Medicine and Surgery	Water Supply
Mills	Weather
Museums	Whaling

It will be appreciated that each of these master headings had in the index a number of subsidiary headings. The nature of these was, of course, determined by the material that cropped up in the newspapers. Beneath the subheadings were grouped a number of particular items with the exact dated reference to the issue of the newspaper. Such a classification may seem unnecessarily elaborate to those not used to making or using indexes, but it is of the greatest importance if the most effective use is to be made by others of the index one has compiled. Indexing is a skilled occupation, and the student anxious to do this particular sort of work would be well advised to have a preliminary talk with someone in his local library before setting out on what is likely to prove a major task. Such an index, however, would be an enormous blessing to his fellow local historians in the future; and in making it he might well turn an honest penny (and please a great number of townspeople) by writing articles in the local newspaper on the more interesting material that comes under his eye during his long labours.

A DICTIONARY OF LOCAL BIOGRAPHY

Arising from the indexing of local newspapers, and a much more manageable task, is the indexing alone of obituary notices of local worthies. By this I do not mean, of course, the indexing of all the

'Deaths' notices, but those obituaries that range from a few lines to a column or so. It is surprising, except to those who have had to make the search, how extremely difficult it is to track down even a Victorian worthy unless one already has a clue from some other source.

In my experience, obituary notices of any worthwhile length do not become a feature of local newspapers until well into the nineteenth century. Finding these notices is a slow job, but the final result —perhaps an index of such notices running from say 1830 to 1939— would be a considerable contribution to local history in itself. It would also be a great standby for people working in other fields, for example that of local painters or architects or writers, besides the usual run of local politicians and officials. Remember, too, that where a town possessed two or more newspapers, you may well find an obituary notice presenting another point of view and fresh facts.

This sort of index may well be an end in itself, but what is also badly needed in this country, and what only local historians can do in adequate detail, is a Dictionary of Local Biography for every county. The *Dictionary of National Biography* serves more or less adequately for figures of national importance, though there are some astonishing omissions, especially of men who helped to create the industries, towns, and cities of the Midlands and the north. One should supplement the *D.N.B.* with the various volumes of *Who Was Who*, and most of all with Frederic Boase's *Modern English Biography*, which contains memoirs of thousands of persons who died between 1851 and 1900.*

Every town and county has produced men and women of local eminence who do not figure in the national works of reference, and who ought to be suitably recorded. Clearly this is a large task, probably beyond the powers of one man and very suitable for a dedicated group, such as a good adult education class, working over a period of years.

Before work begins, there must be prolonged discussion about the principles of inclusion and exclusion. A group of people with varied and specialised interests will do better than a single individual, however catholic his knowledge and tastes. The subject might be broken down, too, into manageable proportions by concentrating on one century to begin with—possibly the nineteenth, with its relatively accessible sources. One must remember that the local obituary notices alone are not sufficient as a source, though they

---

* First published between 1892 and 1921, and reprinted by Cass, 1965.

form a good start: many men and women of distinction have lived and died unnoticed by newspaper editors.

Lastly, I need hardly say that the final writing must be as impartial as it is humanly possible to be, however disagreeable the character under scrutiny may have been. Obituary notices tend to gloss over sins and faults, and many a local scoundrel has finished up with a fulsome column of praise for his charitable works. The Victorians tended to be less mealy-mouthed than we are, but the prize for a candid obituary notice must surely go to this one in the *Exeter Flying Post* for 14 January 1803:

> Thursday last, at his house in this city, Norton Nelson Esq. formerly of Gatcombe, near Totnes.—We are sorry to add, that this is a man whose character affords not even a *solitary instance*, which entitled him to praise or respect: forbidding in his manners, and of the most depraved mind, he lived and died universally despised and execrated, by everyone who holds virtue in respect and vice in abhorrence. We would have said *De mortuis nil nisi bonum*, but we think it a homage due to honest worth not to permit such a character as this to pass, without marking it with our severest indignation.

This is straighter speaking than we can ever hope for again, but reading between the lines of some Victorian obituaries one catches a glimpse of odious characters amid a heap of verbiage. Thus Henry Hooper, mayor of Exeter for the second time in 1856–7, 'achieved the distinction of being the only mayor who was never thanked, even perfunctorily, for his service to the city'. He was widely and rightly thought to have used his years on the council in feathering his own nest at the expense of the community. He would be a prominent candidate for inclusion in a dictionary of local biography for Devon.

RECONSTRUCTING THE OLD TOWN

In the earlier pages of this book, although I made it clear that I regarded local history as a hobby that gave a great deal of pleasure to a great number of people, I also uttered the criticism (pp. 29–30) that local historians were too often preoccupied with facts and correspondingly unaware of problems. This is still a valid criticism, though in the past twenty-five years or so the standards of local historical writing have risen remarkably. Nevertheless, I now feel that my view was a little too severe. There is still room for the kind of local history which gives pleasure but leads nowhere in particular.

One of the purest pleasures as we grow older and the world changes (usually for the worse in our eyes) is to reconstruct the topography of one's native town, or adopted town, as it was say a hundred years ago. It is an almost completely useless occupation; but it yields pleasure to the writer and this is communicated to many readers of his own generation. It solves no problems and it raises none (perhaps a few) but every tiny fact about the old town pleases those of us who have reached a certain age when the contemplation of the past affords more satisfaction than the contemplation of the future. It is a stage which the young naturally do not understand and indeed perhaps despise; but even they will one day find themselves in that not unhappy position. In the meantime, those of us who can look back forty years or more derive a peaceful satisfaction in remembering how things used to look, what interesting personal shops and pubs there were then (each one with its own special character—all gone now); where the old cabs used to stand, and the vanished chapels and now even the vanished cinemas: and all those little back-waters now erased for some hideous car park filled with coloured inanimate objects, where scores of children once played their cheerful homemade games with little or no bought equipment.

But the best of memories fades and becomes unreliable when tested against objective facts. We need not depend on inaccurate elderly memories alone. Old maps and old directories, prosaic though they sound, provide the skeleton of accurate facts: then come the reminiscences to clothe the dry bones with flesh and make them live again. Take, if you can, the 1:500 plan of your town, made at some date between 1855 and 1895. A few towns were done on the 1:1056 scale and 1:528 (see the key maps on pp. 29–30 of *The Historian's Guide to Ordnance Survey Maps*). Even in non-industrial regions the coverage of towns is remarkably uneven, indeed inexplicable. Thus sixteen towns in Devon were done on the 1:500 scale, but only five in Norfolk. Some of the Devon towns were really quite unimportant—such as Crediton, Bideford, and Totnes to make invidious distinctions: nevertheless, they were planned on this very large scale for some reason. If you are fortunate enough to have a town that has been done on such a scale, the next thing is to track down the original sheets. This is more difficult for various reasons. The Map Room in the New Bodleian has a complete collection for the country, and so presumably has the Map Room at the British Library. The sheets are too large to be photographed life-size, as it were, but a photographic reduction to half-scale is perfectly satisfactory and much more manageable on the average-sized working-table.

The study of these sheets (incidentally some of the peripheral sheets are almost completely blank and hardly worth photographing unless you have a developing town with new streets already marked out in the fields) should be married with a good directory of as near-contemporary date as can be found. Here local librarians will help.

Let me take a few examples of varied towns to show what can be done. The little town of East Dereham in mid-Norfolk was surveyed and published in 1882 in no fewer than seventeen sheets, and there is a good White's *Directory for Norfolk*, published in 1883. One could hardly get nearer than that. What I have to say now about my sample towns is scarcely more than random notes—a native will get vastly more out of the exercise—but will serve to show what kind of information to expect from these maps. On the northern edge of East Dereham ninety years ago there stood the Quebec Windmill (corn), of octagonal plan upon a mound. Looking round the town as a whole, the public buildings include the Post Office, Fire Engine Station, Banks (all named, including the old country banks), Corn Hall, Schools (distinguishing boys', girls' and infants') and Assembly Rooms. The large Market Place affords clear evidence of in-filling at some past date. The parish church (St Nicholas) had seats for 1,460 people, and the town plan shows a detailed plan of St With-burga's Well standing detached near the west end of the church. The industrial buildings are at first sight an astonishing range for a small agricultural town, but they all fit into the picture when one reflects about it. They include many smithies (some very large), three iron works, a carriage works, two agricultural implement manufactories (*sic*), timber yards, brick works and brick fields, leather works, large breweries, and a covered saw pit. A notable feature of the town map is the number of malthouses, some of them very large indeed. On the edge of the town several streets are marked out but not yet built up. Several bowling greens show the favourite male sport, but Theatre Street had no theatre at that date. Lewis's *Topographical Dictionary of England* (1835 edn) tells us that the theatre then was 'a small but neat building of brick . . . opened every alternate year by a regular company of performers'. Presumably by the early 1880s this spasmodic entertainment had entirely ceased. Lewis's account ties up well with the map of 1882. Indeed, the whole *Dictionary* is almost the local historian's bible. One could formerly

12.3 East Dereham, Norfolk

East Dereham is of interest not only as a Victorian market town. It has literary associations, for William Cowper was buried here and George Borrow was born nearby. Moreover, the church of St Nicholas is famous for its great bell tower, which stands detached from the rest of the building, a few yards to the south of the chancel. Bells had previously hung in the fourteenth-century central tower. In 1501 Richard Pynnes left a bequest of £40 for a new bell-tower 'if it should be built within ten years after my decease'; other bequests continued up to 1536. The church is also noted for its font of 1486 which depicts the seven sacraments, an art-form that is restricted to East Anglia. Within the churchyard is the well of St Withburga, a place of pilgrimage in the Middle Ages. The saint founded a local monastery and was buried here in 654.

pick up its tattered two volumes or so for a pound or so, but I imagine it is now a valuable possession, for nineteenth-century topography and history above all.

Stamford in Lincolnshire was surveyed in 1885 and published in the following year. The 'historic area' is covered in four sheets, but the peripheral sheets also contain a good deal of topographical detail. Large individual houses are all named, also all terraces however small, and many minor houses such as Ermyn Cottage. This is useful where houses have changed their name, as so often. I once lived in a Victorian house in Leicester (built *c*.1886) which started life as Newhurst—a typically Victorian name—but later became The Bosphorus when, as I discovered, it was bought by a Greek. I dropped this name and was satisfied with no. 39. But the naming of houses on old maps and in older directories is frequently a valuable clue to some piece of family history or town topography.

The Stamford map shows the ancient urban parish boundaries, since it was a town with several parish churches; these are invaluable for the study of medieval topography. A good deal of the Castle earthworks is marked, now erased for the inevitable car park. The town map shows an impressive number of breweries and malt-houses, and of course inns, taverns, and public houses, all nicely distinguished and named. This in itself is curious as the map of Woodbridge in Suffolk (11 sheets, dated 1881) shows nothing but hotels and inns, no public houses at all. There is clearly a bit of social history here. Presumably the public houses of Woodbridge had all upgraded themselves.

Many sites of vanished and formerly important medieval buildings are shown and named on the Stamford map, but in my experience the identification of vanished buildings on these large-scale maps, in any old town, needs checking and some corroborative evidence.

Now we turn to three industrial towns as a final sample: Halifax, Burslem, and Walsall. Here are riches indeed for the devout local historian. Halifax was not surveyed on the 1:500 scale, but on the 1:1056 (five feet to the mile) as early as 1849, published in 1852 in thirteen sheets, beautifully engraved. One could pore over it for hours at a time. All mills are named and described accurately (e.g. silk, woollen, cotton, and several other types), collieries (including old coal pits), quarries (mostly sandstone), iron foundries, dyeworks, and so on. A huge variety of Sunday schools are named, with denominations and usually the number of children catered for. Many large mill-owners' houses are named, with details of their

12.4 The Old Town Hall, Burslem

Burslem was the first of the Potteries villages to grow into a town, and it alone has a recognisable centre. In *The Old Wives' Tale* Arnold Bennett wrote, 'Bursley has the honours of antiquity in the Five Towns. No industrial development can ever rob it of its superiority in age, which makes it absolutely sure in its conceit.'

The market-place is dominated by the old town hall of 1852–57, designed by G. T. Robinson of Leamington in confident classical style with giant columns and pilasters and a portico.

grounds; and many blocks of streets evidently in course of building or merely marked out on the ground. All round the edges of the town there are scattered bits of housing development, showing in some places a bit of planned growth, in others quite haphazard building on odd bits of land. Even the street-names are so characteristic of the age, for example the new layout which included Labour Street, Temperance Street, Health Street, Freedom Street, all adjacent with their hopeful names. Even looking at them on the map one cannot help feeling a little sardonic at the optimism of urban builders and town councils: and if these are so hopefully named, what about Bleak Street in Burslem on the 1879 map? The mind boggles if even the Victorian optimists thought it was bleak.

The Halifax map shows a considerable number of industrial buildings besides mills, and a few—a very few—cultural amenities, the theatre, the Mechanics' Institution, and of all things a riding school, for daughters of rich mill-owners, no doubt. The map of 1852 should be married to the *Post Office Directory for the West Riding*, dated 1857, for the fullest study of a vigorously growing textile town in the mid-century.

Burslem, in the Potteries, was surveyed in 1878, and published in 1879 when the local boy Enoch Arnold Bennett was twelve years old. Again we see the detailed pattern of a town growing into the surrounding fields. Housing patterns of all kinds are visible, working-class houses, of course. There are dreadful names like Primitive Street, called after the large Primitive Methodist chapel. Market Street was short, and ended at that date in a field. Unfinished streets abound, with some houses already built but many plots not yet taken up. Urban growth is datable in many places: Regent Street, Nile Street, Pitt Street, Peel Street; and Wellington, Russell, Waterloo and Adelaide all tell the same story. Collieries are shown, and left amid the growing débris we often see old farms named and still being worked before mining subsidence destroyed their drains and thus their fields. And besides the coal-tips, there are huge holes in the ground, the clay pits from which came millions of industrial and domestic bricks in this teeming mass of towns called the Potteries. Many shafts were already marked as 'Old'—ironstone, limestone, and coal.

Dozens of chapels lie all over the place, with their denominations shown and their human capacity, some seating as many as 1,250 people. The 'Ragged School' stood immediately next to a burial ground: another school adjoined a brickworks. Banks are shown, of course, sometimes with minute details of their internal layout, such as the Liverpool and Manchester District Bank. The old Market Place is shown, with again clear evidence of in-filling: the Market Hall and Town Hall both inserted into what was originally an open space. Industrial buildings abound, scattered apparently at random though no doubt the result of some past choice. Most are Earthenware Manufactories, of course, with bottle-kilns shown as circles: an almost lost landscape now. Potteries were not the only industrial activity. There were tileries, and places that made stacks of encaustic tiles for resounding Victorian churches, and sewer pipes for more lowly concerns; and many other specialised factories. Almost everywhere one can see the relics of the older life being slowly engulfed, such as Port Vale Corn Mills adjacent to a Sagger Manufactory. Country streams still flowed through untouched fields on the urban edge, but the clay pits, the brickworks, and the houses were catching up in the 'seventies. The mansions of the well-to-do stood near, but not too near, all this activity, such as Newport House, where the lawns and gardens ran down to the banks of the famous Trent and Mersey Canal. There must be special directories for The Potteries in the numerous local libraries today.

And lastly, of this cursory sample, the industrial town of Walsall, an ancient market town set upon a rock of limestone. So says Lewis in 1835, in his full and at times idyllic description of the town, which is nevertheless also full of useful information to the social and economic historian. It was surveyed on the 1:500 scale in 1885 and published in the following year. Its special character is immediately evident from the first sheet one picks up. The central area shows tinning and polishing works, a carriage lamps manufactory, an iron, brass, and silver foundry, leather works, tube works, a clothing manufactory, and factories where they made brushes and saddles and ironmongery for coaches. On the same map, evidence of a fast-growing town, a great number of Courts with no names but only a number. Several sheets show this dreary type of urban in-filling. On the outer sheets we see the familiar picture of unfinished streets running out into the country, and also of isolated, sporadic development in bits and pieces stuck down apparently at random but clearly dictated by some now unknown choice. Many streets planned also, but only just begun in 1885.

The sheet for the central area shows no fewer than thirty-three inns and public houses. Seven of these were dignified with the title of inn, the other twenty-six were public houses. All but three small public houses are named, and their names would revive many memories for old customers—the Jolly Bacchus, the Paul Pry, the

Leathern Bottle, the inevitable Blue Pig, the Queen's Head, the Old Still, and a score of others with an individual life and clientèle. No doubt they all made their own beer and ale, and their old customers all swore it was the best in the town. The historian of inns and public houses would have a splendid time with these maps, for they would correct many a hazy memory. Again, the appropriate directory would fill in the names of the landlords or licensees, though not many alive today would remember them. Still, they might have 'heard their fathers tell' of that generation.

Every one of these towns is different: their special character shows up at once on these huge-scale maps. Armed with these sheets that show every lamp-post and pillar-box, every tree in wealthy gardens, every detail, however humble, of urban life of a hundred or so years ago, the elderly local historian can end his days happily reconstructing the town he once knew, or that his old father had wandered round as a young man.

I3 WRITING AND PUBLISHING

WRITING

I assume that the local historian who has spent some years studying every detail about the past history of his chosen place, or some special aspect of it which more particularly appeals to him, will wish to see the results of his labours in print. The great problem which will arise before beginning to write is: What kind of reader has one in mind? For this will determine to a very large extent the treatment of the subject. If one is dealing with a special aspect of local history, for example the financial history of a town or a study of the public health of a particular community, the question does not arise very seriously. But if one intends to write a complete history of a town or a parish one has to envisage two distinct kinds of reader. In a purely local history of what one may call, without disrespect, an antiquarian kind, in which one puts in all sorts of details about local families, local events, local houses, and topography, one must expect to interest mainly the inhabitants of that place and a few people outside who happen to know it. In other words, one is writing for a very limited public, able to appreciate this kind of detail.

On the other hand, one may hope to write an historical study of the origins, the growth, the long period of stability, and perhaps the subsequent disintegration, of a particular English community. In this kind of history again one is writing for a limited public, but the treatment will be very different from that in a history written to interest local people only. One will omit a vast amount of the purely local detail about people and places which may be of great interest in itself, but only if one happens to know those people and places. The writer of this second kind of local history will have to concentrate much more upon a continuous theme in his history, selecting only that detail which illustrates the general point that he happens to be making and omitting all other detail, however interesting in itself, which does not help the argument forward.

It is perhaps too rigid to say that one must write one kind of local history or the other. An able writer will probably be able to compromise between the two approaches, but even he will have to be continually on his guard lest he should satisfy neither kind of reader —one because there is not enough loving detail, the other because there is rather too much of it. This is a difficult question which each local historian must resolve for himself before he begins writing.

There is much one could say about the technique of writing, but in the field of local history it is probably better not to attempt much general advice of this kind. The great bulk of local history is written by amateurs whose time for writing, or for continuous periods of writing, is severely limited by all the other duties they have to perform. They are not professional writers and they have to push on with their writing as and when they can. All the same, we all hope when we commit our work to paper that it will be read by an appreciable number of people.

This desirable result does not follow automatically. The writer must take considerable pains with the way in which he sets out his work, and he must put himself in the place of the reader who may be reading about a place he does not know personally. An elementary point, therefore, is that any local history should contain at least one adequate map, clearly drawn, and if possible pulling out clear of the pages of the book, showing all the places mentioned in the text. More than one map may be necessary. Most historians, including local historians, are inclined to be blind where maps are concerned. One can hardly have too many in a book, and they should, if possible, be drawn and lettered by a skilled cartographer. Writers may well find their publishers unsympathetic (or worse) on the point of how many maps a book needs, but they should stick to their guns, even to the extent of trying to raise additional funds to cover the cost of the necessary maps and plans. It is as horrible a crime to publish a local history without a map (or maps) as it is to publish without a full index.

As to the mechanics of writing, I cannot do better than refer the local historian who wishes to make a good job of his book to the final chapter in C. G. Crump's *History and Historical Research*

(1928), in which he discusses the pitfalls and difficulties of setting out one's work, and offers a good deal of useful advice. This book is no longer in print. One occasionally comes across a copy in a secondhand bookshop, and if so the local historian should acquire it.

Among the points made by Crump is what he calls 'the natural disposition of the beginner to over-estimate the mental equipment and the power of attention of his reader. He will endeavour to write for experts and examiners, and forget that even these luckless and criminal classes are human'. One practical consequence of this is that the local historian may be reluctant to say he does not know the answer to a particular question, or the meaning of something he has seen in the fields or streets of his chosen territory. But as Crump says, 'an admission of ignorance by the writer will often be the very thing that the reader is looking for'. Other faults follow through over-estimating the mental equipment of one's readers, such as the tendency to wrap up simple statements in high-sounding jargon, or indeed to avoid simple statements altogether because they are felt to reflect upon the mental equipment of the writer. The opposite fault, that of writing down to the reader, is even worse. One may be tempted to do this in producing, for example, a village history or a history for school children, and it is rank bad manners. It assumes that your reader is incapable of understanding clear English, and it usually means that the writer is incapable of producing it.

There is no simple answer to these problems of writing, but Crump offers the useful advice that you should write to please yourself.

> Write to please yourself, as if you were to read what you are writing. Do your own criticising as you go along. If you despair and desire to burn all you have written, select your kindest friend and ask her to read your work and tell you how it is getting on. Never destroy what you have written and begin over again, unless you are sure that you can do it better; and if you decide that this is necessary, use in the new version all that you can save in the old one. Remember that every time you rewrite what you have written you will lose something valuable, and therefore make sure that you will gain more than you lose.

There are, further, two ways of writing a book or an article: either one may aim at producing the final result at the first attempt, or one may write a first draft and then revise this until perhaps it is almost unrecognisable. Few writers are so gifted that they can succeed with the former method. Most of us, and especially perhaps most local historians (who are not professional writers), can only hope to produce after much struggling a first draft; and then to sit down with it after an interval, read it through as a whole, and make the necessary corrections of fact, deletions, and perhaps filling-in of gaps, until the second version is complete.

The effort of starting to write on a somewhat complicated subject is one that most people naturally shrink from. One finds oneself doing everything except getting on with the job, especially if on sitting down one's mind appears to be, not a blank, but a welter of unassimilated facts, so that all one can do is to write two lines and then cross them out, then make a fresh start and cross that out, and so on until one tends to give up and go out and do something in the garden. Even the most practised writers experience this initial difficulty in starting the day's work, but there is a simple solution to it. Even if we think we are writing confused rubbish for the first twenty minutes or half an hour, we should plough on without bothering too much about getting the writing word-perfect or one's meaning crystal clear. Ignore all the imperfections and go on relentlessly, until at last, after writing perhaps one side of a sheet of foolscap, the mind suddenly gets into working order and everything begins to flow more easily. At the end of the morning, on reading through what you have written, you may well decide to cross through the whole of the first page or so of the manuscript because it becomes clear that halfway down the second page you have really got into your stride. All this is precisely like a bowler's run at cricket. No bowler would do much if he had to bowl from a standing position. He has to get steamed up with a more or less long run; and so has the writer as he begins the unnatural occupation of pushing a pen for hours on end.

Another useful hint, if one is writing a longish book or even a longish article, is to leave off the day's work without completely exhausting the subject in hand; above all, not to complete a chapter if it can be avoided, at the end of the day, so that one is forced on the next day to begin a fresh chapter with all the mental struggle that this will involve. If you break off at a point in the middle of a subject and make a brief marginal note about how you intend to go on, the next day's writing will begin much more easily, especially if one has read through, before beginning writing, all that was written the day before in order to get the mind working along the right lines.

There is much else one could say of a practical nature but this is hardly the place for it. Perhaps, however, there are one or two points I ought to make which bear particularly upon the writing of local histories. Always give the exact reference for your statements unless they happen to be fairly common knowledge. Nothing is more maddening to the reader of any work of scholarship than to read some extraordinary fact or statement and not to be given the authority upon which it rests. If the author of such a statement has died in the meantime (or, more likely, lost his notes) the statement may be almost valueless if there is no means of checking it. At the same time you should not overload the text or the bottom of the page with a parade of footnote references for simple statements. You must use your own judgement in all these matters and no one is infallible. It is essential when giving references to ensure that they are full enough to enable the reader to track the original sources down if he wishes: that is, the full title of the manuscript collection, where it is housed, and precisely where in the collection the particular information is drawn from. It ought not to need saying that references should be absolutely accurate; but it is astonishing how slap-dash many authors are in this respect. There is no excuse for this sort of inaccuracy. One does not need a university training to get one's facts right, especially facts of this nature.

One final point as regards writing: always be careful to make a clear distinction in your writing between facts which are based upon some authority, and opinions which you may feel called upon to express about some difficult question in your local history. There are periods in the history of a town or a parish, especially perhaps the pre-Conquest period, for which there are no documentary sources, or for which the documentary sources are vague or contradictory, and yet one cannot pass over this period or problem in complete silence. Some kind of opinion must be expressed. So long as it is made clear that it is an opinion, and the evidence for holding it is clearly set out, a later worker in the same field may be able to test it and eventually to elevate it to the status of a fact. For the rest, the writer should now turn to Crump's final pages. Writing is a difficult and laborious process and advice on the subject tends to make it sound even more difficult, but the local historian should not be discouraged by this. The pen is a tool like any other craftsman's tool and the more one uses it the better one becomes at it.

PUBLISHING

It may be that the local historian is content merely to go on browsing amongst the sources, adding detail to detail for year after year, without wishing to face the labour of writing a book on the subject.

13.1 Balderton Hall, Shropshire

Balderton Hall was erected in the 1570s or 1580s by William Nicholas on a typical Elizabethan plan. The central hall is reached by an off-centre entry, but is not open to the rafters in the medieval style. Nicholas's original building was L-shaped, with a parlour wing, but he later added the kitchen wing on the other side of the hall. The timber-framing of the two wings differs in pattern. The chimneys are Victorian additions in 'Tudor Gothic' style. William Nicholas went bankrupt after speculation in a timber business, and within the next hundred years the property changed hands seven times. Richard Gough's *History of Myddle* gives a vivid account of the varied characters who lived here, from the pious rector of Hodnet to Michael Chambre, who had 'nothing commendable in him but that hee was well descended, and that hee was so blasted by his vitiouse life that hee was a person of noe accompt'.

Writing is a heavy labour, and it is not surprising that so many local historians never bring themselves anywhere near completing a book. Yet one wants to feel that all the work that one has put into the study of some place is going to see the light of day in some form or other. Indeed, this may be the necessary spur to our efforts to keep on with the job and get it finished. It is the easiest and pleasantest thing in the world to go on browsing peacefully amongst your notes. If you know you are never going to publish anything, and you are content to browse in this way, at least ensure that your notes are legible and in good order so that somebody else coming after you can make use of them. So many local historians die, leaving behind them masses of notes in quite illegible handwriting, often with no clear indication where the notes have come from; and the result is so much waste paper. Such notes are unusable by anyone else. You should therefore aim at publication in some form or another.

A few local historians possess sufficient means to enable them to publish their own work in a suitable form. Sir Matthew Nathan's history of the small Somerset village of West Coker appeared in this way in 1957. It was the sort of local history we should all like to see for our own chosen field, running to well over five hundred pages and handsomely produced by the Cambridge University Press. On an even more monumental scale was Dr Cunliffe Shaw's *History of Kirkham-in-Amounderness*, published privately in 1950. By far the best history of the town of Dartmouth was published by Mr Percy Russell in something of the same way in 1950. But these are idle dreams for the great majority of us, for no commercial publisher will produce a local history nowadays unless it is heavily subsidised. The cost of doing this oneself is usually prohibitive. There are, however, compromise solutions to the problem. Some local historians have put a good deal of their town or parish history into print in instalments, either printed and published independently or published as a series of articles in the Transactions or Proceedings of the local Historical or Antiquarian Society. Some complete village histories have been published in this way over a period of years.* This method is harder to employ nowadays than it used to be because most local societies have been forced to ration their space severely, but a competent local historian will always be recognised and an enterprising editor of the local historical journal will always be glad to come to some arrangement whereby a sub-

---

* The Cricklade Historical Society represents another method of publication. The Society published nine papers, covering the entire history of the town, between 1948 and 1957.

stantial article relating to one town or parish may appear at suitable intervals.

The Department of English Local History at the University of Leicester, founded in 1948 as the first department of its kind in any university, also offers a possible channel of publication. It publishes from time to time monographs (Occasional Papers) of some eight to ten thousand words on a wide range of subjects, but intending contributors should write in the first instance to the Professor of English Local History at the University for advice and guidance. It also awards annually the John Nichols Prize (of the value of £25) for the best essay in English local history on any subject chosen by the candidate; and it reserves the right to print the prize essay in the series of Occasional Papers published under the aegis of the Department by the University Press. Several of these prize essays have been so published.

The publication of local histories nowadays may seem a depressing subject, but it is better to face the facts of economics at the start. It is a complete waste of time to approach any commercial publisher with a local history unless you are prepared to pay most of the costs yourself. The one good side of all this is that it forces local historians nowadays to write concisely, or it should do so if they are to have any hope of publication. Nearly all of us tend to put too much into a local history. To be forced to produce a shortened version is generally all to the good. We think every single fact about a place is precious, and we hate to see it go back into the limbo from which we rescued it in some Record Office. In other words, we lose all sense of proportion about our work. If the harsh facts of economics force us to say in ten thousand words what we have splashed over into thirty thousand it will be a far better book in the end. If you cannot bear to prune your own roses get some knowledgeable friend to do it for you. Sometimes the Women's Institute is a possible channel of publication.* The Women's Institute of Ashton, a small village in Northamptonshire, compiled and published in 1954 an admirable history of the village during the past hundred and fifty years or so, liberally illustrated with old photographs, line drawings, and large clear maps. You may be fortunate enough to live in a village where the Women's Institute is equally enterprising.

The local historian who thinks he (or she) has a good market—for example, for the history of a small town which has never been

---

* Women's Institutes, organised on a county basis, have a similar (or even better) organisation at their disposal through their branches, for advertising, gathering orders, and distribution.

written before or so long ago as to be rare and out-of-date—can avoid some of the commercial risks of publication by adopting the pre-publication subscription method. The total costs of printing, binding, and distribution (e.g. postage costs nowadays) should be ascertained from a reliable local printer, the size of the edition determined, and the final retail price decided on this basis. This is too big and intricate a subject to discuss in detail here. A talk with a good local printer is the only way to avoid trouble and possible calamity.

If the costs of printing by orthodox means are prohibitive, even by the pre-publication method of subscription, then another method should be tried. This is offset-lithography, which is being increasingly used by local societies as well as individuals. Several good local histories have been produced in recent years by this method, and several firms now specialise in such work. Their advice should be sought in advance. If it is decided to go ahead, the publication could still be accompanied by advance subscriptions for copies, provided the outcome is certain. I have been told also, but have no personal experience of it, that many firms such as estate agents already possess the necessary apparatus for this kind of printing, and a sympathetic businessman in a small town might well be willing to produce a local history at a nominal cost.

If you find for some reason that none of these methods of publication is open to you, you should prepare half a dozen copies of your history in typescript and distribute them to key places where they will be of value to other workers, or of interest to other readers. A copy should go to the local record office, another to the library of your local historical society (if it is not a moribund institution), another copy to the county library, and another to the reference library of your county town. The important thing is to make your work available to others in some form or other.

In the original edition of this book, I ended by suggesting that the frustrated parish historian might well seek a channel for publication in the *Victoria County History* if his county is actively in preparation. A great number of counties show no signs of life, but even where the work is going forward I am advised that the *V.C.H.* does not offer much scope for those who are not full-time workers on its central or local staffs. Over many years the work of compiling the topographical articles for the *History* has become highly specialised and is controlled by a group of memoranda and similar documents which vary, of course, from time to time. To end on a less discouraging note, however, anyone who is working on a county where the *V.C.H.* is

active, and is willing to share his knowledge, should get into touch
with his County Editor or directly with the General Editor at the
Institute of Historical Research, Senate House, London W.C.1.
At the present time of writing, the following counties are actively
in preparation: Cambridgeshire, Essex, Gloucestershire, Middlesex, Oxfordshire, Shropshire, Somerset, Staffordshire, Sussex,
Wiltshire, and the East Riding of Yorkshire. Other counties may
be added from time to time.

In the first pages of this book I made it clear that I was writing, not
for the specialist or the professional historian, but for the great
army of amateurs in the field of local history. I quoted too some
remarks by Samuel Butler to show that amateurs have no excuse for
doing bad work. There is much to be said for being an amateur.

The distinguished Swiss historian, Jacob Burckhardt (1818–97),
in his *Reflections on History* had this to say:

> The word 'amateur' owes its evil reputation to the arts. An artist must
> be a master or nothing, and must dedicate his life to his art, for the
> arts, of their very nature, demand perfection.
>
> In learning, on the other hand, a man can only be a master in one
> particular field, namely as a specialist, and in some field he *should* be a
> specialist. But if he is not to forfeit his capacity for taking a general
> view, or even his respect for general views, he should be an amateur
> at as many points as possible, privately at any rate, for the increase of
> his own knowledge and the enrichment of his possible standpoints.
> Otherwise he will remain ignorant in any field lying outside his own
> speciality and perhaps, as a man, a barbarian.
>
> But the amateur, because he loves things, may, in the course of his
> life, find points at which to dig deep.

13.2 Whaley Bridge, near Stockport

Whaley Bridge is a product of the Industrial Revolution, a typical small northern town built
of local gritstone and set amongst the bleak hills of the Pennines. Such places have a rough
grandeur and a period-piece attraction that can be as compelling as the appeal of settlements
with much longer histories.

In 1800 the Peak Forest canal was completed as far as Buxworth Basin and Whaley Bridge.
The Marple aqueduct and a flight of sixteen locks took it along its 14½-mile route from the
Ashton canal at Dukinfield Junction. In 1831 the canal terminus at Whaley Bridge was linked
with the Cromford canal by the Cromford and High Peak railway, which rose in a series of
inclines to a height of 1,264 feet at Hurdlow. A spectacular series of four inclines took the
railway down 750 feet to Whaley Bridge. Stationary steam engines provided most of the
power, but the final incline was worked by a horse gin. The railway was closed in 1967.

The covered dock building in the canal basin enabled barges to enter the central section and
railway wagons to come alongside. It was built in 1832 and extended in 1916. Some of the
atmosphere of the era of canals and early mineral railways can still be captured at the basin,
and the town retains its nineteenth-century town hall, hotel, Wesleyan chapel, Sunday school
and Mechanics Institute.

Burckhardt's deepest sentiments were such as to appeal especially to local historians, though he established his great reputation in a much wider field. He was born in Basle, then an ancient little city of only twenty thousand people, like my own in south-western England at that date. He saw all the faults of a small, purse-proud town and vacillated between other places for some time; but he returned for good to his native town at the age of forty as Professor of History. The university was small and possibly undistinguished; but he remained there for the rest of his life, even refusing in 1872 an invitation to the most prestigious Chair of History in Europe at that time, that vacated by Ranke at Berlin. For Basle was his ancestral city, and his published *Letters* reveal how much he loved it despite all its faults. In his retirement, 'as the days take on a mellower light, and the apple at last hangs really finish'd and indolent ripe upon the tree' he drank his favourite wine, the noble Chateauneuf du Pape, with old friends and moved into a serene and happy old age. He took Sunday afternoon strolls, followed by supper, in his beloved Basle countryside, and returned to his piano for a couple of hours. He might truly have echoed the Horatian epitaph which I used at the start of this book:

> *It is that corner of the world, above all others,*
> *Which has a smile for me.*

APPENDIX I

The following tables are derived from different sources. They show the ranking of the leading provincial towns over a period of rather more than five hundred years. Though they offer a good general guide to the economic vicissitudes of some fifty towns, they must be used with a certain amount of caution. Some of the difficulties involved in setting out the tables are noted here:

1334

The major difficulty here is the inclusion of suburbs which were an integral part of a town at this date. I have included the suburbs of Bishop's Lynn (King's Lynn), Exeter, and Stamford in the respective totals, but other towns may also need adjustment in this way. Only the local historian, familiar with the topographical history of his town, can settle this question for himself. In some cases the assessment includes the outlying 'members' of a borough, and the ranking of the town itself is inflated accordingly. Ely and Peterborough are probably much over-rated here. The large and wealthy parishes of the Marshland around the Wash constitute a special difficulty. Some, like Pinchbeck (Lincs) and Terrington (Norfolk), were more highly assessed than half the towns in the list. But I have excluded all these cases, including more doubtful ones like Wisbech, on the ground that they were not towns or that the urban area was small in relation to the surrounding parish. It should be noted that Chester and Durham are not taxed in this list. Chester certainly would have ranked high had it been included.

1377*

Most of the difficulties discussed above for the 1334 table apply to this table also. The local historian will also bear in mind that this is an exceptional period for population statistics, in the middle of half a century of devastating outbreaks of plague which hit different towns with varying force. Some of the changes in ranking since 1334 would therefore be abnormal, e.g. Newcastle and Great Yarmouth. In the case of Newcastle the drop was temporary (see the 1523–27 table), but at Great Yarmouth it was a more permanent fall from which there was little or no recovery until about 1600. It will be noted, too, that where poll-tax assessments or certificates are missing for particular places, it has been necessary to make an estimate of the population in 1377.

1523–27

Here, too, there are difficulties about what suburbs to include in the urban totals which can only be resolved in each case by the local historian, but the ranking in this list is unlikely to be changed by any such adjustments. For some towns the necessary assessments to the subsidy do not survive in their completeness and I have made an estimate on the basis of what remains. Certain towns and districts were excluded from the subsidy (see p. 119, footnote). It is possible to make a good placing for Newcastle, but Chester, Durham, Dover, and possibly Ludlow should be somewhere in the table also. Chester would have ranked fairly high in the table.

1662

This table is based upon the figures of Mr C. A. F. Meekings, of the Public Record Office. The figures relate to taxable hearths only but are all comparable with each other. They also relate to administrative areas. A number of places included a country district which might be of considerable size, such as York or Shrewsbury. A number of other places had liberties and precincts within their built-up area which lay under the jurisdiction of surrounding hundreds. If these adjustments are made, some changes in ranking follow: thus York becomes 3rd, Canterbury 8th, Chester 16th, and so on. But the exact placing of his town is again a matter for the local historian, who will know what to include and what to exclude. It ought to be said, too, that the local historian who is working on one town must examine all the surviving hearth tax assessments for his chosen place, above all those that include the names of those who were exempt for one reason or another. Only in this way will he get a complete picture of his town. In my experience the assessments for 1670 and 1674, where they survive, are among the most valuable of all.

1861

These figures are taken from the census report of 1861. Where a town was both a municipal and a parliamentary borough, and these areas were not co-terminous, the municipal limits have been chosen in each instance. Similarly, where a town was both a municipal borough and a civil parish, and the areas were not identical, the municipal limits have been taken as defining the town.

THE RANKING OF PROVINCIAL TOWNS 1334–1861

1334 (Tax quota in shillings)		1377* (Taxpaying populations)	
1. Bristol	4400	1. York	7248
2. York	3240	2. Bristol	6345
3. Newcastle	2667	3. Coventry	4817
4. Great Yarmouth	2000	4. Norwich	3952
5. Lincoln	2000	5. Lincoln	3569
6. Norwich	1892	6. Salisbury	3226
7. Shrewsbury	1881	7. Lynn	3217
8. Oxford	1828	8. Colchester	2955
9. Salisbury	1500	9. Boston	2871
10. Boston	1467	10. Beverley	2663
11. Lynn (incl. South Lynn)	1360	11. Newcastle	2647
12. Ipswich	1291	12. Canterbury	2574
13. Hereford	1209	13. Bury St. Edmunds	2445
14. Canterbury	1199	14. Oxford	2357
15. Beverley	1140	15. Gloucester	2239
16. Gloucester	1098	16. Leicester	2101
17. Winchester	1030	17. Shrewsbury	2083
18. Southampton	1022	18. Great Yarmouth	1941
19. Coventry	1000	19. Hereford	1903
20. Cambridge	932	20. Cambridge	1902
21. Stamford (incl. Stamford Baron)	918	21. Ely	1772
22. Spalding	840	22. Plymouth	1700 (est.)
23. Exeter (incl. Exe Island)	812	23. Exeter	1560
24. Nottingham	741	24. Hull	1557
25. Plymouth	693	25. Worcester	1557
26. Hull	667	26. Ipswich	1507
27. Scarborough	667	27. Northampton	1477
28. Derby	600	28. Nottingham	1447
		29. Winchester	1440

* This table is based upon figures compiled by Professor Beresford of the University of Leeds.

THE RANKING OF PROVINCIAL TOWNS (contd.)

1334 (Tax quota in shillings)			1377 (Taxpaying populations)	
29. Reading	586		30. Scarborough	1393
30. Bampton (Oxon.)	c. 580		31. Stamford	1218
31. Rochester	570		32. Newark	1178
32. Newbury	550		33. Ludlow	1172
33. Northampton	540		34. Southampton	1152
34. Leicester	533		35. Pontefract	1085
35. Colchester (with hamlets)	523		36. Reading	1050 (est.)
36. Bridgwater	520		37. Derby	1046
37. Newark	520		38. Lichfield	1024
38. Peterborough (c.m.*)	510		39. Newbury	1000 (est.)
39. Cirencester	500		40. Wells	901
40. Bridgnorth (c.m.)	488		41. Bridgnorth	900 (est.)
41. Bury St. Edmunds	480		42. Cirencester	900 (est.)
42. Ely (c.m.)	476		43. Barking	880 (est.)

1523-7 (Subsidy paid: to nearest £)			1662 (No. of hearths taxed)	
1. Norwich	1704		1. Norwich	7302
2. Bristol	1072		2. York	7294
3. Newcastle	——†		3. Bristol	6925
4. Coventry	974		4. Newcastle	5967
5. Exeter	855		5. Exeter	5294
6. Salisbury	852		6. Ipswich	5020
7. Ipswich	657		7. Great Yarmouth	4750
8. Lynn	576		8. Oxford	4205*
9. Canterbury	552		9. Cambridge	4133*
10. Reading	c. 470		10. Canterbury	3940
11. Colchester	426		11. Worcester	3619
12. Bury St. Edmunds	405		12. Deptford	3554
13. Lavenham	402		13. Shrewsbury	3527
14. York	379		14. Salisbury	3498
15. Totnes	c. 317		15. Colchester	3414
16. Worcester	312		16. East Greenwich	3390
17. Gloucester	c. 307		17. Hull	3390
18. Lincoln	298		18. Coventry	3301
19. Hereford	273		19. Chester	3004
20. Great Yarmouth	260		20. Plymouth	2600 (est.)
21. Hull	256		21. Portsmouth	2600 (est.)

* c.m. = *cum membris*

† Not taxed.   Position estimated from population.

* Excluding the colleges.

THE RANKING OF PROVINCIAL TOWNS

1523–7 (Subsidy paid: to nearest £)			1662 (No. of hearths taxed)	
22.	Boston	c. 240	22. Lynn	2572
23.	Southampton	224	23. Rochester	2271
24.	Hadleigh	c. 224	24. Lincoln	2211
25.	Wisbech	c. 220	25. Dover	2208
26.	Shrewsbury	c. 220	26. Nottingham	2190
27.	Oxford	202	27. Gloucester	2174
28.	Leicester	199	28. Bury S. Edmunds	2109*
29.	Cambridge	181	29. Winchester	2069*
30.	Stamford	c. 180	30. Sandwich	2033
31.	Northampton	180	31. Maidstone	1900
32.	Windsor	178	32. Leeds	1798
33.	Plymouth	163	33. Leicester	1773
34.	Maldon	c. 150	34. Northampton	1610
35.	St. Albans	c. 150	35. Chatham	1588
36.	Chichester	138	36. Ely	1554
37.	Winchester	132	37. Chichester	1550 (est.)
38.	Long Melford	c. 120	38. Gateshead	1532
39.	Sudbury	c. 120	39. Southampton	1500
40.	Rochester	117	40. Derby	1479
41.	Nottingham	112	41. Ludlow	1467
42.	Nayland	c. 110	42. Warwick	1467

1801 (Census population)		1861 (Census population)	
1. Manchester (incl. Salford)	84,020	1. Liverpool	443,938
2. Liverpool	77,653	2. Manchester (incl. Salford)	441,171
3. Birmingham	73,670	3. Birmingham	296,076
4. Bristol	63,645	4. Leeds	207,165
5. Leeds	53,162	5. Sheffield	185,172
6. Plymouth (incl. Devonport)	43,194	6. Bristol	154,093
7. Norwich	36,832	7. Plymouth (incl. Devonport)	113,039
8. Bath	32,200	8. Newcastle	109,108
9. Portsmouth (incl. Portsea)	32,166	9. Bradford	106,218
10. Sheffield	31,314	10. Stoke-upon-Trent	101,207
11. Hull	29,516	11. Hull	97,661
12. Nottingham	28,861	12. Portsmouth	94,799
		13. Preston	82,985

* 1664 Lady Day Assessment.

THE RANKING OF PROVINCIAL TOWNS (contd.)

1801 (Census population)		1861 (Census population)	
13. Newcastle	28,366	14. Sunderland	78,211
14. Exeter	17,398	15. Brighton	77,693
15. Leicester	16,953	16. Norwich	74,891
16. Stoke-on-Trent	16,414	17. Nottingham	74,693
17. York	16,145	18. Oldham	72,333
18. Coventry	16,034	19. Bolton	70,395
19. Ashton-under-Lyne	15,632	20. Leicester	68,056
20. Chester	15,052	21. Blackburn	63,126
21. Dover	14,845	22. Wolverhampton	60,860
22. Great Yarmouth	14,845	23. Stockport	54,681
23. Stockport	14,830	24. Bath	52,528
24. Shrewsbury	14,739	25. Birkenhead	51,649
25. Wolverhampton	12,565	26. Southampton	46,960
26. Bolton	12,549	27. Derby	43,091
27. Sunderland	12,412	28. Coventry	40,936
28. Oldham	12,024	29. York	40,433
29. Blackburn	11,980	30. Rochdale	38,114
30. Preston	11,887	31. Ipswich	37,950
31. Oxford	11,694	32. Walsall	37,760
32. Colchester	11,520	33. Wigan	37,658
33. Worcester	11,352	34. Halifax	37,014
34. Ipswich	11,277	35. Macclesfield	36,101
35. Wigan	10,989	36. South Shields	35,239
36. Derby	10,832	37. Ashton-under-Lyne	34,886
37. Warrington	10,567	38. Great Yarmouth	34,810
38. Chatham	10,505	39. Tynemouth	34,021
39. Carlisle	10,221	40. Exeter	33,738
40. Dudley	10,107	41. Gateshead	33,587
41. Kings Lynn	10,096	42. Northampton	32,813
42. Cambridge	10,087		

SELECT BIBLIOGRAPHY

Since the first edition of *Local History in England* (1959) the subject has attracted enormous interest among amateurs and professionals alike. The battle to achieve academic respectability has been won, but Local History is still a field in which amateurs can make positive contributions and get a real sense of achievement out of their research and study. Each year sees a huge output of books, pamphlets and articles, many of them inspired by the writings of William Hoskins. So varied is the subject matter that it is difficult to keep abreast of all significant developments; indeed, it is sometimes hard to determine just what is significant. Any select bibliography must be an individual choice. This one seeks to reflect the spirit of the Hoskins approach and to offer guidance to the beginner. Many of the works listed below have their own bibliographies to guide the student further.

CHAPTER 1

The concerns of the Department of English Local History, which Hoskins founded at Leicester University, are expressed in H. P. R. Finberg, *The Local Historian and His Theme* (1952) and A. Everitt, *Ways and Means in Local History* (1971). V. Skipp makes a persuasive analysis of the current scene in 'Local History: A New Definition and Its Implications', *The Local Historian*, 14, nos 6 and 7 (1981). Many useful articles can be found in *The Local Historian*'s quarterly volumes and in the regional journals which have been founded since Hoskins first wrote, namely *Northern History, Midland History, Southern History* and the *Bulletin of Local History: East Midlands Region*, as well as in numerous local society transactions.

Advice on sources and approaches in addition to the books quoted in the text is given in: A. Rogers, *Approaches to Local History* (1977); A. Rogers (ed.), *Group Projects in Local History* (1977); J. West, *Village Records* (1962); J. Ravensdale, *History on Your Doorstep* (1982); A. Macfarlane, *Reconstructing Historical Communities* (1977); and R. Storey and L. Madden, *Primary Sources for Victorian Studies* (1977). Several local record offices have published their own guides on how to read early documents. Of general use are: F. G. Emmison, *How to Read Local Archives, 1550–1700* (1967); H. E. P. Grieve, *Examples of English Handwriting, 1150–1750* (1959); K. C. Newton, *Medieval Local Records: A Reading Aid* (1971); E. A. Gooder, *Latin for Local History* (1978); and R. E. Latham (ed.), *Revised Medieval Latin Word List* (1965).

CHAPTER 2

W. G. Hoskins, *The Midland Peasant* (1957) was the forerunner of modern studies of rural communities, such as M. K. Ashby, *The Changing English Village, 1066–1914* (1974). The approach of the rural sociologist, most notably W. M. Williams, *The Sociology of an English Village: Gosforth, Cumberland* (1956) has also been influential. An outstanding study of Welsh rural society is D. Jenkins, *The Agricultural Community in South-West Wales at the Turn of the Twentieth Century* (1971). Richard Gough's *History of Myddle* (edited and introduced by D. Hey, 1981) is now available in paperback and forms the basis of D. Hey, *An English Rural Community: Myddle Under the Tudors and Stuarts* (1974).

The anthropological approach, which widens traditional concerns by investigating attitudes and beliefs, is used in K. Thomas's two masterly national surveys, *Religion and the Decline of Magic* (1971) and *Man and the Natural World* (1983). A framework for this sort of approach at a local level is provided by C. V. Phythian-Adams, *Local History and Folklore* (1975). the best study of the social as well as the economic aspects of early-modern local society is M. Spufford, *Contrasting Communities* (1974), an analysis of three very different Cambridgeshire parishes. Modern statistical methods are applied to this approach in K. Wrightson and D. Levine, *Poverty and Piety in an English Village: Terling, 1525–1700* (1979). A very good recent study of a different kind of community is M. Prior, *Fisher Row: Fishermen, Bargemen and Canal Boatmen in Oxford, 1500–1900* (1982).

The concerns of modern local and regional historians are also well expressed in: C. W. Chalklin and M. A. Havinden (eds), *Rural Change and Urban Growth, 1500–1800: Essays in English regional history in honour of W. G. Hoskins* (1974). J. Thirsk (ed.), *Land, Church and People: essays presented to Professor H. P. R. Finberg* (1970); J. Thirsk, (ed.), *Agrarian History of England and Wales, IV, 1500–1640* (1967); C. Dyer, *Lords and Peasants in a Changing Society* (1980); and J. H. Bettey, *Rural Life in Wessex, 1500–1900* (1977).

Recent county historians have been principally concerned with the period from the Reformation to the Civil War. Interest was stimulated by A. Everitt, *The Community of Kent and the Great Rebellion* (1966) and followed by: J. T. Cliffe, *The Yorkshire Gentry from the Reformation to the Civil War* (1969); A. Fletcher, *A County Community in Peace and War: Sussex, 1600–1660* (1975); P. Clark, *English Provincial Society from the Reformation to the Revolution: religion, politics and society in Kent, 1500–1640* (1977); B. G. Blackwood, *The Lancashire Gentry and the Great Rebellion, 1640–60* (1978); and C. Holmes, *Seventeenth-Century Lincolnshire* (1980). See G. E. Aylmer and J. S. Morrill, *The Civil War and Interregnum—sources for local historians* (1979).

CHAPTER 3

Essential background reading for the study of nineteenth-century rural communities is supplied by the two volumes of G. E. Mingay (ed.), *The Victorian Countryside* (1981). H. J. Dyos and M. Wolff, *The Victorian City: images and realities* (1973) provides a similar two-volume service for those working on urban societies. See also G. Best, *Mid-Victorian Britain, 1851–75* (1971). Good local urban studies include: H. J. Dyos, *Victorian Suburb: a study of the growth of Camberwell* (1961); B. H. Harrison and B. Trinder, *Drink and Sobriety in an Early Victorian Country Town: Banbury, 1830–1860* (1969); and A. Henstock, (ed.), *Early Victorian Country Town: a portrait of Ashbourne in the mid-nineteenth Century* (1978). R. Moore,

Pitmen, Preachers and Politics: the effects of Methodism in a Durham mining community (1974) is one of the most interesting local studies to have appeared in recent years. Good regional works include J. Obelkevich, *Religion and Rural Society: South Lindsey, 1825–1875* (1976) and R. J. Olney, *Rural Society and County Government in Nineteenth-Century Lincolnshire* (1979).

Great advances have been made in the study of oral history, and since 1972 the Oral History Society has had its own journal. The pioneer works of G. E. Evans are still the most readable, from *Ask the Fellows Who Cut the Hay* (1956) to *The Days We Have Seen* (1975). P. Thompson, *The Voice of the Past: Oral History* (1978) states the case for this approach, as does E. Roberts, 'Oral History and the Local Historian', *The Local Historian*, 13, no. 7, pp. 408–16 (Aug. 1979). Oral History is used effectively in the publications of the Ruskin College History Workshop, notably: R. Samuel (ed.), *Village Life and Labour* (1975); R. Samuel (ed.), *Miners, Quarrymen and Saltworkers* (1977); and S. Alexander, *St Giles Fair, 1830–1914: popular culture in the industrial revolution in nineteenth-century Oxford* (1970). Work of a similar nature is summarised in R. Chaplin, 'Ordinary Men: recent work in social history', *The Local Historian*, 12, nos 3–4, pp. 131–5 (Nov. 1976). The Society for the Study of Labour History has published its own bulletin since 1960.

The attraction and use of old photographs is demonstrated by G. Winter, *A Country Camera, 1844–1914* (1973) and N. McCord, 'Photographs as Historical Evidence', *The Local Historian*, 13, no. 1, pp. 23–36 (Feb. 1978).

CHAPTER 4

The study of place-names has undergone such radical revision in recent years that the local historian cannot rely upon older works. M. Gelling, *Signposts to the Past* (1978) explains the new interpretations. Modern approaches to the study of settlement history are applied in P. Sawyer (ed.), *Medieval Settlement* (1976), which has a comprehensive bibliography. D. Hill, *An Atlas of Anglo-Saxon England* (1981) is useful for the beginner, and 'Recent Work on Anglo-Saxon Charters' is discussed by M. Gelling in *The Local Historian*, 13, no. 4, pp. 209–16 (Nov. 1978).

C. V. Phythian-Adams, *Continuity, Fields and Fission:the making a midland parish* (1978) is a persuasive study of the origins of a

Leicestershire community, and P. D. A. Harvey, *A Medieval Oxfordshire Village, Cuxham, 1240–1400* (1965) is a model for medievalists. Recent work on the origins and development of open-field systems is best represented by A. R. H. Baker and R. A. Butlin (eds), *Studies of Field Systems in the British Isles* (1973) and R. Russell, *The Logic of Open Field Systems* (1974). Enclosure of open fields and commons is considered by J. A. Yelling, *Common Field and Enclosure in England 1450–1850* (1977) and W. E. Tate, *The English Village Community and the Enclosure Movements* (1967). These and many other matters related to agrarian history are the subjects of numerous articles in *The Agricultural History Review* (1953 onwards). The volumes of *The Agrarian History of England and Wales* (in progress) are indispensible reference works for the rural historian.

CHAPTER 5

D. P. Dymond, *Writing A Church Guide* (1977) is full of sensible advice for anyone wishing to undertake this task. The three volumes of H. M. and J. Taylor, *Anglo-Saxon Architecture* (1965 (2 vols), 1978) and W. Rodwell, *The Archaeology of the English Church* (1981) are basic to an understanding of origins and early structures. P. F. Ryder, *Saxon Churches in South Yorkshire* (1982) is a good example of what can be done at a regional level. J. Harvey, *The Perpendicular Style* (1978) is equally rigorous for a later period, and M. Chatfield, *Churches the Victorians Forgot* (1979) illustrates interior arrangements of 'unrestored' churches. Amongst the best of the numerous general works on English parish churches are C. Platt, *Parish Churches of Medieval England* (1981) and R. Foster, *Discovering English Churches* (1981).

Comparative studies of nonconformity are represented by A. Everitt, *The Pattern of Rural Dissent in the Nineteenth Century* (1972) and C. Binfield, *So Down to Prayers: studies in English nonconformity, 1780–1920* (1977). For 'Recusant History' see L. Brooks, *The Local Historian*, 15, no. 5, pp. 288–95 (Feb. 1983). An introduction to 'The 1851 Census of Religions Worship' is provided by R. W. Ambler in *The Local Historian*, 11, no. 7, pp. 375–81 (Autumn 1975).

M. Seaborne, *The English School: its architecture and organis-ation, 1370–1870* (1971) and W. H. G. Armytage, *Four Hundred*

Years of English Education (1964) provide background. On literacy see D. Cressy, *Literacy and the Social Order* (1980) and M. Spufford, *Small Books and Pleasant Histories* (1981).

CHAPTER 6

The most influential work on the topography of medieval towns has been M. W. Beresford, *New Towns of the Middle Ages* (1967). C. Platt, *The English Medieval Town* (1976) combines modern archaeological, topographical and historical work and is a basic text. M. D. Lobel (ed.), *Historic Towns: maps and plans of towns and cities in the British Isles,* two volumes (1969, 1975) carefully maps and analyses selected places. See also M. Aston and J. C. Bond, *The Landscape of Towns* (1976). M. W. Beresford and H. P. R. Finberg, *English Medieval Boroughs: a hand-list* (1973) was extended in *Urban History Yearbook 1981,* pp. 59–65.

The antiquity of some of our towns is discussed in A. Everitt, 'The Primary Towns of England', *The Local Historian,* 11, No. 5, pp. 263–77 (Feb. 1975). Two studies which relate topography and architecture are Royal Commission on Historical Monuments, *The Town of Stamford* (1977) and V. Parker, *The Making of King's Lynn* (1971). For a later period see F. M. L. Thompson, *Hampstead— Building a Borough, 1650–1964* (1974).

CHAPTER 7

The second edition of C. Gross, *A Bibliography of British Municipal History* (ed. G. Martin, 1966) lists relevant works published before the mid-1960s, and the annual volumes of *Urban History Yearbook* (1974 onwards) contain articles and reviews of all important recent work. The liveliest debate concerns the fortunes of late-medieval towns, on which the major contribution is C. V. Phythian-Adams, *Desolation of a City: Coventry and the urban crisis of the late middle ages* (1979).

A great deal of work has been done in recent years on early-modern towns. Good local studies include D. Palliser, *Tudor York* (1979) and A. Dyer, *The City of Worcester in the Sixteenth Century* (1973). For general surveys see P. Clark and P. Slack, *English Towns in Transition, 1500–1700* (1976), and J. Patten, *English Towns, 1500–1700* (1978). A number of stimulating essays are collected in P. Clark and P. Slack (eds), *Crisis and Order in English Towns, 1500–1700* (1972) and P. Clark (ed.), *Country Towns in Pre-Industrial England* (1981).

B. Jennings (ed.), *A History of Harrogate and Knaresborough* (1970) and R. Fieldhouse and B. Jennings (eds), *A History of Richmond and Swaledale* (1978) trace the history of towns over a long period of time. Important works on later periods include: C. W. Chalklin, *The Provincial Towns of Georgian England: a study of the building process, 1740–1820* (1974); D. J. Olsen, *The Growth of Victorian London* (1976); and D. Fraser (ed.), *A History of Modern Leeds* (1980).

CHAPTER 8

The study of landscape history has expanded enormously since the publication of William Hoskins's seminal work, *The Making of the English Landscape* (1955). The county volumes in the Hodder and Stoughton series now cover about half of England. Methods of study are outlined in W. G. Hoskins, *Fieldwork in Local History* (2nd edn) (1982, with bibliography by C. Taylor) and in C. Taylor, *Fieldwork in Medieval Archaeology* (1974). M. W. Beresford, another great exponent of landscape history, recounts his adventures in *History on the Ground* (1957) and with J. K. St Joseph uses aerial photographs to good effect in *Medieval England: an aerial survey* (1979).

H. C. Darby (ed.), *A New Historical Geography of England* (1973) provides general background. Particular aspects of fieldwork are dealt with in: M. W. Beresford and J. G. Hurst (eds), *Deserted Villages* (1971); A. Aberg (ed.), *Medieval Moated Sites* (1978); T. Rowley, *Villages in the Landscape* (1978); C. Taylor, *Fields in the English Landscape* (1975); C. Taylor, *Roads and Tracks of Britain* (1979); O. Rackham, *Trees and Woodland in the British Landscape* (1976); and the same author's *Ancient Woodland* (1980), which treats the subject in more depth, using East Anglian examples.

In 'The Making of the English Landscape—25 years on', *The Local Historian*, 14, no. 4, pp. 195–201 (Nov. 1980) C. Taylor summarises changes in thinking since the publication of Hoskins's book as: the English landscape is much older than we have ever conceived, and its basic origins are prehistoric not Saxon; change, not stability, is the main feature of the landscape; and the development of the landscape is much more complex than we used to think. He expands these views in *Village and Farmstead: A History of Rural Settlement in England* (1983). M. Aston, 'The Making of the English Landscape—The Next 25 Years', *The Local Historian*, 15, no. 6, pp. 323–32 (May 1983) suggests that the principal aim should be to define major landscape phases.

CHAPTER 9

The study of vernacular architecture has become increasingly technical and specialised and needs to be related more to social-and-economic history. The subject has its own journal, *Vernacular Architecture*, and is often featured in other journals, notably *Medieval Archaeology, Post-Medieval Archaeology* and *Archaeological Journal*. R. W. Brunskill, *Illustrated Handbook of Vernacular Architecture* (1971) explains the techniques, and M. W. Barley, *The English Farmhouse and Cottage* (1961) combines documentary and architectural evidence to show historical development. E. Mercer, *English Vernacular Houses* (1975) and A. Clifton-Taylor, *The Pattern of English Building* (1972) are readable, informative and well-illustrated.

Hoskins's pioneer essay, 'The Rebuilding of Rural England, 1570–1640', *Provincial England* (1964) has been very influential, but now needs to be modified in the light of R. Machin, 'The Great Rebuilding: a reassessment', *Past and Present*, 77, pp. 33–56 (1977). For urban building see M. Laithwaite, 'The Buildings of Burford: A Cotswold Town in the Fourteenth to the Nineteenth Centuries' in A. Everitt (ed.), *Perspectives in English Urban History* (1973), and the booklets produced by the Ludlow History Research Group, such as M. E. Speight and D. J. Lloyd, *Ludlow Houses and Their Residents* (1978) and D. J. Lloyd, *Broad Street—its houses and residents through eight centuries* (1978).

M. Girouard, *Life in the English Country House* (1978) links social and architectural history and shows how houses were used over the centuries. Vernacular architecture would benefit from widening its concerns this way. Sir J. Summerson, *Architecture in Britain, 1530–1830* (1953) and the county volumes of Sir N. Pevsner's magnificent *Buildings of England* series are well-known reference works. Those interested in labour history should consult J. Tarn, *Working Class Housing in Nineteenth-Century Britain* (1971) and S. D. Chapman (ed.), *The History of Working Class Housing: A Symposium* (1971).

CHAPTER 10

M. Flinn, *British Population Growth, 1700–1850* (1970) and E. A. Wrigley (ed.), *Introduction to English Historical Demography* (1966) provide introductions to a subject which is basic to many local studies. Those who wish to pursue demography seriously must refer to E. A. Wrigley and R. S. Schofield, *The Population History of England, 1541–1971* (1981) and to the journal *Local Population Studies* (1968 onwards).

J. Hatcher, *Plague, Population and the English Economy, 1334–1530* (1977) relates population levels and the incidence of disease to the late-medieval economy before parish registers begin. The effects of plague and famine are discussed in a Local Population Studies supplement, *The Plague Reconsidered: a new look at its origin and effects in sixteenth and seventeenth century England* (1977) and in A. B. Appleby, *Famine in Tudor and Stuart England* (1978). See also P. Clark, 'Migration in England during the late-seventeenth and early eighteenth centuries', *Past and Present*, 83, pp. 57–90 (May 1979). V. Skipp, *Crisis and Development: an ecological case study of the Forest of Arden, 1570–1674* (1978) places demographic research firmly in the wider context of economic history. For a later period see M. Anderson, *Family Structure in Nineteenth-Century Lancashire* (1971).

CHAPTER 11

The modern study of surnames is largely the work of two scholars: R. McKinley, *Norfolk and Suffolk Surnames in the Middle Ages* (1975), *The Surnames of Oxfordshire* (1977), *The Surnames of Lancashire* (1981); and G. Redmonds, *Yorkshire, West Riding: English surname series* (1973) and 'Surnames and Place Names', *The Local Historian*, x, no. 1, pp. 3–7 (Feb. 1982).

For family history see D. Steel, *Family History* (1980),

beginners' guides such as G. Hamilton-Edwards, *In Search of Ancestry* (1974) and M. Mander, *Tracing Your Ancestors* (1976), and the wider treatment of Sir A. Wagner, *English Genealogy* (1972).

CHAPTER 12

This is covered in the bibliography for other chapters.

CHAPTER 13

R. Parker, the author of the best-seller, *The Common Stream* (1978) gives an amusing and realistic account of his experiences in 'I didn't mean to do it', *The Local Historian*, 12, no. 8, pp. 391–4 (Nov. 1977). Sensible advice is given in J. Batley 'Publishing Local History: a practical approach: 1. Preparing your material', *The Local Historian*, 12, no. 7, pp. 360–4 (Aug. 1977); '2. Format and Style', 12, no. 8, pp. 424–9 (Nov. 1977); '3. Seeing it through the press', 13, no. 3, pp. 163–7 (Aug. 1978); and '4. Publication and Marketing', 13, no. 4, pp. 227–32 (Nov. 1978).

Good advice can be found in D. Dymond, *Writing Local History: A Practical Guide* (1981), which every local historian should consult before putting pen to paper.

INDEX